Walking the Appalachian Trail

Larry Luxenberg
Photographs by Mike Warren

STACKPOLE
BOOKS

Published by
STACKPOLE BOOKS
5067 Ritter Road
Mechanicsburg, PA 17055

Printed in the United States of America

10 9 8 7 6 5

First Edition

Cover design by Mark Olszewski
Back cover map by Sandra M. Blair
Cover photograph by Mike Warren. From Millbrook Mountain
    in the Delaware Water Gap, New Jersey.

Library of Congress Cataloging-in-Publication Data

Luxenberg, Larry.
    Walking the Appalachian Trail / Larry Luxenberg ; photographs by
Mike Warren. — 1st ed.
        p.   cm.
    Includes bibliographical references.
    ISBN 0-8117-3095-6
    1. Hiking—Appalachian Trail. 2. Appalachian Trail—Description
and travel. I. Title.
GV199.42.A68L68 1995   94-26376
796.5'1'0974—dc20   CIP

To my parents,
who were with me every step of the way

Contents

Foreword

T
HE SUBJECT OF THIS BOOK IS NOTHING LESS THAN AN APPA-
lachian Trail continuum through time and space. In time, it runs
from the trail's beginning in one man's dream, passing through the
present to an ever-expanding vision for the future. In space, of course, it
stretches from the southern Appalachians in Georgia to Maine's lodestar
mountain. The author has designed an approach to this vast subject that illu-
minates the trail by means of a light refracted through the seasonally shifting
prism that is the annual flow of A.T. thru-hikers. In the process of becoming
one of the most visible manifestations of the Appalachian Trail experience,
this itinerant community has created over the years a mystical fellowship that
becomes at times otherworldly in its pervasive sense of apartness from the
quotidian concerns of all the rest of us. A society in motion, it has evolved its
own set of rituals, none of which is more clearly calculated to separate the
initiates from the others than the now near mandatory assumption of "trail
names" by those who would fully enter the fellowship. Luxenberg dutifully
acknowledges this rite by so regularly citing trail names along with the legal
ones that the reader is brought up short when some occasional thru-hiker is
identified by only one name rather than the pair that we have quickly come
to expect.

At least part of the reason for these apparent omissions is that the use of
trail names by thru-hikers did not become universal until the early 1980s.
Before that, for a time, there had been a mix of the trail named and
unnamed. Another possible reason is that, after leaving the trail, some hikers seem embarrassed about this aspect of their adventure. They avoid mentioning their own trail names to the uninitiated or, in extreme cases, actually
deny the use of such names, even though other hikers may confirm their
existence. The use of trail names is, in any case, a fascinating phenomenon,
and their endless variety is an invitation to the collector and cataloguer. At
some time I expect we will see a thesis produced by some doctoral candidate
in sociology analyzing this singular ritual.

Another of the key underpinnings of this society, and one that does as much as any to hold it together through its annual flourishing, is its communication mechanism, which is based on the registers found at most shelters and some other sites along the trail. The combination of these communal journals, the constantly shifting configuration of the major northward flow of hikers, the smaller trickle of southbounders, and the occasional trail-stop people all serve to facilitate a communications network of startling efficiency. Few secrets exist, it would seem, in the peripatetic world of those who follow the Katahdin lodestar.

Even though the visionaries who created the Appalachian Trail did not apparently foresee this annual tide of end-to-enders, it seems inevitable that they would emerge. By creating a trail that goes from one point to another, however far the distance might be, an implicit challenge was extended. Every hiker who sets out from one end or the other, and indeed even those who, bit by bit, complete the trail over time, are responding to that challenge. The thru-hikers serve as a textbook example of the "if you build it they will come" dictum.

Still, there are those who cavil at the attention lavished on thru-hikers. It is argued that while thru-hikers each year number in the hundreds, other uses of the trail (mostly day-hikers) number in the hundreds of thousands. While this is unarguably true, it may be more appropriate—if we must resort to bean counting—to make our comparisons in terms of miles per hiker. Each thru-hiker logs something over 2,000 miles of trail use, the equivalent of perhaps 200 day hikers. By this measure, 150 thru-hikers may equal the trail use of 30,000 day hikers. Moreover, in addition to the modest number of those who each year successfully negotiate the entire trail, there is some unknown but surely much larger number of thwarted aspirants, ranging from those who abandon the quest within a day or two to those who heart-breakingly come within the very sight of the northern mountain itself. The trail miles walked by these uncounted dreamers can never be known but must be vast.

It is my own feeling, however, that such reckonings miss the point. The length of the A.T. is part of its essence, and surely nothing embodies that aspect more purely than the individual who seeks to know it all, either in pieces or in a single journey. The trail is there for all: the afternoon stroller, the day hiker, and the weekend backpacker, as well as the end-to-enders. But the crowning mystique will always settle on those who have experienced it in its entirety.

Has reading Larry Luxenberg's surprisingly moving work made me want to set out some day to do the whole trail myself? I think not. At my age there are still too many other things I want to crowd into the few remaining years to be willing to commit half a year to this one adventure. But I will always hold in special regard that disparate but growing battalion of seekers who have seized the dream, and thereby both changed their lives and validated the Appalachian Trail.

—*Maurice J. Forrester, Jr.*

Acknowledgments

No THRU-HIKE OF THE APPALACHIAN TRAIL IS POSSIBLE WITHOUT helping hands along the way. It's just as true for books about the trail. Several hundred strangers, usually with no notice, have given generously of their time, letting me share their precious memories of life on the trail. It has been a privilege to meet so many wonderful people; renew some old friendships; and again ponder the power and fascination of the A.T.

The ATC staff was especially helpful, notably David Startzell, Brian King, Jean Cashin, Laurie Potteiger, Jan Skadberg, Teresa Tumblin, and Amy and Don Owen. Reading the back issues of the *Appalachian Trailway News* has renewed my appreciation for the work of editor Judy Jenner.

Ruth Blackburn, Ray Hunt, and George Zoebelein, all former ATC chairs, shared their unique perspectives with me. Ruth Blackburn spent a day walking me through PATC and A.T. history.

Frank "the Hawk" Logue, former ALDHA coordinator, offered early encouragement. Ron Keal, his successor, gave me valuable suggestions about hikers to contact. Bert Gilbert, who hosted a four-star ALDHA work trip, proved that he not only swings a mean chain saw but is no slouch with a skillet.

Holly "Doc" Leeds and Frank "Red Blaze" Shea introduced me to the record-breaking thru-hiker class of 1990.

The staff at Hemlock Overlook made my visit pleasant and productive. They included Steve "Offshore Steve" Gomez, Keith "Wolf" Kimball, Frank "the Merry Slav" Krajcovic, Dan Nellis, and John "Indiana John" Stevenson. Warren Doyle, Jr., the director, and his father, Warren Doyle, Sr., were helpful at many points along the way.

Art Hehn, Janet Malcolm, and Nancy and Norm Sills do not appear in these pages but loom large in my memory of the friendliness and generosity of the A.T. community.

Arthur "A. B. Positive" Batchelder arose before dawn and drove halfway across New England to talk about the trail and join me on a wild goose chase.

Bob "Rerun" Sparkes regaled me with stories of trail personalities.

June and Bill Harless called to my attention the pioneering hikes of Robert MacMullin.

Ed Miller and Steve Tai offered frequent encouragement.

Sam Waddle, the definition of a "trail angel," gave me some helpful tips and clippings from his encyclopedic collection. Lucy and Bob Seeds and Esther Allen shared their memories of Grandma Gatewood. Dick "Lo-Tec" Cieslik made available his huge file of research on Grandma's hiking career and his enthusiasm for her story.

Liz, Geoff, Greg, and Henry, my Maine A.T. family, provided the highlight of my hike. And thanks also go to my other 1980 hiking friends, among them Pat "Wool Hat Kid" Jacobs, Marilyn and John Pasanen, and Rick Hancock, and to the memory of John Kuzniak.

Special thanks to Noel "The Singing Horseman" DeCavalcante, Maurice Forrester, Jr., Roly Mueser, Bill "Sprained Rice" O'Brien, Al "A.T. Al" Sochard, and Pieter "The Cheshire Cat" Van Why for reading the manuscript and offering many helpful suggestions. Roly also made available his comprehensive research on thru-hikers and encouraged me at key points along the way. Karen Berger and Dan Smith offered author kinship.

Ken Scott and Mildred and Maurice Forrester, Jr., made my two young sons welcome at a Keystone Trails Association meeting. Thurston Griggs gave me several insights into pioneer A.T. hikers.

Mike Schroeder and Steve Johnson offered encouragement early in my hiking career. Mark Lynch accompanied me on many day hikes on the A.T.

Sally Atwater and Valerie Gittings of Stackpole Books took a chance and made a difficult task easier.

Mike Warren, known to others as a top photographer of the A.T., is an old friend of the family who has taught me much about hiking and other matters over the years.

My older brother, Stan, first suggested thirteen years ago that I talk to A.T. hikers and do a book about them. I may be slow, but I do listen to him. My mother-in-law, Muriel, sister, Deb, and sister-in-law, Sara, also provided steady encouragement.

My family, with great humor, absorbed massive amounts of information about the A.T., endured vacations focused on research, and gave up the hiking, canoeing, and camping trips they have come to expect. My son, Seth, as a first- and second-grader, climbed Katahdin with me, came up with the title, reminded me who said what, and critically read the manuscript. His brother, Eli, patiently accompanied me to a half dozen interviews and listened to many of the stories again and again. My daughter, Adina Robin, learned to say "A.T." before her second birthday and let me know when it was time to wrap up an interview at Abol Bridge. My wife, Frieda, gave unwavering support and made this, as so much else, possible and enjoyable.

A Day in the Life of a Thru-Hiker

THE APPALACHIAN TRAIL IS A 2,147-MILE-LONG FOOTPATH FROM Georgia to Maine, which follows the ridgetops of the fourteen states through which it passes. Each year, as many as two hundred back-packers hike the full length of the trail. They are called thru-hikers. One such thru-hiker was Darrell Maret, who covered the distance in 1980.

What follows is the first section of Darrell "The Philosopher" Maret's report to the Appalachian Trail Conference, informing them that he had hiked the entire A.T.

Wake to birds singing and an illuminated tent. Reach into pack for morning snack as glance over guidebook for preview of the day's trail. Pack up, pleased to see clear skies, gulp a quart of water from nearby spring, move out by 7:30. If going for 20 miles, push for 10 by 12, but today needs no hurry.

Walk the forest corridor: the beaten path, the bordering trees, the white blazes. Climb a few mountains, wonder when it will get easy—it never will—take numerous breaks alongside streams and vistas. Chat with hikers about trail conditions, bemused by outra-geous estimations of Yahoos as to time and distances, stop to make first acquaintance with certain wildflowers, take a few pictures for souvenir-sake.

What madness is this? Trees turning to ice cream cones and rocks into hamburgers? Could it have been that last water source? No, it is being overdue for a recivilization. Thank goodness there is a town by way of the next road.

Standing beside the road, disgusted with all those drivers who can't recognize a good person deserving a lift. Finally catch a ride with either a local or a short-term backpacker. The strange sensation of riding in a fast motion.

In town, stay at the hostel, the church, the hospice, the monas-tery, the firehouse, the community center, the fraternity house, the mountain inn, the boarding house, the hotel, the motel, or the home of a former Georgia-to-Mainer. That long, hot luxurious shower. Being clean for the first time in a week. Buying a quart of ice cream and a Coke on the way to the laundromat. Writing letters as wait for clothes. Sitting with only shorts and boots on—but the local ladies have seen this before. By the post office for mail. To grocery store for provisions. The contrast: at home being careful to buy few calories, less fat and no preservatives, but on trail the desperate need of fats, calories, and preservatives. To a restaurant, cafe, kitchen for a dinner that really isn't so great but tonight tastes the best ever had.

The legs begin to tighten. Going up steps is excruciating. General soreness and fatigue. Isn't several months and a thousand miles enough for the body to adapt to the trail? Feels like just returned from a weekend of overexertion.

Talk with fellow-hikers about experiences, about news of the trail, about who is skipping sections, who has dropped out, where the speed-demons are up ahead. Make phone calls home to loved ones. Arrange and pack food: discard boxes, give away excess commodities, anxiously wonder if have enough, when lift pack wonder what can do without.

Lay down to sleep . . . but bed uncomfortable, too soft. Toss and turn. Finally admit defeat and get out of bed, grab the airing out sleeping bag, and take to the floor. That is better, but still an uneasiness—those unusual sounds of a town!

Up early for big breakfast, mail packages and letters at post office, stop by store for one last splurge, resume course by noon. Pleased with self, less than 24 hours off trail.

If gained by town and recuperation, then why this slow going? Because it is the law that it is always descent with light pack into town, and ascent with an almost intolerable burden on the way out. The problem is only compounded by that last half-gallon of ice cream over-indulgently consumed at the store.

Ah, but provisions for a week, a hundred miles of trail stretching toward the horizon, and every step being a step closer to Katahdin. A life more worthwhile even the gods could not dream of.

A Day in the Life of a Thru-Hiker

Springer Mountain: The Beginning

*The days pass, and never return, and the South still waits for you.
Take the adventure, heed the call, now ere the irrevocable moment
passes! 'Tis but a banging of the door behind you, a blithesome step
forward, and you are out of the old life and into the new!*

The Adventurer to the Water Rat,
from *Wind in the Willows*
by Kenneth Grahame

No one ever began an Appalachian Trail thru-hike with
more panache than Robie Hensley. In the hiking community he
has only one name: "Jumpstart." After retiring as postmaster of
Chuckey, Tennessee, Robie began a search for new challenges. On his second flight on a hazy, blustery day, Robie parachuted out of a small plane
piloted by son Steve. He landed eight thousand feet below among the rocks
and dense tree cover at the very top of Springer Mountain, Georgia, not
far from the plaque marking the southern end of the 2,147-mile long
Appalachian Trail (A.T.).

Hensley's story is only one of countless fascinating journeys. Each year
as many as two thousand people start out to hike the whole A.T. Nearly
two hundred report to the Appalachian Trail Conference (ATC) that they
have done so. It's anyone's guess how many others hike the trail and never
report it.

Most backpackers who set out to hike the entire trail in one year begin
at the small visitor's center at the base of Amicalola Falls ("Tumbling Waters"

in Cherokee). In a few strides, they will enter some pretty woods and begin climbing the steep, rugged eight-mile approach trail to Springer Mountain. The first mile parallels the falls, which drops 729 feet in seven cascades, making it the highest waterfall east of the Rocky Mountains. When the early hikers passed through Amicalola Falls State Park, it was a park in name only, with one narrow road. Today, although the park continues to be developed, it is still surprisingly remote and wild.

Usually hikers begin by signing their first trail register at Amicalola. These huge notebooks in which people share their thoughts are the heart of the trail's efficient grapevine. They reveal hikers who are nervous but enthusiastic. Reality has yet to sink in. Not until the Katahdin Stream ranger station register, more than two thousand miles away in Maine, will such widespread high spirits be evident again. In the meantime, there will be complaints and miseries, joys and sorrows, blisters, cold, hunger and thirst, panoramic views, and an abundance of good fellowship.

Sometimes the A.T. does not meet hikers' expectations. Within days, the hardships lead many to abandon the trail. Among them are some who dreamed of the A.T. for a decade or more. Bad weather, steep climbs, hard ground, and aching bones all take a toll.

"The first time on Springer, I had a daunting feeling," said Leonard "Habitual Hiker" Adkins. "What am I doing here? Maine's a ways up there. I was excited and full of self-doubts. I was questioning why I was there. On the approach trail, I thought, 'If this is what it's like the whole way, I'm in trouble.'"

"It felt strange," said Bill "Stats Godric" Gunderson, a 1989 thru-hiker. "I didn't know anybody. It's like going off to college. Suddenly you're tossed into a new world."

Mitch "Breeze" Keiler arrived at Springer with his mother, brother, and a grandfather who had built some of the A.T. in the 1930s. "I felt a minor panic attack when they left," Mitch said. "I walked two hundred yards down the trail and sat down and had a snack. I felt like I was the biggest fool on earth one minute, like I was going to do it the next. Soon I picked myself up, and by the end of the day I'd met a lot of lifelong buddies."

"Your first week you think, 'I'm way down in Georgia and I'm already exhausted,'" said Henry Phillips. "No wonder so many people drop out the first week. Then the second week, blisters set in. In Georgia, it's straight up and straight down. Six miles is a big deal. You think, 'How am I ever going to get to Katahdin?' But then you start wondering just what's around the next bend. You know if you stay in one place, nothing exciting is going to happen."

Pieter "the Cheshire Cat" Van Why, who came to the A.T. as a novice backpacker, found everything so new and wonderful that the initial stretch was magical.

Since 1958, Springer has been the southern end of the A.T. The previous terminus, Mount Oglethorpe, is a more dramatic mountain, but construction of a gravel logging road on Oglethorpe led to vandalism; pungent chicken farms along the route also helped persuade the Georgia Appalachian Trail Club (GATC) to find a different trailhead.

In many ways Springer is a more appropriate place for the trail to start. Here a hiker abruptly enters the wilderness of the Chattahoochee National Forest and remains in forest so lush with understory that it prompted one early thru-hiker to call the A.T. "the long, green tunnel."

Although it's revered among hikers for its prominent role on the A.T., Springer, at 3,782 feet, is an otherwise anonymous mountain. Unlike its northern counterpart, Mount Katahdin, Springer has little history or myth associated with it. Katahdin, with its panoramic views, stands alone, the centerpiece of the Maine wilderness. Springer is just one of many beautiful mountains in a rugged part of north Georgia. Springer's twin distinctions are that it unites the two branches of the southern Blue Ridge Mountains and is the southern end of the A.T.

No one seems sure how Springer Mountain got its name. The most common story is that a family named Springer lived on the mountain in the nineteenth century. According to Whit Benson, former GATC president, local legend held that the mountaineer was not of outstanding repute. In fact, when the trail shifted from Mount Oglethorpe, GATC looked into this story and investigated earlier Cherokee names for the mountain. Nothing satisfactory came of this effort, however. Springer had been the name on all twentieth century maps and the name by which local people knew the mountain. Whatever the origins, Springer is quite a change from a prior name, Penitentiary Mountain.

A.T. founder Benton MacKaye's first map of the proposed trail route put the southern end on North Carolina's Mount Mitchell, at 6,684 feet the highest peak in the east. Other sites considered for the southern terminus were Lookout Mountain in Tennessee and Cohutta Mountain in Georgia. MacKaye showed a spur trail running the whole way to Stone Mountain near Atlanta.

Legend has it that a backpacker can equip himself with the gear he finds abandoned on the first few miles of the trail—but don't count on it. Sonie "Light Eagle" Shams, a 1988 thru-hiker who now is a ranger at Amicalola, says that on a single trip up to Springer she picked up an insulated down jacket, two wool sweaters, 150 feet of climbing rope, and a lot of fuel.

One day two girls left Amicalola for Springer Mountain, each carrying a gallon of Coleman fuel—maybe enough to get them to Maine. The staff tried to dissuade the girls. "But you can't tell a person you don't need it," Sonie said. "You can tell them there's going to be fuel at Neels Gap [forty miles away]. How much are you going to use here to there?"

Twenty-eight miles and maybe three days after starting the A.T., hikers reach Blood Mountain. They've survived the first big temptation to quit, the highway crossing at Woody Gap, where one can hitchhike into Suches, Georgia, and a bus home. The summit of Blood Mountain, 4,461 feet, the highest point on the A.T. in Georgia, offers views far into the distance.

The mountain takes its name from a battle between the Cherokee and Creek Indians. The Cherokee inhabited the northern half of Georgia into Virginia until most were forced to march west to Oklahoma in the deadly 1838 Trail of Tears. Of the sixteen thousand who began the winter march, four thousand died en route. The Cherokee left their mark along the way in names such as the Chattahoochee (stone and marked or flowered) and Nantahala (Land of the Noon-Day Sun) national forests, through which the A.T. runs in Georgia and North Carolina. Neels Gap was formerly Walasi-Yi (Place of the Frogs or Frogtown Gap) but was renamed after an engineer who put a highway through the gap in 1930. The Walasi-Yi Center, built as a lodge for Civilian Conservation Corps (CCC) workers in 1933 and converted to an inn in 1937, has been serving hikers for decades.

Pressure to push the Cherokee out grew intense after the discovery of gold in streambeds near Dahlonega, Georgia, in 1828, resulting in what is billed as America's first gold rush, although North Carolina claims a slightly earlier one. Tourists can still pan for gold in the area. The gold was "so pretty, there was no other gold in the world like it," a local miner claimed. "It was so pure, as pure as 98.6 percent right out of the ground." Gold was so plentiful here that in 1838, the same year as the Trail of Tears, a U.S. branch mint opened in Dahlonega. The name Dahlonega is said to be the Cherokee name for "precious yellow or gold." World War II marked the end of large-scale mining in the Georgia mountains.

Once hikers make the steep descent from Blood Mountain into Neels Gap, good fortune awaits. Here Dorothy and Jeff Hansen have been operating Mountain Crossings at Walasi-Yi (Wall-la-see-e) Center for ten years. Hikers not as prepared as they thought, or unexpectedly weary, find a place to stay, good food, a warm atmosphere, expert advice, and a store well equipped with practical backpacking gear. They will pass through a breezeway, the only place on the A.T. where the trail goes under a roof.

Dorothy Hansen thru-hiked in 1979 and Jeff has been an outdoor educator most of his life. Their staff includes experienced hikers such as 1987 2,000-miler Wayne "Sky" King. Jeff is renowned on the A.T. for examining hikers' packs and helping them discard much of what they thought was already the barest of essentials. Each year, from the Hansen place alone, the eight hundred or so hikers who visit send home four thousand pounds of gear—10 percent of pack weight. Some shed as much as thirty pounds. Many continue to prune pounds as they go. As Pieter Van Why points out, "It's all too easy to end up with a seventy-two-pound pack full of lightweight backpacking gear." Among the ridiculous items discarded at Walasi-Yi have been scuba gear, hardbound books, big hatchets, and large iron pans. Either the heavy gear or the people carrying it are soon gone from the trail.

Jeff Hansen believes hikers have gotten better at picking gear each year, but mentally they are no better prepared than ever. Yet most experienced hikers say that attitude and determination are the keys to a successful thru-hike. Equipment problems, after all, can be overcome. Jeff says that too many people believe that "if I just get my equipment right, all that's left is the walking." They don't understand that what's inside their head is more important than what's on their back. "It's you walking the trail, not the gear," he adds.

The north Georgia mountains are so rugged that the elite Army Rangers have based their mountain training programs there since 1952. Hikers are well advised to camp at or near the first four shelters along the trail because Ranger training includes frequent night patrols, which can cross the A.T. The Rangers try to avoid hikers and in particular the shelter areas. Hikers can take comfort knowing that if Ranger trainees stumble on civilians, they receive a lower grade. Hikers can also be assured that what these Rangers go through in their seventeen-day stint in these mountains is infinitely more difficult than the thru-hikers' transit. Rangers arrive at Camp Frank D. Merrill (named after the commander of Merrill's Marauders during World War II) by parachute and, as Jumpstart found out, there's not much open country here. While at Camp Merrill the soldiers learn rap-pelling, patrolling, and other skills. They get little food or sleep. A typical Ranger loses as much as forty pounds during his sixty-eight-day training program, twice what an average A.T. hiker loses in five to six months on the trail.

Robie "Jumpstart" Hensley

*E*xcept for a faded T-shirt with a picture of a parachutist and the label *"Jumpstart," nothing about Robie Hensley looks extraordinary. Still vig-orous at seventy, he's tackling new trails and challenges. I caught up to him in mid–March 1993, shortly after the big blizzard. He'd spent much of the day on top of a neighbor's tree doing some trimming, after having done some rock work building a fireplace for his daughter. "Other hikers think I'm either crazy or unique," Robie said. "Even now when I'm on the [Pacific Crest] trail in Califor-nia, I'll run across hikers and they all know about my jump. I'm surprised at the number of hikers who've heard of me."*

On March 9, 1986, when Robie "Jumpstart" Hensley planned to begin his first A.T. thru-hike, Springer Mountain was fogged in. Son Steve, pilot-ing a Cessna 182, took a look at the drop site and returned to the airport. An hour and a half later they tried again. By this time the fog had cleared, but the wind was still fierce. Robie's daughter Sherry, son-in-law Dave, and Dave's brother Don, waiting on top of Springer with Robie's backpack, launched a red smoke grenade to guide him to his landing site. To Steve, the jump target looked like "a postage stamp on the side of the mountain." He considered refusing to let his father jump but figured he'd just find another pilot. "Robie is a very determined man," he wrote in the introduction to Robie's *Appalachian Trail Journal.*

Because of the high winds, Robie jumped two miles upwind of Springer. "Even then, I had to hold against the wind until I got to the little clearing on top," Robie said. "I got caught in a downdraft and dropped in the trees, right near the start of the trail, within a stone's throw of the top marker. There was nothing but woods as far as you could see." His canopy was caught in two trees, leaving him "dangling between them like a grasshopper in a spider web." Recalling the jump, he said, "All it took was guts. I wouldn't attempt it again under those conditions."

Newly married, Robie returned to the trail in 1988 for a second thru-hike, this time with his wife, Lana. His family was relieved when this time he started the trail like everyone else, walking up Springer Mountain.

Robie had tried to take up parachuting several times earlier but gave up when people at the local club told him he was too old. "I finally started jumping when I was fifty," he said. "I've done nearly five hundred jumps. I quit logging my jumps at four hundred." Once he did a demonstration jump in Tennessee for President Reagan. He likes to drop in—literally—on neighbors who are having a cookout, and even at seventy he does about a dozen jumps a year. One year, he made an unscheduled jump into the Gathering of the Appalachian Long Distance Hikers Association (ALDHA) at Pipestem, West Virginia. His only jumping injuries have been several sprained ankles, a small broken bone in his leg, and bruises. "I wasn't scared in the first place when I started jumping," he said. "I just decided that when your time comes, that's it. Till then, I'll do what I want to do."

He first became interested in the A.T. in the 1930s when he worked for the Civilian Conservation Corps near the trail and hiked a little of it. After retiring, he welcomed the challenge of hiking long distances. Already a scuba diver and skydiver, he wanted something else. During World War II, the military rejected him several times because he had flat feet, convinced that he wouldn't be able to tolerate walking with a pack. Since he retired in 1985, he's backpacked more than six thousand miles.

On that first thru-hike, Robie didn't have to subsist on peanut butter and jelly sandwiches and macaroni and cheese like most hikers. Instead, Steve flew over the trail five times and dropped hot food, such as roast beef, pizza, and fried chicken.

Robie also obtained food along the trail. Most hikers dismiss the notion of gathering edible plants, hunting, and fishing along the trail. For one thing, the fourteen to fifteen miles that most single-year thru-hikers average per day doesn't leave much time or energy for gathering food. For another, it would be a logistical nightmare to obtain hunting and fishing licenses and information for all fourteen states through which the trail passes. Steve "Offshore Steve" Gomez, probably as devoted a fisherman as anyone who's ever hiked the trail, didn't even attempt to fish during his thru-hike. Another avid hunter and fisherman, Henry Phillips, says, "It's a big misconception that you can find your own food as you go along, do the Euell Gibbons thing. There's no place in this country where you can do that."

Robie probably picked up more food along the way than nearly any other hiker. Although he had never backpacked a day before hiking the A.T., he had hunted and fished and was quite comfortable in the woods. On his thru-hike, Robie saw a cornucopia where others saw nothing but brambles and brush. He carried fishing equipment and caught fish; captured and ate bullfrogs, crawdads, and snakes; picked hickory nuts and a wide assortment of berries, mushrooms, fruits, and other edible plants; gathered clams from a lake in Maine; and in late summer and early fall found corn, grapes, and apples.

His journal is sprinkled with delightful down-home country humor. Trying to hitchhike for a long time in southern Virginia, he wrote, "I thought I might get a blister on my thumb from waving it in the air." At Charlie's Bunion, a mountain in the Smokies with a sheer drop: "I thought if a fellow fell from here he'd have to take his lunch to keep from starving to death before he hit bottom." On a rainy day in Maine, it was "so foggy the birds were walking."

Robie wrote articles en route for his hometown newspaper, and some of his readers sent him encouraging mail. "I felt that I was hiking for them, for all those people who, for whatever reason, wanted to be out there but couldn't be. I kept feeding them all my experiences. That encouraged me so much I never felt alone."

To avoid severe cold and snow at the northern end of the trail, he took a bus from Harpers Ferry, West Virginia, near the trail's midpoint, to Mount Katahdin and began hiking south. Near the end of his trip, he wrote, "I think I'll be living my life differently when I return to that faster world." Speaking of the changes that came from hiking the trail, he said, "I got rid of a lot of things. If there was malice or hatred, I got rid of it. You get your priorities in order. You look inside, see who this person is, where you want to go."

When he finished the trail at Harpers Ferry, he'd changed so much that his daughter didn't recognize him. He was forty-two pounds lighter and had a long, white beard.

Summing up, he wrote, "Now that I've reached my destination, I realize it wasn't the destination that was important: it was the journey. It was hard work, but rest and food have never been as sweet. I've been in bad weather and on dangerous terrain and have discovered that strength and youth aren't as valuable as persistence is. And mostly I've just been overwhelmed by beauty—every day, every direction I looked. I won't ever forget it."

Who Are the Thru-Hikers?

What are these,
So wither'd and
so wild in their attire,
That look not like
th' inhabitants o' th'
earth, And yet are on't?

Macbeth, by William Shakespeare

P EOPLE USED TO CALL AN A.T. THRU-HIKE "THE ADVENTURE OF A
lifetime." Now, it's more like a jumping-off point into the world of
adventure. In 1989, Noel "the Singing Horseman" DeCavalcante
completed an A.T. thru-hike. In 1990, he paddled the Mississippi River for
three and a half months. That same year, one of Noel's 1989 hiking companions, Carol "Lagunatic" Moore, happened upon Jim "the Geek" Adams,
who was hiking the A.T. with his cat, Ziggy. The Geek was near the end of
what he called "the ultimate triathalon vacation." He and Ziggy had paddled
the Ohio and the Mississippi the previous fall. After hiking the A.T., they
would complete their adventure by bicycling from Maine to their starting
point in Pennsylvania. Eventually, the Geek and the Singing Horseman got
in touch with each other and traded tips for the rest of their adventures.

Who are these 2,000-milers and why do they hike the A.T.? Moreover,
why do they, and the thousands of other hikers, maintainers, and "trail
angels" who make up the A.T. community, feel such a strong attachment to
the trail?

Common to the 2,000-milers is a spirit of adventure. They are energetic wanderers, open to their dreams. Each requires a powerful impetus to keep going six months, up and down steep mountains, through all kinds of weather. Everyone who backpacks the A.T. experiences discomfort. Only those who can shrug off the miseries and savor the joys of the trail will last.

"The thru-hikers I've met seemed alive," said three-time 2,000-miler Albie Pokrob. "They had a spark in their eye, a wild look, full of life."

As of 1993, nearly three thousand people had reported to ATC that they hiked the entire trail, either in one trip or over many years. Nearly three-quarters have completed their trip since 1980, and 98 percent have done the trip since 1970. Myron H. Avery, one of the principal architects of the trail, was the first to complete it, in 1936, hiking sections over nine years. In 1948, Earl V. Shaffer became the first person to hike the entire trail in one trip—a true thru-hiker.

Thru-hikers are a remarkably diverse group. The youngest to hike the entire trail was Michael Cogswell, who was six in 1980 when he hiked with his parents, Jeffrey and Reina. Jeffrey had previously bicycled across the United States and canoed the Pacific. In an article Jeffrey wrote after they completed the A.T. (in eight and a half months), he quoted Michael as saying, "I learned that anytime I can't do something, all I have to do is try harder."

Ernie Morris completed the trail in 1975 at age eighty-six. He did it in several long stretches over four years, always carrying a heavy backpack. Thru-hikers have come from as far away as England, Australia, Hawaii, and Alaska. The trail has been home to twins, brothers and sisters, fathers and sons, mothers and daughters, married couples, groups of college students, speed-hikers, free spirits, and more serious sorts. In recent years, about 20 percent of the thru-hikers have been women. The handicapped have been well represented, including a blind man (two others did half the trail), a three-time hiker with multiple sclerosis, a deaf person, and at least one with a hip replacement. Occupations range from none to retired admiral to Supreme Court justice. Many thru-hikers hold advanced academic degrees, including Ph.D.s, and many dissertations have been written about the trail and related subjects. Doctors, surgeons, and nurses are not unknown, nor are teachers, Alaskan fish canners, engineers, clergymen, or those pursuing "alternative lifestyles." A large number are retired military men. Eagle Scouts are common. Some are artists, singers, rangers, and outdoor educators.

What you generally will not find are genuine mountain men. Many

"Years ago, they hiked the Appalachian Trail from end to end,
and they never let you forget it."

thru-hikers can't even identify poison ivy. Few of today's hikers have grown up on farms or even in rural areas. Roger Brickner, who has met more 2,000-milers than all but a handful of people, says thru-hikers hail mostly from the suburbs.

Not surprisingly, long-distance hikers tend to be introverts. Dr. O. W. "Red Owl" Lacy, a psychologist, has studied the personalities of 2,000-milers and trail activists for more than a decade, compiling profiles of more than eight hundred hikers, including five hundred thru-hikers. He found that introverts are twice as common among 2,000-milers as among the general population. In the population at large, two-thirds to three-quarters are extroverts. Among hikers, two-thirds are introverts. "That's an overwhelming discrepancy. It's a clear-cut and well-established profile," said Dr. Lacy (who completed the trail in 1980 after a decade of walking bits and pieces). Particular types of introverts that are rare in general are common among 2,000-milers. At the other end of the spectrum, few thru-hikers are extreme extroverts. It makes sense, because even hikers who complete the whole trail with a partner usually walk alone a large part of the day.

Although "everyone needs to extrovert a little every day," too much socializing drains introverts and energizes extroverts. "The introvert gets his or her energy from the inner world of ideas and feelings and images," says Dr. Lacy. "Extroverts get their energy from the outer world of activity, of people and things. The large majority of the population prefers to see the world in terms of facts, what's tangible. But among hikers, two-thirds prefer to see the world in terms of possibilities."

Perhaps the archetypal personality of a long-distance hiker was that of Henry David Thoreau. He was an independent loner, a lover of nature, a dreamer. Although he didn't take many long hikes, he was comfortable for long periods with his own company. Throughout his life, he had trouble reconciling himself to the dictates of society.

Since few extreme extroverts are on the trail, they stand out. One day in April 1980, Rick Hancock, Jeff "the Chief" Laverdiere, and Al "A.T. Al" Sochard decided to hike under a full moon north from Hot Springs, North Carolina. "We did it," Rick said, "and we wanted everyone to know we did it." What they did was hike twenty miles to Little Laurel Shelter, arriving well after midnight singing a loud chorus of "When the Saints Come Marching In." They roused a packed shelter and a half dozen hikers tenting nearby. "Just about everybody was mad at us," Rick said. "Looking back on it, we shouldn't have done it."

Despite the extreme physical effort needed to complete the trail, most thru-hikers do not possess special athletic prowess. In fact, strong athletes are more likely to aggressively challenge the trail and exit with injuries than are the frail and the cautious. Most 2,000-milers say attitude and determination are far more important than strength and conditioning. Women less than ninety pounds have hiked the trail with full backpacks. An early thru-hiker, Grandma Gatewood, said "Head is more important than heel."

As part of their pilgrimage, most thru-hikers assume a new identity—a trail name. Trail names on the A.T. go back at least to the early seventies, but they caught on in the late seventies, when the number of hikers increased dramatically. Now trail names are almost mandatory. Examples of actual trail names are included as chapter headings in this book. Some fit so well that after a while it's hard to recall the hikers' given names. Trail names reflect a sort of split personality, in which one's trail identity is far removed from one's other life in, say, the corporate world. Trail names are so widespread that one can hike with someone for weeks and not know the name his parents would use.

"It's dropping one persona and taking on another," said Leonard

"Habitual Hiker" Adkins. "In high school and college, people get nicknames. Trail names show that you are being accepted into the club. You're freer to become someone you always wanted to be."

Greg "Pooh" Knoettner, assistant ATC field representative in New England, earned his trail name when he left the A.T. in 1989 to attend his sister's college graduation in upstate New York. On his way back to the trail, he was waiting for a train at Pennsylvania Station in New York City. He set his pack down too hard and a big glass jar of honey inside the pack shattered. The honey went over everything, Greg recounted. "So I'm sitting on the ground in my grungy thru-hiker clothes in Pennsylvania Station, taking things out and licking them off and putting them down next to me. I felt like a derelict. Then some guy, faking a foreign accent, came up to me and said 'Rockefeller Station. How do I get to Rockefeller Station?' I knew from my days living right across the river in New Jersey so I started explaining to him. Then he said, 'No. Write down.' I wrote it down and gave it to him. Then he said 'thank you' and disappeared. I looked down and my camera equipment was gone. My jacket was gone. I'd been scammed. He and somebody else had robbed me and it was all because of this stupid jar of honey." Like Winnie, Greg the Pooh is now known for his love of honey.

Why thru-hike? More often than not, people turn to the trail at times of radical change in their life: when they're graduating from school, considering a new career, retiring, or dealing with personal trauma such as divorce, loss of job, or the death of a close friend or relative. Some are disillusioned with a job or just burned out. One thru-hiker did the trail after both his divorces. Others hike the trail for the physical and mental challenge, to see if they can attain a goal that demands dedication and focus. Still others want to get closer to nature and to enjoy the trail community. Paul "Lucky, Lucky, Lucky" Holabaugh said just once in his life he wanted to get into the woods and see what life was like for the pioneers.

Often, the origin of a desire to hike the trail is murky. It is, after all, hard to remember the origin of a dream. Sometimes it's a chance remark by a friend, a newspaper article, an earlier encounter with the trail that is nurtured in the dim recesses of the mind for decades until it one day pops out unbidden with surprising force. Many began thinking about the A.T. after spotting a highway sign at a trail crossing. For others, it's more of a spur-of-the-moment decision; before they know it, they are on the trail in Georgia carrying a heavy backpack north.

As a teenager, Laurie "Mountain Laurel" Potteiger saw a slide show by a thru-hiker. He said that when he reached a town, he'd eat a whole pie. "When I heard that," said Laurie, "I said, 'This thing's for me.'"

For Gordon "Old Man" Gamble, a retired AT&T engineer, hiking the trail was a dream nurtured for fifteen years until retirement made it possible. He used the time wisely, planning his thru-hike meticulously to ease the stress on his frail, sixty-six-year-old body and arthritic knees.

Barb Briggs, a 1986 thru-hiker from New Hampshire, first met a 2,000-miler in 1985. After talking to him for a while, "I figured if he could do it, I could do it," she said.

Some thru-hikers had previous backpacking or outdoor experience. But at least as many others had backpacked only a few days before they did the A.T. A few thru-hikers had never backpacked as much as a day before they journeyed to Springer Mountain. According to Roly Mueser, who did a detailed study of A.T. thru-hikers, some 10 to 20 percent had little or no backpacking experience before starting the A.T. Many are the only hikers in their families. Many thru-hikers feel that inexperienced backpackers have as good a chance as veterans to complete the trail. If, as two-time thru-hiker Phil Pepin says, mental attitude is 90 percent of the requirement for the trip, those with a powerful desire have an advantage over those with technical skills but less commitment. Indeed, much of the useful backpacking knowledge can be acquired en route, for the A.T. is like a university of hiking. On this trail, one finds some of the world's most experienced backpackers, many of whom know every trick in the books and some that aren't there. Being a novice doesn't preclude a successful thru-hike, but most hikers stress that you should prepare extensively before starting.

In the 1970s, it was not unusual to find teenagers hiking the trail alone. Most hikers were either college-age or younger, or retirees; few were in their thirties or forties. Recently, teenagers on the trail have become rare; hikers in their middle and senior years are common. Elmer Hall thinks the trend of teenage hikers in the seventies was part of a wave of rebellious youths traveling the world. As for the older hikers, Jean Cashin of ATC attributes it partly to downturns in the economy. People who lose their jobs frequently turn to the trail as a cheap place to review their options and gather their resolve.

Another trend is that more women are hiking the trail. Many hike with a husband or boyfriend, but some have no partner. Of the three thousand people who had completed the trail by 1993, more than three hundred were women.

Bill "Stats Godric" Gunderson

*A*t *the ATC's biennial meeting in Dahlonega, Georgia, Bill "Sprained Rice" O'Brien told me Stats had just set up his seventy-five-foot-long map of the A.T. and I should go see it. He said to be sure to climb the ladder to get the best viewpoint. Painstakingly done, Bill Gunderson's map gives the best perspective I've seen on Appalachian Mountain terrain. "I started without realizing what I was getting into," Bill said.*

Perhaps Bill Gunderson's fascination with elevation profiles has a simple explanation. After all, he's spent his entire life in the flat areas of Chicago and Minnesota.

By chance, Bill came across the A.T. during a New England bus trip in 1985. He saw a line on a map that represented the A.T. Curious, he got out in Vermont, hiked over Killington, and thought it was great. During the next few years, he continued to hike. Finally, in 1989, he thru-hiked the A.T.

A year later, in November 1990, he started doodling on a detailed map of Virginia. "I didn't have a great plan," he says. "It was doodling that kept building on itself." He picked 1,000-meter contours (about 3,500 feet) to color in. He was curious about the highland areas. There were many near Mount Rogers but few around Roanoke and none near the A.T. Large areas of West Virginia were at that elevation; but his gazetteer ended and he was curious to see how far those areas went.

He ordered the U.S. Geological Survey maps of North Carolina, Georgia, and West Virginia to see the areas above one thousand meters. But that elevation didn't show much in the Northeast, so he lowered his hurdle to seven hundred meters, where red spruce starts. He started coloring the forests green; he chose red to show the low, flat ridges of Pennsylvania. Looking at the area these elevations would cover, he decided it would be too much work to do the south. But, being incomplete, it "looked stupid," he said. "I gritted my teeth and started coloring in the western slopes." He ordered more maps, and his living room filled up.

He'd order ten U.S. Geological Survey maps at a time. He'd finish those and order more. A year later, after devoting most of his spare time to the map, he was finished. It had grown to seventy-five feet, consisting of 135 topographic maps from Alabama to Canada. On each, he had painstakingly colored in areas bounded by the contour lines. He used six colors, each representing three hundred meters (nearly a thousand feet) of elevation change.

The overall effect is striking. "Seeing it as a whole really showed me the complexity of the mountains," Bill said. Nowhere else can one get such a detailed and compelling perspective on the Appalachian Mountains. One sees the steep drop-offs, the great gorges carved by rivers, and the serpentine ridge pattern from the Alabama foothills to the higher peaks of Tennessee, North Carolina, and New England. It's like looking at the earth from a spaceship orbiting at one hundred miles up.

Bill deliberately refused to put in state lines or political boundaries. He said, "I'm just interested in the mountains and where the ridge lines are." For Bill, one of the map's clear lessons is that there are "a lot of other mountains to know, love, and protect" besides the ones the A.T. touches. Although it's two thousand miles long, the trail corridor is only one thousand feet wide.

Bill had hiked a little before his thru-hike. His main "shakedown" trip was a ten-day backpacking trek on the A.T. in 1988. He decided after that to do the whole trail. The contrast between those two years "was really wild," he said. A drought in 1988 put Watauga Lake, Tennessee, forty feet lower than usual. One could walk across part of the lake bed, saving a half mile of hiking. In 1989, it was so wet one couldn't even walk on the trail.

All through the south in 1989, Bill faced severe weather. He was in the worst hailstorm of his life near Woody Gap, Georgia. For the first week and a half, he was hit with seven inches of snow, and it was always below freezing. After Hot Springs, North Carolina, it was "cold and wet." One day in early May, when he was hiking into Damascus, Virginia, it never rose above thirty-eight degrees. The bad weather strengthened the camaraderie of the hikers.

At Brown Mountain Shelter, near Lynchburg, Virginia, his spirits reached low ebb after four straight days of rain. "My feet were tired of being wet," he said. But he'd quit his job and wasn't prepared to drop off the trail. "To save embarrassment, I wasn't going to renege for any minor reason," he said.

He reached McAfee Knob in Virginia just as the sun was setting and found the view to be one of the best on the trail.

Bill's worst day began when he hiked from Upper Goose Pond, Massachusetts. He left his guidebook there and had to walk back a mile to retrieve it. On a rough, relocated stretch of trail he cut his hand. An overhanging branch almost poked his eye out. He thought, "What else can go wrong?"

In the Maine wilderness, he broke his pack and spent two days getting it fixed. Meanwhile, his trail friends had gone ahead, and he wanted to find them to finish the trail together. He hiked twenty-six miles past Abol Bridge into Baxter State Park. He came to a rocky stream, but it was so dark he couldn't see a thing. He camped right on the trail. Early the next morning, Bill made it to Daicey Pond, where most thru-hikers stay the day before climbing Katahdin. He didn't see his friends, but he started up. "I ran up the mountain, I was so happy to be there."

On top, he saw no one except a father and son, both celebrating their birthdays that day with a cherry pie. Bill joined their celebration, and later located his friends back at Daicey Pond and climbed again with them the next day.

Of finishing the trail, Bill said, "I was sad. It was a letdown. The trail became part of my life. I wanted it to keep going." After being home for a week, he went to an ALDHA gathering. From there, he finished forty miles of trail that he'd skipped. The continuing trail ties helped him gradually acclimatize to the outside world.

One thing Bill especially misses from the trail is the way "the wind was always in my face when I slept." He adds, "I'm still sleeping on the floor. I rarely sleep in a bed. It keeps me in trail shape." After the trail, he "kept looking for blazes. Traffic seemed strange, how quickly it moved and how much there was." He has tried to stay "self-propelled," relying on bicycling and walking for transportation.

After his hike, Bill became involved with prairie restoration. "I've learned to value grasses a lot more. I'm not so fond of trees. On top of a mountain in the East, you feel big. You never really feel the size of the Earth as you do on the plains. I have changed my values. I appreciate the Appalachians, but I have learned to appreciate the Midwest, the unlimited horizons."

A History of the Trail

Make no little plans: They have no magic to stir men's blood.

Daniel H. Burnham

A S A YOUNG MAN, BENTON MACKAYE CONCEIVED OF A TRAIL connecting the ridgetops of the Appalachian Mountains from New England to the South. The idea of a long-distance trail was shared by others, including J. Ashton Allis, Will Monroe, James Taylor, and Allen Chamberlain, who had made detailed proposals for trails in the Northeast. Existing trails included the Long Trail in Vermont, several trails in the White Mountains of New Hampshire, such as the Crawford Path, dating to the early nineteenth century, and heavily used trails along the Hudson Valley and the Hudson Highlands in New York. All of these were later incorporated into the A.T.

MacKaye's concept had crystalized in his mind for several decades. In later years he gave differing accounts of what inspired him. The most accepted account involves a six-week hiking trip he took after graduating from Harvard in 1900. While atop Stratton Mountain in Vermont, he visualized a ridgetop trail spanning the Appalachians. At other times, MacKaye said the A.T. idea may have come to him on one of his youthful expeditions in the New England mountains or while listening to a talk by Southwest explorer John Wesley Powell.

Born in Stamford, Connecticut, in 1879, Benton spent his boyhood roaming the hills near Shirley Center, Massachusetts, where he lived much of his life. He received a master's degree in forestry from Harvard in 1905, and his first job in the White Mountains helped lead to the area's designation as a national forest in 1911. MacKaye became a revered figure in A.T. circles, and his desk and library were put on display at Harpers Ferry by retired colonel Lester Holmes, first ATC executive director.

MacKaye conceived the A.T. as more than a hiking trail; he saw it as the backbone of a recreational network for people crowded into cities along the eastern seaboard. He believed the purpose of the trail was to "extend the primeval environment and to set bounds to the metropolitan environment." He also hoped to tie in cottage industries to provide work for impoverished mountain people. Only elements of his proposal survived. But surely, he would be proud that today nearly the entire trail corridor is protected and is the focus for protecting surrounding lands.

In July 1921, two friends persuaded MacKaye to write an article, which appeared that October in the *American Institute of Architects Journal*. MacKaye did not simply propose ideas in the article and then vanish. Had he done that, there would have been no A.T. Instead, he waged a highly focused campaign to locate and inspire trail activists and to lay the groundwork for an organization capable of completing this monumental task. These trail pioneers were few in number but large in spirit, and totally dedicated to the cause. Within weeks of the article's publication, MacKaye and his new friend, Clarence Stein, were mailing out reprints. MacKaye also traveled the East Coast promoting his proposal. He met with Allen Chamberlain and attended a New England Trail Conference meeting.

In 1922, MacKaye asked Chamberlain to suggest hikers whom he could contact in Washington, D.C. He eventually met with a half dozen, including Dr. Lawrence Schmeckebier, who later became president of the Potomac Appalachian Trail Club (PATC). That spring, MacKaye attended one of the first meetings of the Palisades Trail Conference, the forerunner of today's New York–New Jersey Trail Conference. Because of these efforts, work on the A.T. began in Harriman Park, New York, in 1922.

From his days at Harvard and working in the White Mountains, MacKaye knew the leaders of many local hiking groups. He would eventually credit many of them as key figures in the early trail work. Others he credited included Verne Rhoades, who was in charge of acquiring land for the Great Smoky Mountains National Park and later head of Pisgah National Forest in North Carolina. Dr. Halstead Hedges did initial scouting of the route in southwestern Virginia, then one of the most remote stretches of the A.T. On March 2–3, 1925, a small group met in Washington, D.C., to form the Appalachian Trail Conference (ATC). Benton MacKaye became the group's field organizer.

Within a year of ATC's formation, the initial surge of activity had slowed dramatically. Arthur Perkins, a retired Hartford lawyer, took the reins and revitalized the project. He also gets credit for attracting to the A.T. Myron H. Avery, a young associate with his law firm. A native of Maine, Avery was an expert on the Katahdin area, where he had first became interested in the A.T. project. Avery succeeded Perkins as ATC chairman after Perkins's death in 1931, holding the post until shortly before his own death in 1952.

Avery and PATC spearheaded the A.T.'s completion. In the A.T.'s early years, PATC built and maintained much of the trail from the North Carolina–Virginia line to the Susquehanna River in Pennsylvania, nearly a third of the A.T.'s length. With the ATC chairman based in Washington, his fellow PATC members became the nucleus of the entire A.T. project. For many years it was difficult to separate the two organizations. The ATC even had its office in the PATC building until moving to Harpers Ferry in 1972. Avery, along with other PATC members, helped form other hiking clubs. Avery was a founder of the Maine Appalachian Trail Club (MATC) in 1935. A Mainer, Walter D. Greene, was the first MATC president and a key force in locating the trail through the Maine wilderness. Avery also helped found the Georgia Appalachian Trail Club and the Smoky Mountain Hiking Club, among others. These were especially important because the South did not have much of an organized hiking community.

Although it is tempting to describe Avery as a one-man band (and he was), hundreds of other people contributed to building the A.T. Without them, and the network of local clubs, it's hard to imagine that the A.T. could have been built so quickly almost from scratch. Half the trail was marked by the time Avery became ATC chairman in 1931. The final two-mile A.T. stretch in Maine was finally completed on August 14, 1937, only sixteen years after the publication of MacKaye's original article. The last link was a densely wooded stretch between Spaulding and Sugarloaf Mountains nearly two hundred miles by trail south of Katahdin. No celebration marked the trail's completion. The only indication was one sentence tucked in a letter to Avery from Leon Brooks, head of the CCC group that blazed and cleared the stretch.

At the 1937 ATC meeting in Gatlinburg, Tennessee, Myron Avery, knowing that the trail would soon be completely linked, said, "Those of us, who have physically worked on the Trail, know that the Trail, as such, will never be completed." That was an apt prophecy, given that the trail was severed the next year and wasn't linked again for more than a decade. In the years since, hundreds of relocations and continual work on existing sections have borne out Avery's remarks.

Looking back, it's hard to overestimate the obstacles those early trail builders faced. Outside of the Northeast, there were few existing trails to incorporate. Maine and southwestern Virginia were "utter wilderness." The Great Smoky Mountains and Shenandoah National Parks, the Skyline Drive, and the Blue Ridge Parkway were yet to be built.

Paul Fink was the last surviving ATC founder. Arch Nichols, who served on the ATC board for almost forty years, credited Rhoades and Fink with locating the trail in the South. Fink had been hiking and studying the Smokies for a decade, when, in 1922, he developed a map for a proposed southern end of the A.T.

Shortly before he died at age eighty-eight, Paul Fink wrote from his nursing home, "I sit in this room, with never a hope of getting out, with thoughts running through my mind of how delightful it would be to be lying by a trailside under a big balsam tree with no sound unless it be the twittering of the birds and the rustle of the breeze in the tree branches above. That, too, is a no-no, but nothing can keep me from thinking and remembering and living over in retrospect some of the joys of years now long gone."

The A.T. has often benefited from favorable publicity. Articles in the *Reader's Digest* in the early seventies and eighties flooded ATC with requests for information. Much earlier, the *PATC Bulletin* described "A Crisis at A.T.C. Headquarters" a year after an article appeared in 1942: ATC stopped counting after two thousand requests for information.

An oft-cited quote describing the A.T. dates from the trail's early days, probably the early thirties:

> Remote for detachment,
> narrow for chosen company,
> winding for leisure,
> lonely for contemplation,
> the Trail leads not merely north and south
> but upward to the body, mind and soul of man.

The author, Harold Allen, is now largely forgotten, except for this quote, but he contributed greatly to the trail's development. Avery thought that as time went on, Allen's contribution would loom larger. A government lawyer like Avery, Allen was active both in PATC and ATC. He edited the first PATC guidebook, *Guide to Paths in the Blue Ridge.* "If there was any publication that needed to be done, he was the one they got," said Ruth Blackburn, a former PATC president and ATC chair. Avery credited Allen with developing the guidebook style that ATC continued to use. At a time when trail markings were sparse and little information was available about the trail, guidebooks were critical in making the trail accessible to the public.

Harold Allen was also a key figure in the creation of Shenandoah National Park. One of the first to advocate a national park in the East, Allen worked hard to preserve the Blue Ridge. With several others, including George Pollack, owner of the Skylands Resort (through which the A.T. passes), Allen helped build support for Shenandoah. Jean Stephenson, founding editor of the *Appalachian Trailway News,* wrote that Allen was truly "the father of Shenandoah National Park." Born in Pittsburgh in 1877, Allen was the great-grandson of William Wilson, a government agent to the Indians. Many of Wilson's holdings were among the land that Allen helped to protect. Ending his career at the I.R.S., Allen was said to have been one of the country's most brilliant trial lawyers. He died in 1939. Myron Avery wrote of Allen, "For me, Harold Allen, the Virginia Blue Ridge and Shenandoah National Park will forever be associated. My earliest acquaintance with the Shenandoah region came through him. His enthusiasm and knowledge of the area soon developed a community of interests and of activity. Without Harold Allen's particular genius, this movement might never have reached the stage where it attracted national attention. Allen has left an indelible impression upon the Appalachian Trail movement."

Few men played a bigger role in building the trail than J. Frank Schairer. A geologist with the Carnegie Institute in Washington, he was equally comfortable in an urban setting or drinking and carousing with mountain people. Some of these people, isolated in remote mountain hollows, were intensely distrustful of outsiders and suspicious of a "government trail." A born raconteur, as well as a scholar, Schairer helped to bridge that gap. A distinguished scientist who won the Medal of Freedom for scientific achievement, Schairer was PATC supervisor of trails from 1930 until he resigned in 1943. Schairer was one of a handful of PATC members who joined Avery and Walter Greene, a Broadway actor and summer resident of Maine, on a trip in 1933 to open the northernmost section of the trail, from Katahdin to Monson,

Maine. This 119-mile section was, and still is one of the wildest parts of the entire A.T. Avery described the section as "utter wilderness," and others thought it too wild for a trail. But they were wrong. Myron Avery was not about to settle for Mount Washington as the trail's northern end. Today, most thru-hikers consider Maine the best section of the entire trail. Signs today warn hikers to carry a ten-day supply of food because they can't resupply between Monson and Abol Bridge, at either end of the section. Yet, ironically, in the early 1930s before the trail was built, so many sporting camps were scattered throughout the Maine woods that a hiker could find meals and lodging every day throughout the entire section.

Another Maine native who made a major contribution to the early A.T. was Jean Stephenson. In addition to trail work in Maine and the Washington area, she authored ATC's first book on standards for trail maintenance, edited guidebooks, and was founding editor of ATC's magazine, the *Appalachian Trailway News*, in 1939. Much of the trail's mystique can be attributed to the *A.T. News*, which has preserved the trail's heritage.

Two people who epitomize the A.T.'s builders are Ruth and Fred Blackburn. Both worked for more than fifty years on the trail, and both served three terms as PATC president. In 1929, Fred saw a notice soliciting workers who were skilled with tools to help on the trail. Having grown up on a farm in Pennsylvania, he was adept at the construction techniques needed to carve a trail out of heavy forests. Ruth remembers many years of weekend work trips along the trail. Typifying the unglamorous work of trail volunteers, Ruth spent more than twenty years at Maryland county courthouses and other offices, poring over tax records and section maps to clear the way for a land-protection preservation effort. She was ATC chair in the 1980s and, at eighty-six, is still active in trail affairs. "The trail project came along at the right time when there was still enough wild country," she said. "If we had to do it now, I don't think we could."

Another trail pioneer was the Reverend A. Rufus Morgan. Reverend Morgan, who grew up and lived much of his life in western North Carolina, had a church near where the A.T. crosses Wallace Gap, North Carolina, about thirty miles from Georgia. The A.T. was in his family. Albert Mountain, known for its steep final ascent, was named for his grandfather, Albert Siler; Silers Bald in the Smokies for his great-great uncle, Jesse Siler; and a Siler's Bald, in the Nantahalas, for his great-grandfather, William Siler. Reverend Morgan left his own mark, namely the A. Rufus Morgan Trail near Siler's Bald on the Mountains to the Sea Trail and an A.T. shelter south of

Wesser, North Carolina. For twenty-five years, he alone maintained as much as fifty-five miles of the A.T. Now, most individual maintainers handle three miles, and few people do more than seven. He served on the A.T. board for twenty-nine years, and his efforts led to the founding of the Nantahala Hiking Club. On his ninety-second birthday, he climbed Mount LeConte in the Smokies for the 172nd and last time.

From the time it was completed, the A.T. remained the longest continuously marked trail in the world until June 5, 1993, when the Pacific Crest Trail usurped that distinction. After the A.T.'s initial completion, trailworkers had only a brief respite. In 1938, thirteen months after the A.T. was linked, a severe hurricane blew through the northeastern United States, downing trees across hundreds of miles of the A.T. Roger Brickner, a 2,000-miler and ATC life member, chronicled the storm in his book, *The Long Island Express: Tracking the Hurricane of 1938*. One of the worst natural disasters in U.S. history, the storm killed nearly seven hundred people and left sixty thousand homeless. More than 270 million trees were destroyed, including one third of Vermont's sugar maples and half of New Hampshire's white pines. A few years later, World War II severely limited trail activities. Most able-bodied men entered the service, and gas and tire rationing restricted transportation to remote areas of the trail. After the war, limited highway construction and resistance from private landowners caused more problems in many trail states. Construction of the Blue Ridge Parkway, which began in 1935, prompted a 118-mile relocation of the A.T. in southwestern Virginia. In the fifties and sixties, proposals to extend the parkway into Georgia and to build ridgetop parkways in Vermont, Virginia, and New Jersey further threatened the trail. Not until 1951, with the opening of a six-mile section across the Tye River Valley between Three Ridges and Priest Mountain in Virginia, was the Blue Ridge relocation completed and the trail fully reopened. Even then, early thru-hikers complained that the trail was inadequately cleared and hard to follow.

Early trail leaders knew that construction of the A.T. was only the beginning. The ATC chairmen who followed Avery, Murray Stevens and Stanley Murray, supported a "greenway," a protective buffer on both sides of the trail (an idea that dates from MacKaye's original article) to defend against homes and roads that were being built near the trail. Without a buffer of protected land, they realized, the trail's continuity and wilderness character would be threatened.

As early as 1945, Congressman Daniel Hoch of Pennsylvania, an early

Walking the Appalachian Trail

member of the Blue Mountain Eagle Climbing Club, introduced a bill to protect the trail. But not until 1968 did a bill pass. Ray Hunt, a 2,000-miler and former ATC chair, recalls that Stanley Murray struggled with the decision of whether to seek federal protection for the A.T. Murray knew that federal help meant loss of control and bureaucratic interference.

Senator Gaylord Nelson, later counselor to the Wilderness Society, finally introduced a bill that became the National Scenic Trails Act of 1968. It designated three national scenic trails, including the A.T., and provided funds to acquire land to protect the trails. At the 1993 A.T. meeting, Senator Nelson recalled that PATC member Cecil Cullander had convinced him that without federal protection the A.T. would not survive. Work progressed slowly until 1976, when David Richie, a lawyer and career National Park Service employee, created a special A.T. project office that he headed until 1987. Low-key and dedicated, Richie took a controversial program, defused most of the hostility, and quietly completed his task. As has happened so often with the trail, a key person came along at a critical juncture. Inspired by his own A.T. work, Richie became a 2,000-miler himself in 1986, hiking sections over seven years.

Today, nearly six thousand volunteers work on the trail each year. In the early days, there were fewer people, but they worked endless hours. Federal employees did work in the national forests and parks, but it was the volunteers who built and maintained most of the trail.

Not until 1968 did ATC hire its first paid employee, Lester Holmes, as part-time executive director. Holmes, discovering that the Park Service had extra space in a building in historic Harpers Ferry, West Virginia, moved the ATC there in 1972 to be closer to the trail. A second employee, Jean Cashin, joined as office manager that year. Currently, she is the ATC information specialist and unofficial "trail mother" and advisor to hikers. In 1976, chairman George Zoebelein moved the conference headquarters a few blocks to its current home on one of Harpers Ferry's main streets.

Today, the ATC is a loose mix of local clubs and thousands of volunteers. But the prominent headquarters in Harpers Ferry has helped create a firm identity for the ATC. In addition to preserving and protecting the trail, ATC manages thousands of acres that the government acquired for the trail corridor. Recently the emphasis has switched from protecting the trail itself to preserving the quality of the trail experience.

Myron H. Avery

*B*orn in Lubec, Maine, in 1899, Myron Avery was a man who provoked *definite opinions; few people were neutral about him. Possessing almost superhuman energy and dedication, he stood out as a leader from an early age. He surrounded himself with talented, capable people, dedicated to their tasks. Bill Mersch, who started as the PATC bus driver on group trips in 1939 and succeeded Frank Schairer as supervisor of trails in 1943, said of Avery: "Myron left two trails from Maine to Georgia. One was of hurt feelings and bruised egos. The other was the A.T. The first will disappear, the second will last."*

After attending Bowdoin College in Maine and Harvard Law School, Avery joined a law firm in Hartford that also included Arthur Perkins, who became ATC chairman. Myron was founding president of the PATC, assistant ATC chair at age twenty-seven, and head of ATC at thirty-one. Myron was in a leadership position for ten of the sixteen years between the publication of Benton MacKaye's article and completion of the A.T.

He could be brusque and abrasive. A Navy veteran of two world wars and a winner of the Legion of Merit, he was used to command. But he loved the woods. He edited guidebooks, wrote more than one hundred articles, and maintained a prolific correspondence, all in precise, beautiful prose. The leading authority on Katahdin, he wrote many articles about the area and co-edited a seventy-page Katahdin bibliography. He also edited the *A.T. Guide to Maine,* the *Guide to Paths in the Blue Ridge,* and *Guide to the A.T. in the Southern Appalachians,* as well as Arnold Guyot's *Mountain Regions of Western North Carolina.* A stickler for details, Avery wrote long, detailed letters correcting some of the early maps of Katahdin. His articles covered recreation in the mountains and woods, camping equipment, trail techniques, and the historical background of the Maine woods.

Avery traveled, directed, and wrote—all for the A.T.'s benefit. He pushed a measuring wheel over all of the trail. On the trail nearly every weekend, Avery made long trips to Maine, the White Mountains, the Virginia Blue Ridge, and the Smokies. On one three-day weekend, he hiked with a twenty-five-pound pack, pushing his measuring wheel seventy miles through a rough section of the Blue Ridge to Apple Orchard Camp. There he helped found the Natural Bridge A.T. Club. Later that fall he helped form two other clubs in Virginia. On another weekend trip, Avery cut sixteen miles of trail in Maryland, and shortly thereafter led a ten-day trip to the White Mountains. He organized work trips and outings, and personally trained many volunteers. He himself maintained a section of trail in Shenandoah, from Panorama to Skyland. By 1936, before the trail was completely finished, he had walked the entire route at least once, most of it twice or more.

For someone who spent much of his adult life at desk jobs, he was amazingly fit. He could hike and do trail work all day, leaving weary rangers by the wayside. Helon Taylor, a longtime supervisor of Baxter State Park and a legendary hiker, recalled some of Avery's feats in an interview with the *A.T. News:* "I thought I was pretty good on the Trail. I was amazed to think that any man could hike faster than I could and push a bicycle wheel at the same time." Helon added, "He knew more about Maine than most anybody I ever met. He could stand and talk and keep you interested for hours."

Avery's roots went deep in Maine. He considered himself a resident and kept a house in Lubec, a seafaring town of two thousand people, throughout his life. Avery, who would come to be considered one of the country's top admiralty lawyers, married Jeannette Lechie in 1925 and had two sons.

A strong personality, Avery quarrelled with both Benton MacKaye and Governor Percival Baxter of Maine, who, like Avery, attended Bowdoin College and Harvard Law School. Avery and MacKaye split in 1936 after an angry exchange of letters, partly over their positions on the building of the Skyline Drive, which would displace the A.T. in Shenandoah National Park. Avery favored the parkway as a way of providing access to hikers, but Mac-Kaye was opposed to such an intrusion in the wild mountains. Apparently, the rift between the two never healed before Avery's death sixteen years later.

At first, Avery welcomed Baxter's establishment of a state park, calling it a "farsighted act." Later, he became convinced that the area was becoming too developed and that the state was not adequately protecting the wilderness. In the mid-thirties, Avery supported making the area a national park. Governor Baxter, however, squelched that effort.

Though not a diplomat, Avery inspired intense loyalty. From his base in Washington, he recruited strong leaders and directed trail work all along the route. His attention to detail, from trail signs to guidebooks to proofreading, combined with a strong opinion of what the A.T. should be, brought the trail to fruition during the difficult time of the Great Depression and World War II. MacKaye is generally seen as the visionary, Avery the implementer, but Avery, too, had a vision, and much of what he accomplished, he created from scratch. He took great pains to attract public interest and make the trail accessible. In 1952, in his final address to ATC, Avery spoke about the appeal of the trail: "The Appalachian Trail does derive much of its strength and appeal from its uninterrupted and practically endless character. This is an attribute which must be preserved. I view the existence of this pathway and the opportunity to travel it, day after day without interruption, as a distinct aspect of our American life."

Shailer Philbrick, who accompanied Avery on the 1933 trip to Maine, said of Avery, "He was so delightful, so quick, and so full of humor. He was fun to be with. One of the greatest men I ever knew."

Fannie Eckstorm, the Maine historian, wrote to Avery about that time conveying the impressions of someone who had just met him. "Mr. Mellinger Henry wrote me an enthusiastic letter about his trip to Washington and of you said, 'Mr. Avery is very self-sacrificing, genial, energetic, hospitable and much concerned about the welfare of others. It is very easy to understand now why the Potomac Trail Club and the A.T. Conference are so successful.'" Robert B. MacMullin, upon first meeting Avery in Washington, described him as having "the body of an athlete, hard as nails, and built for endurance." Avery spent two days in 1938 briefing MacMullin for a month-long backpacking trip on the southern part of the trail. During World War II, MacMullin frequently joined Avery on weekend trail maintenance trips in New York. "Myron was a remarkable man, a born leader, and his body and soul were dedicated to the Appalachian Trail," MacMullin wrote in his autobiography.

David Bates in "Breaking Trail in the Central Appalachians," describes Avery as writing thousands of letters on behalf of the trail. On one night alone, he wrote forty, and the next night twenty more. Dozens of people believed Avery was interested in every detail of their work; they would write to him each time they went on the trail, making requests as small as for a gallon of paint to blaze the path. The ATC, PATC, MATC, and Maine State Library all have extensive collections of his correspondence.

"It's clear you either loved the guy or hated him," said David Field, former president of the MATC. "Reading his letters, you could see he was pushy and abrasive. He was determined to accomplish the goal of completing the Appalachian Trail. He tread on some toes.

"Avery was dealing with enormous difficulties at the Conference. People thought the trail couldn't be put through Maine. There was talk of ending it at Mount Washington. Avery said simply no, it's got to go to Katahdin. And he found the way to do it.

"Avery was the right man for the times. The difficulties facing the conference absolutely demanded strong and even autocratic leadership. It was the only way it would have gotten done.

"He was capable of writing a letter full of sharply edged words," David said. Some of the recipients were game wardens, fire wardens, and people around sporting camps. "He would browbeat these people. He would write these haranguing letters—why haven't you done this? and when are you going to do that? and we've got to get this done. Not everybody reacts well to that kind of incentive, but he got the job done.

"Avery made a lot of friends and a lot of enemies. He was what it required at the time, not just for Maine but for the whole trail."

Upon Avery's death, the obituary in the *A.T. News* said, "His interest never waned, he never became complacent, and if he ever became tired or discouraged he never disclosed it to another. Workers in many fields of endeavor will miss the keen intelligence, dynamic energy, ever-fresh enthusiasm, and the selfless and kindly spirit which inspired everyone to carry through his or her appointed task."

Avery died July 26, 1952, on the lawn of the Annapolis Royal Hotel in Nova Scotia while on vacation. The *A.T. News* attributed his death to the "nerve fatigue" he'd had for a year because of the demands of his profession: "To his Navy work he gave himself unstintingly; it was this that drew too deeply on even his iron constitution. He was definitely a 'war casualty' even though he died on a peaceful lawn instead of a field of battle."

Pioneer Thru-Hikers

There is no reason for boasting of walking as though it were a special talent or virtue possessed by an endowed few.

John Kieran, 1953

T HE A.T. WAS DESIGNED TO BE SO LONG THAT IT WOULD SEEM TO have no end. Initially, there was no thought of anyone walking the entire length in a single season, even at the originally intended length of 1,200 miles. Just before Earl Shaffer's 1948 thru-hike, an article in the *A.T. News* debunked the notion that anyone could do a thru-hike (even though six people had done the whole trail in bits and pieces). But when adventurous souls are told a task is impossible, they immediately begin to find ways to do it.

People harbored dreams of a thru-hike long before anyone succeeded, and some attempted to go the distance before Earl. After his hike, the ATC greeted Earl with incredulity. Only after Earl showed hundreds of slides and his journal and discussed the trail in detail did Myron Avery and Jean Stephenson accept his account. For years after, Benton MacKaye and others derided thru-hikes as "stunts."

Earl Shaffer faced formidable obstacles in 1948. Trail maintenance had been spotty for a decade; the hurricane of 1938 and neglect during World War II had left the trail in poor condition. Blazes and trail signs were neither abundant nor clear. Guidebooks were obsolete. Because of a mix-up at the post office, Earl never received the guidebooks he'd ordered from ATC. Instead, he made do with regular oil company road maps and a few local maps of national parks and forests. No one knew how long the trip would take, when one should start, how to resupply, or what weather to expect. Equipment was primitive.

The year after Earl's hike, *National Geographic* did an article on his trip and the trail. This article, and other publicity, brought new thru-hikers to the A.T. In the fifties and sixties, thru-hikers were a close-knit group, hiking and corresponding with one another. Yet the first gathering of thru-hikers was not until the 1972 ATC meeting in Plymouth, New Hampshire. During the twenty-four years between Earl's hike and the Plymouth meeting, only thirty-two people had hiked the trail in one season. Today, that many people arrive at Katahdin in a busy September week.

Earl, who was ATC corresponding secretary for five years, began advising potential thru-hikers in the fifties. In the next couple of years after his hike, several people attempted thru-hikes, but no one was successful until 1951, when Gene Espy became the second thru-hiker. Chester Dziengielewski and Martin Papendick became the first to hike from Maine to Georgia and William Hall did 1,750 miles that year, also southbound. Earl met or corresponded with all three of them. He hiked with Hall in Pennsylvania for three days and said that Hall, whose average pace was four miles per hour, was one of the strongest hikers he'd ever met. Earl—a powerful hiker in his own right—felt worn out when he left Hall at Caledonia State Park. In 1952, George Miller, seventy-two, became the fifth person and first senior citizen to thru-hike, covering the trail in 139 days.

When Dick Hudson hiked the trail between 1966 and 1970, he met so few hikers that he can still recall nearly all of them. "I had the trail to myself," he said. On his longest stretch, in 1969, he met four hikers in two and a half weeks while covering three hundred miles in Virginia.

In 1955, Emma "Grandma" Gatewood became the first woman to hike the trail alone and in one continuous trip. Two years later, Dorothy Laker became the second. Oddly enough, they were also the first people to do a second thru-hike, both finishing with three two-thousand-mile trips. Not until the seventies would another woman hike the trail alone. The first woman to hike the trail in sections was Mary Kilpatrick, who hiked with her husband and friends and finished in 1939. Mildred Lamb, who like Mary was from Philadelphia, hiked the trail in 1952 with her husband, Dick. They hiked from Mount Oglethorpe to the Susquehanna River, then jumped to Katahdin and hiked south. This was also the first "flip flop," hiking the complete trail in different directions instead of in one continuous line.

Grandma Gatewood, who was sixty-seven when she completed her thru-hike, brought a great amount of attention to the trail. The exploits of this gentle-looking great-grandmother captured the country's fancy.

Not until Ed Garvey hiked the trail in 1970 did another hiker get such attention. His trip and his book afterward, *Appalachian Hiker*, came at the start of a growing wave of interest in hiking and backpacking. In 1970, ten people completed the trail, six of whom were thru-hikers. In 1972, *National Geographic* published its first book on the trail, and *Reader's Digest* ran an article on the A.T. Jean Cashin recalls that the ATC conference was swamped with inquiries after the *Reader's Digest* article. In 1973, eighty-eight people became 2,000-milers. Among them was Warren Doyle, who thru-hiked in a record time of sixty-six and one-third days. He has completed the trail eight times since then.

In recent years, two more hikers have attracted great publicity to the trail. Dan "Wingfoot" Bruce has thru-hiked six times and section-hiked once, all since 1985. He also has written *The Thru-Hiker's Handbook*, with mile-by-mile information for A.T. hikers. In 1987, he spearheaded the "Golden Anniversary Expedition." To mark the fiftieth anniversary of the trail's completion, he arranged for ceremonies as he passed through towns.

In 1990, Bill Irwin became the first blind person to walk the entire trail. His near miraculous feat thrilled people around the world.

The most famous person who ever hiked the whole A.T. received little attention for it. Justice William O. Douglas completed section-hiking the A.T. in 1958, the eighteenth 2,000-miler. Born in the Midwest, he overcame infantile paralysis and acquired a love for the mountains while growing up in the Pacific Northwest. While serving a record thirty-five years on the Supreme Court, he continued to hike. In 1954, with the help of many PATC members, Justice Douglas staged a well-publicized walk on the C&O Canal along the Potomac River. The walk led to the eventual defeat of a proposal to turn it into a parkway and preserved it as a scenic trail, including a short stretch of the A.T. In *Of Men and Mountains*, his account of growing up, he wrote, "I learned early that the richness of life is found in adventure. Adventure calls on all the faculties of mind and spirit. It develops self-reliance and independence. Life then teems with excitement. But man is not ready for adventure unless he is rid of fear. For fear confines him and limits his scope. He stays tethered by strings of doubt and indecision and has only a small and narrow world to explore."

Gene Espy

*A*t sixty-six, still active and involved in the Georgia Appalachian Trail
Club, Gene displayed his equipment and discussed his 1951 pioneering
trip at the 1993 ATC meeting in Dahlonega. During that hike, a man in
Virginia showed Gene a newspaper article about the A.T. and told him he'd be the
second man to hike the trail after Earl Shaffer. Espy said, "It surprised me. I
thought it had been hiked lots of time before."

In 1951, the first Eagle Scout from Cordele, Georgia, Gene Espy,
twenty-four, became the second man to thru-hike the A.T. Gene was a Navy
veteran of World War II who "always wanted to do something different." As
a young man, he had taken a long bicycle trip and a long river trip. In 1945,
he hiked in the Smokies for a week.

In late 1950, he decided it was time to hike the A.T. Jean Stephenson
of ATC lent him her personal guidebooks and maps. Gene left the last day
of May and finished the end of September, four months later. He started
late, because he had to wait for his partner to finish high school. On the hike
from Mount Oglethorpe, then the southern terminus, his partner quickly
learned that he didn't like carrying a backpack. He took a side trail to get off
at Amicalola Falls; from then on, Gene was alone.

"I didn't tell my family I was going to hike the whole trail," Gene said.
"Nobody knew where I was. If I had gotten hurt, it would have been two or
three months before somebody would have seen me. There wasn't anybody
hiking. I practically had the whole trail to myself," he said. Many times he
went for a week without seeing another person. In places, the trail had rock
climbs where today switchbacks make it easier. "A blind man and his dog

wouldn't have had a chance then," he said. "I had trouble following the trail myself."

Speaking of recent speed hikes, Gene said, "To each his own. But to me, it's like going in the Smithsonian and out the other door. What did you see? It was strictly a vacation for me." If he took a side trail, he backtracked to where he had left the A.T. He was unable to do about twenty miles of trail, however, because he couldn't find the A.T. or faced other problems, such as flooding from beaver ponds. "I gave it the good hardest try," he said.

His pack was a steel-framed World War II Army pack purchased for five dollars at a surplus store. His pack weight varied from forty to fifty pounds. On his earlier trip through the Smokies, he had taken five blankets instead of a sleeping bag and learned that "what you put in your pack wet, you pull out wet." Those wet blankets got very heavy and weren't warm. This time he took a sleeping bag.

Two pairs of 100 percent Wigwam cushioned athletic socks lasted him the whole trip. "I washed my feet and socks every night," he said. "I knew the hike depended on my feet." He wore a chamois shirt that was in tatters by Unicoi Gap, Georgia, less than a week into his hike. His late start meant that the A.T. was "a trail in name only." The summer growth of scrub brush had reclaimed the footway, and there were few other hikers then to trample the growth.

Gene carried a four-pound Boy Scout tent. Shelters then were far less common; a 250-mile stretch in southern Virginia had none. "I always picked up stones or sticks before I got to a shelter to scare the animals out," Gene said. Since the shelters were rarely used, animals would take up residence largely undisturbed by man.

Sometimes he'd be invited to spend the night in a barn on one of the small farms tucked up in remote mountain hollows. Much of the trail then was on rural roads near farms. As late as the mid-seventies, some two hundred miles of the trail were on roads. Now only quite short stretches of road-walking remain; however, the trail crosses more roads and goes by more stores than it did then, according to Gene.

He carried the relevant guidebook section in his cap for easy access. He also carried a miner's carbide light (but no flashlight), a collapsible drinking cup, an L. L. Bean hatchet (to cut tent poles), a metal canteen, and two SOS pads. "I'd take sand and clean off my pots, then pinch off a piece of SOS to finish the job. Two pads lasted the whole trip."

"Any time I had a chance to get a good meal, I did, whether at a restaurant or at people's homes," he said. He found half a cherry pie in a garbage can in Virginia. "That was good eating," he said. And not many thru-hikers would have turned it down.

For cooking, he had a black Primus gas stove, and he didn't bother making a single fire the whole way. He put wires on the stove to make a tripod and used a Boy Scout cook kit. He used dehydrated food he'd mailed from home and powdered milk he bought in grocery stores. "I'd start to mix it at night, and it would be good by morning."

Before the hike, he bought three pairs of Maine guide shoes from L. L. Bean and two pairs of paratrooper boots, which he found too heavy to use. In Port Jervis, New York, he used fish cord and a needle to sew the tops of his shoes. He went into a store there and they wouldn't take a twenty-dollar traveler's check. "They were scared of it," he said. Gene's appearance—he didn't shave on the trail—might have frightened them. Beards weren't popular then, particularly in the South, where they were viewed as evidence of a drifter or bum. One person who saw the bearded Gene, then twenty-four, said "That sure is a spry old man."

In contrast to the Port Jervis store was a backwoods store in the South that used spring water to cool off drinks. The place had a dirt floor and no electricity, but the people there took his traveler's check with no difficulty.

One of Gene's most unusual campsites was atop the fifty-five-foot-high fire tower then standing on Hawk Mountain, Georgia. On top was a platform and a locked trapdoor to the observation deck. He decided to sleep on the tower after hearing wildcats fighting in the area, but there was nothing to prevent him from rolling off the high landing. Gene used his shoelaces to tie one end of his sleeping bag to the tower and his belt to tie the other end. "I slept good," he said.

It was raining at the deep gorge of the Nantahala River when he arrived in the afternoon, and the downpour continued the next day. He stayed two nights, one of six times on the trip that he stayed twice in the same place. "I got caught in enough storms without going into one intentionally," he said.

A warden at a North Carolina game refuge learned that Gene was carrying a pistol in his pack and disabled the gun. Later, Gene found a note inviting him to the warden's cabin for a trout dinner. At Hot Springs, North Carolina, Gene sent the pistol home.

Farther north, Gene met a moonshiner carrying a shipment. The moonshiner asked him, "How much are they paying you to hike the government trail?" Sometimes, if you asked for white gas for your stove, they'd think you were asking for white lightning—moonshine. "I tried to avoid the moonshiners," Gene said. "I didn't want to see a still and have someone hurt me."

At Damascus, Virginia, just across the North Carolina line, Gene went into a drugstore. He sat on a stool and ordered toast with syrup and a milkshake.

When Gene finished eating, he asked how much he owed. Police chief Orville "Corney" McNish, who also ran the store, said "You're all right. You don't have to pay."

The chief picked out a handful of postcards. He told Gene to fill out the cards and he'd put stamps on them. He said, "You've got a long way to go. Save your money." Later Corney put him in a police car and showed him the sights.

After the ride, the chief said, "It's getting so late, why don't you stay at headquarters?" He gave Gene "a right nice clean cell."

He also gave Gene a note for the woman who opened the store in the morning. It said, "Give this man what he wants for breakfast. He's O.K. The Chief."

Because of his disheveled appearance, Gene had trouble hitchhiking into towns. One evening, he decided to go to the back door of the Skylands Lodge in Shenandoah, Virginia, for a meal. "The man there said, 'I don't sell anything out the back door' and shut it." So Gene walked in the front door, causing quite a stir. "I ate a big meal despite the stares. He had his chance," Gene said.

At the Smith Gap Shelter (no longer on the A.T.) in Pennsylvania, he met Chester Dziengielewski, who was hiking the trail from north to south. Chester had tried to hike the trail in 1950 but had run out of money. His pack weighed twenty pounds. He carried a copy of the New Testament. After he'd read a page, he'd tear it out to save weight. Gene was just as weight conscious. According to Louise Williams, when Gene was leaving Snowden, Virginia, he lightened his load by trading two nickels for a dime.

Farther north, in the White Mountains of New Hampshire, it grew cold and windy. Gene arrived at the huts just after they closed for the season, but fortunately they left food and kept one open room for "survivors."

During his trip, Gene killed fifteen to twenty rattlesnakes and five copperheads. He used a twelve-year-old walking stick he'd cut as a Boy Scout to check for snakes in the brush along the trail. In North Carolina, he found a three- or four-foot snake. "I whacked him with the stick and broke off the handle, and the snake wasn't dead either. I believe if you see a rattlesnake, you should kill him," Gene said. Today, poisonous snakes are so rare along the trail that few hikers kill them.

He saw several hundred deer along the way, but no moose. Many of the deer were bedded down right on the trail. Near Katahdin, someone snapped a picture of a deer eating out of his hand. "I told people I was out in the woods so long, it thought I was another animal," he said. What he didn't tell them was that shortly before, he'd given the deer some of his leftover food. In the South, he saw bird's nests in roots right on the trail. One time, a black-snake chasing a mouse went right between his legs.

After Gene finished his hike, he sent a postcard to his mother from Millinocket, Maine. But his story had already gone out over the Associated Press newswire. A news announcer in Georgia, who knew Gene, broadcast the report. A neighbor heard the radio report and called his mother. "That's the way she learned I finished the trail," he said.

During the trip, Gene lost twenty-eight pounds, and he was not a big person to begin with. His trip cost four hundred dollars, three hundred dollars for equipment and food and one hundred dollars for a new suit, a shave, and the trip home.

Gene was the tenth hiker to do the whole trail and the second thru-hiker. "I did it the easy way," he said. "I was strictly on my own."

A graduate of Georgia Tech, Gene works as an engineer in Georgia. In 1981, he backpacked from Mount Oglethorpe to Springer Mountain. It was the first time he'd backpacked since his 1951 thru-hike.

Today, Gene still has his gear, and it's in remarkable shape, considering what it went through. In his den, he displays several mementos from the trip, including his walking stick and completion plaque. "He never throws anything away," says his wife, Eugenia.

"I keep account of where my stuff is," Gene says. "Doing the A.T. was one of the highlights of my life."

Gene first met Earl Shaffer in 1952 and they've remained friends. When Earl's book, *Walking with Spring* came out in 1983, Earl autographed a copy for Gene: "to the second of the crazies."

In Gene's favorite account of the trip, the *Sun* of Lewiston, Maine, called his trip "a feat of endurance . . . [by] a man of fortitude." The paper concluded, "The young man set his sights on a distant goal and reached it, and who can say there isn't something worthy in that?"

Emma "Grandma" Gatewood

The Reward of Nature

If you'll go with me to the mountains
And sleep on the leaf carpeted floors
And enjoy the bigness of nature
And the beauty of all out-of-doors,
You will find your troubles all fading
And feel the Creator was not man
That made lovely mountains and forests
Which only a Supreme Power can.

When we trust in the Power above
And with the realm of nature hold fast,
We will have a jewel of great price
To brighten our lives till the last.

For the love of nature is healing,
If we will only give it a try
And our reward will be forthcoming,
If we go deeper than what meets the eye.

Emma Gatewood

*I*n May 1993 I stopped at Harpers Ferry, West Virginia, on my way home from Trail Days in Damascus, Virginia. None of the people I hoped to see were there and I idled away an hour in Benton MacKaye's library. Then Emma "Grandma" Gatewood's youngest daughter, Lucy Seeds, arrived, delivering some of her mother's hiking equipment and other memorabilia for the ATC archives. A half-dozen of us, thrilled to be so close to an A.T. legend—especially to those well-worn high-top Keds—carried the things in and plied Lucy with questions. Several months later I talked with another of Grandma Gatewood's daughters, Esther Allen.

By all accounts, Emma "Grandma" Gatewood was a spunky lady with a hiking style all her own. Her first hike on the A.T., an abysmal failure, earned her a stern rebuke from rangers in Maine. She regrouped the following year, 1955, and at age sixty-seven she walked into the A.T. record books and national prominence. By 1969, she had hiked ten thousand miles, more than any other woman. She was the best-known walker of her generation. At a time when long-distance backpackers were rare and few people lived a vigorous retirement, the sight of an old woman hiking alone in high-top sneakers, with a duffel bag slung over her shoulder, created a national stir. The fledgling *Sports Illustrated*, as well as many newspapers, chronicled her trips. She was a guest on several network television shows, where her accomplishments were recounted again and again. She was the first woman to hike the A.T. alone and in one continuous trip, the first person to hike the trail more than once (three times in all), and only the eighth person to finish a thru-hike. Perhaps her greatest legacy, though, is that she proved you don't have to be a young male athlete to enjoy the trail.

Grandma kept right on hiking. She hiked parts of the A.T. for seven out of ten years. She completed two thru-hikes and in 1960 abandoned another in the south because she grew tired of contending with massive tangles of brush left in the wake of big snowstorms. In 1964, at age seventy-seven, she walked five hundred miles in New England, finishing a third A.T. trek that was pieced together. Ready for more, she said at the time, "I'd hike it again if I had someone to go along."

Grandma is a beloved figure along the trail, and people still point out with pride that she stayed in their homes.

Grandma Gatewood was known as a workaholic, even among the hardworking farming people in southern Ohio, where she spent most of her life.

Born October 25, 1887, in a log cabin in a hollow along Raccoon Creek, in Gallia County, Emma Rowena Caldwell was the eighth of fifteen children. Her father lost a leg fighting in the Civil War. She married at nineteen and had eleven children. By the time she first hiked the A.T., she was a great-grandmother with twenty-three grandchildren and two great-grandchildren. Her first great-great grandchild was born in 1973, several weeks before her death at age eighty-five.

Besides raising her children and doing all the cooking and domestic chores, she worked with the men in the fields.

Grandma Gatewood's formal education in a one-room school ended at eighth grade, but she had the practical knowledge and self-sufficient attitude useful in farm life. Her store of medical lore made her prized among her neighbors. She had, as well, a better-than-common knowledge of plants and often arose at 4:00 or 4:30 A.M. to tend her treasured flower beds by kerosene lantern light before getting tied down with the day's chores. She was an accomplished quilt- and rugmaker, poet, and prolific correspondent. Lucy said that a typical day's entry in Grandma's diary would say that she mowed the grass, worked in the garden, fixed the underpinnings of some trailers, dug up potatoes, and on and on. At the end she'd write, "I'm tired."

Grandma had always been a walker, partly because other transportation was not always available. And so when she saw a 1949 *National Geographic* article on the A.T. and Earl Shaffer's thru-hike, "I immediately knew this was something I had to do." She went to work as a practical nurse, so she could get Social Security, then began hiking. By 1954, with her children grown, she was ready to try hiking the A.T.

Without telling anyone, she headed for Maine, climbed Katahdin on the first day, then headed south. "I got lost right off the bat," she said. Seeking water, she had taken a side trail down to a small lake. The water looked so nice, she decided to take a bath. When she came out, she stepped on and broke her glasses. She repaired the glasses with some tape, but by then she'd forgotten which way she'd come. Although she didn't know it, rangers had been following her progress, and when she didn't appear down the trail, they started looking for her.

She began following a trail that eventually petered out in thick brush and vines. Remembering an old rowboat back on the trail, she headed that way, figuring she could take refuge under it if it rained. She set signal fires to alert search planes but finally decided she was going to have to walk out. She was out of food, and the blackflies were torturing her. She decided, "If I'm going

Walking the Appalachian Trail

to perish in the woods, I didn't want it to be here." She started trying to find her way back.

After three days and two nights, she came upon four rangers looking for her. She told them, "I wasn't lost, just misplaced." They told her, "Go home, Grandma."

"I told them if I couldn't walk from Maine to Georgia, I'd try Georgia to Maine." She wasn't eager to encounter the blackflies again, but she figured by the time she got to Maine "it would be cold and their tails would freeze off."

Later, when she saw herself in a mirror, she knew why the rangers wanted to send her home. She had disheveled hair, swollen feet, taped glasses, and a black eye from an insect bite. She later said, "I looked worse than anything drug out of the gutter."

In May, she went to Mount Oglethorpe, Georgia, alone and without a map, but more determined than ever to hike the A.T. Grandma's family knew she was "going for a hike in the woods," but they did not learn of her true intentions until she had completed seven hundred miles. She later told them she hadn't wanted anyone to try to talk her out of going. After talking to some reporters, she realized she'd better alert her family before they read about her in the papers. "I was beginning to wonder what she was up to," her daughter Esther said. "But I never worried about her. We knew Mama could do whatever she put her mind to."

She carried only the bare essentials in a handmade duffel bag slung loosely over her shoulder. (Before her first long trip she had read a list of what experts said to bring and decided that if she were to carry all that gear she wouldn't even want to start.) She had sewn a yard of denim from old jeans into a duffel sack with a drawstring closure. The bag was big enough that she didn't have to cram things into it and she could carry it comfortably. Generally her load ranged from fourteen to seventeen pounds and never more than twenty-five.

On steep places she'd pull up or lower her sack with the fifteen feet of nylon rope she carried or drag it behind her if she had to crawl. "The nicest thing about the bag was that I didn't have to keep unstrapping it when I had to jump across a wide crevice or climb over those big rocks on the mountain sides," she said. She'd rejected a backpack. In those days, packs were less comfortable than today. They lacked hip belts, so most of the weight rested on the shoulders. She said, "I didn't like those backpacks. I saw too many blistered shoulders from them."

She carried a light cotton Indian blanket and an old shower curtain for bedding, a plastic rain cape, an old sweater, a lumberman's jacket, and clothes to change into for visiting in town. Her "cooking utensils" consisted of a stainless-steel tumbler, a spoon, and a nine-tool Swiss Army knife.

With rare exceptions, she carried food she could eat cold, such as raisins, nuts, cheese, bouillon cubes, crackers, sausage, powdered milk, canned meats, and candy mints for quick energy and to settle her stomach.

On her first trip, she cooked only six times and made fires about every three weeks to dry out wet clothes or warm up. On cold nights, she would heat rocks in the fire, then put them under her bedding to keep warm. If she woke up cold during the night, she'd reheat the rocks. Sometimes she'd pile leaves in her denim sack and use that for her mattress.

She carried a walking stick and sang, usually hymns. She always wore her trademark high-top Keds that the company began supplying her after her early walks. On her first thru-hike, she wore out four pairs of canvas-topped shoes and three pairs of sneakers. Her bunions made hiking boots uncomfortable. Besides, they weren't made for women back then. In sneakers, she never had a blister. Also sneakers dried quickly, and an A.T. backpacker often walks in the rain or on wet trails.

Grandma had only bad experiences with tents, so she stopped using them. She sought refuge where she could, sometimes sleeping on or under picnic tables. The trail then included a lot of roadwalking, and it was often closer to farms and ranger stations than it is today. She relied heavily on the generosity of others, seeking help often for lodging, food, and difficult stream crossings.

She used ingenuity to compensate for meager equipment. Part of an old tire became an arch support and a plastic fork became a comb. She knew plants and herbs and used them for tea, seasonings, and medicines. Remembering that her father had put a hat of sassafras leaves on his horses to ward off flies, she would break off sassafras and stick it inside her visor, letting the leaves droop down over her ears.

She normally avoided the shelters, except in severe weather. Shelters were scarce and so were hikers, so animals often took up residence in the shelters, which had become filthy and rundown. Grandma also thought it might be dangerous for a lone woman to stay there.

A tough, disciplined, and confident woman, Grandma said, "I'm not afraid of anything in the mountains." But she did worry about falling. She sprained a knee hiking through the rugged Kinsmans in New Hampshire, and the knee plagued her the rest of the hike. She had to rest overnight in Maine and cut her daily mileage from twelve to eight.

When she became discouraged on her first thru-hike, she told herself, "If I go back, I'll just have to work hard anyway. After the hard life I've lived, this trail isn't so bad." When people advised her not to go because she was too old, she said, "As long as I can still chop wood and climb on top of the trailer to paint, I'm not too old to hike." After one hike, she said, "It was easier than building fences or chopping wood or taking in tobacco or hauling in the corn."

By the time Grandma Gatewood reached Roanoke, Virginia, on her first thru-hike, the press had discovered her. Word of her had spread rapidly along the trail. Now, at least once a week someone wanted to photograph or interview her. Mary Snow began writing about the trip for *Sports Illustrated,* which called her the "Pioneer Grandmother."

In Maine, the rangers, having been alerted, this time found Grandma and rowed her across streams.

The day before climbing Katahdin to complete her 1955 hike, she fell and broke her glasses again, bruised her face, and sprained her ankle. She climbed Mount Katahdin anyway on a cold and windy day. "It took me a long time to get to the top," she said. "When I signed my name in the register, I never felt so alone in my life." Atop Katahdin, she sang "America the Beautiful." "I did it," she told herself. "I said I'd do it, and I've done it."

She had lost twenty-nine pounds, and her feet had swollen two sizes. Her longest day had been twenty-eight miles and her shortest, eight. Besides the seven pairs of shoes, she wore out four raincoats. (She often wore raincoats to protect herself from the brush.)

Soon after she finished, the *Today Show* flew her to New York for an appearance. She also appeared on NBC's *Jack Smith Show.* They paid her two hundred dollars, which was how much her A.T. trip cost, so she liked to say she broke even.

After she finished her first-thru hike, she expressed surprise at how difficult the trip had been and indicated no desire to repeat it. Her biggest complaint was that in many places the footway was heavily overgrown. The brush was so dense and the trail so narrow in places that she had to fight her way through.

Sports Illustrated quoted her: "There were terrible blow downs, burnt-over areas that were never re-marked, gravel and sand washouts, weeds and brush to your neck, and most of the shelters were blown down, burned down, or so filthy I chose to sleep out of doors. This is no trail. This is a nightmare. For some fool reason they always lead you right up over the biggest rock to the top of the biggest mountain they can find. I would never have started this trip if I had known how tough it was, but I couldn't and I wouldn't quit."

Grandma remarked she'd done the hike for a lark. "The books said it was so lovely that I couldn't resist hiking it."

Later, she said that before her first hiking trip, "I felt ridiculous. But I wanted the satisfaction of doing something I wanted to do, by myself. Just as I pleased. I couldn't swim. Couldn't drive a car. Didn't have the money to travel by bus."

Many times she pointed out that she had always liked to walk and, when she had the chance, to seek out broader horizons. "I didn't get started sooner because when you're raising a family of eleven, you don't just run off when you want to." As to why she chose the A.T., she said, "I just decided that I'd had enough aimless walking. I needed a goal. There was something that no woman had done and it would give me something to shoot for."

Asked why she liked to hike, she said, "I want to see what's on the other side of the hill, then what's beyond that. The forest is a quiet place and nature is beautiful. I don't want to sit and rock. I want to do something.

"I find a restfulness, something that satisfies my type of nature. The woods make me feel more contented."

An opinionated woman with firm views on religion and politics, the attention late in life did not change Grandma, according to her children. "I'm just an ordinary farm woman," she said. She continued hiking and working hard until just before her death.

In the summer of 1959, at age seventy-one, she walked the 2,000-mile Oregon Trail from Independence, Missouri to Portland, Oregon, carrying an umbrella to ward off the hot prairie sun. She completed the trip in three months, averaging twenty-two miles a day, losing thirty pounds en route, and wearing out five pairs of shoes. Grandma called this trip the most grueling of her life and the most satisfying.

Large crowds dogged her footsteps as she arrived in Oregon. Exhausted from the long trip and tiring of cameras in her face, she asked the press to stop for a while. When more photographers rushed in front of her, she knocked down a camera and bopped a photographer over the head with her tattered blue umbrella. Instantly she regretted it, hugged him, and broke into tears. It took several minutes to calm her with a hamburger and glass of ice water.

Despite this incident, she had a warm welcome in Portland, with thousands of people greeting her. The mayor proclaimed opening day of the Oregon Centennial "Grandma Gatewood Day." Oregon Governor Mark Hatfield declared an Ohio Day in her honor, and she received the key to the city. She also received another umbrella to replace the broken one, which went on permanent exhibit at the Portland Historical Museum. The centennial committee put her up at a famous hotel, plied her with gifts, and flew her to California. There she visited a sister and appeared on the *Art Linkletter Show* and on Groucho Marx's *You Bet Your Life*. She finally returned home on a Greyhound bus by way of Canada.

At eighty-one she walked from Harrisburg, Kentucky, to Springfield, Illinois. Besides the A.T., she hiked the Baker Trail in western Pennsylvania several times, the C&O Canal towpath, and the Horseshoe Trail; she walked up to the Adirondacks and Canada. She considered the Long Trail in Vermont the rockiest and most dangerous of her hikes. Grandma was a founder of the Buckeye Trail Association and donated blue paint for its first blazes.

One of her favorite trails in Ohio was from Old Man's Cave to Ash Cave in Hocking Hills Park. In 1979 it was dedicated as a national recreation trail and named after her. Every winter a special hike on this trail is dedicated to her memory.

She enjoyed traveling around the country by bus and in 1973 completed a 48-state bus tour at age eighty-five. A few weeks later, after putting in a garden at her home in Ohio, she told a son who lived nearby that she felt ill. He took her to the hospital, where she died the next day, shortly after humming the "Battle Hymn of the Republic."

Surprises and Misconceptions

*Being taken by its narrowness for chosen company is indeed one
delightful aspect of the Appalachian Trail. One easily recognizes those
whom the trail has chosen. One senses kindred spirit. Some folk say the
chosen are a special breed. I mean if you enjoy, if you can really get
into going up mountains where you can might nigh stand up straight
and bite the ground or can thrill in downward descent where a person
wants hobnails in the seat of his pants; I mean you be a special breed!
Mountain wilderness lovers are chosen company.*

Bruce Otto, 1974 thru-hike report to ATC

I CAN'T EXPLAIN WHAT IT WILL BE LIKE," SAID ROSS "RIDGERUNNER"
Geredian. "They're never really going to know what it's like till they get
out there." The A.T. offers surprises, even for veteran hikers, and
beginning long-distance backpackers find new discoveries around every
bend. Hikers learn about people and nature, and what they have inside
themselves.

It's possible that no one ever had a worse start to a backpacking career
than Keith "Wolf" Kimball. His first trip in 1989 was an attempted thru-
hike. He had a 1978 data book but no maps or guidebooks. He had never
read a book on the A.T. and didn't know anybody who backpacked.

"I went to backpacking stores and bought junk," he said. "My total load
was eighty-five pounds." He even carried two backpacks.

On May 15, Keith started in Maine. He mistakenly walked to Abol
Bridge instead of Baxter State Park, which meant he had to walk eighteen

extra miles. On that walk he learned a little about what he'd need; he mailed home twenty-five pounds of gear from Abol.

Among the supplies he kept: three boxes of pancake mix, at two pounds each; three pounds of spaghetti; and several glass jars of jelly, which are heavy—and messy if they shatter.

He started with five sets of clothes. An experienced backpacker might have one spare set. All his clothes were soaked within a few days. He wore logging boots. They were waterproof, chain saw–proof, insulated with a steel tip, but much too heavy for backpacking.

After climbing Katahdin and resuming his southbound trip, Keith was hurt only six miles south of Abol Bridge. At Rainbow Ledges, he slipped on some rocks and fell a couple of feet. His ankle was twisted, and he couldn't walk on it. He spent twenty-six days—an almost biblical time scale—covering one hundred miles of wilderness, without seeing another hiker. Today, an experienced northbounder can do that section in five days, although rangers at Baxter suggest preparing for ten days.

The rest of the stretch became a saga of determination and mule-headed perseverance. He could have hobbled back to Abol Bridge, but he decided to press on. "I wasn't going to go home and tell them I walked seventeen miles and quit," he said.

He spent many nights in the rain because he couldn't make it the full distance between shelters. He counted twenty-three days of rain out of the first twenty-six. On top of that, it was blackfly season, when all but the hardiest or greenest outdoorsmen stay clear of the Maine woods.

By Monson, Maine, Keith's ankle had healed. "I'd sworn as soon as I hit Monson, I'd quit," he said. "But I spent one night in Monson and decided to continue. I got cleaned up and felt better. I got good food in me. People in the town cheered me on. I figured it was worth another shot. It really inspired me."

By Garfield Ridge, in the White Mountains of New Hampshire, he met his first thru-hiker. "It made me feel better," Keith said. "I knew I wasn't the only crazy person doing this." He'd gotten his pack down to thirty pounds by then.

He ended the trip in September at Delaware Water Gap, Pennsylvania. He had only fifteen dollars in cash and the bus ticket home cost seventeen dollars. He called home, and his mother refused to pick him up, thinking he was joking, so he walked the one hundred miles home to Levittown, Pennsylvania.

"It was a tough trip," he said. "I had sixty-seven days of rain out of a hundred, then I stopped counting. It was wet. I thought it was tough but fun. I liked the challenge. People were really friendly, but I was very lonely."

Now, Keith is an experienced hiker who travels with an extremely light pack of ten to fifteen pounds, including food for five days, a sleeping bag, and a tarp. In winter, he carries thirty pounds. Once he carried only a fanny pack for five days. "That's kind of tough," he said. "I've done without every piece of equipment in my pack, including my pack," he added. He's completed the A.T. twice and done part of a third trip. In the summer of 1993, he hiked the Pacific Crest Trail in four months.

Most hikers come to the A.T. expecting a wilderness experience. The physical and mental challenge of completing the trail is often the attraction. It's a surprise to most of them that their biggest pleasure is often the sense of community forged by their fellow hikers and the trail angels. As long as there have been hikers, there have been people—trail angels—willing to help them.

Although there are occasionally curmudgeons, more common are the people who hold out cold drinks or offer a bed for the night. "It restores your faith in mankind," said two-time thru-hiker Phil Pepin. "There are a lot of good people out there."

For most of the A.T.'s past, long-distance hikers have been sparse. Dick Hudson, who finished the trail in 1970, remembered every long-distance hiker he met in the four years he hiked. Since then, long-distance hiking on the A.T. has grown rapidly. In 1990, the record year, 212 people reported finishing the A.T. Thousands more backpack shorter stretches.

Despite the increased number of long-distance hikers, the trail still appears wild to most of them; however, if you begin at Springer Mountain at peak time—late March to mid-April—there's lots of company. (Of course, it's all relative. A crowded shelter on a rainy night may house only eight people, but it's a long way from solitude.) Then, as you go north, the crowds thin out. Some people think of better things to do with their summer, and others speed up or fall behind.

It surprises some how quickly strong friendships form among hikers. "I don't know what it is, but if they have a backpack on and you're heading in the same direction, it's like you've just met your next friend," said Connor "Carolina Cookers" Coward. "It's like a ritual or initiation that ties you together. It was the closest I've ever felt to people."

"It's because you don't know each other's backgrounds," said Dorothy

Hansen. "Everybody's a hiker and you're all equal in the eyes of the trail." As for why the bond is so strong, she suggested that "it's because it's such an elemental thing we're doing out there, sharing the essentials and the really vital parts of living in such close proximity. Maybe it's the relative anonymity of it, too. It's safer sometimes to talk to somebody out there than to somebody in your regular life. Maybe it's the common goal and common dreams. Almost everybody is there for a little bit of soul searching."

Another possible explanation is that although most hikers are in an introspective mood, they prize whatever company they have.

Many hikers, worried about doing the trail alone, try to find a partner before they start. But anyone who shows up at Springer in April soon finds hiking companions, though it is admittedly hard to form durable hiking partnerships when hiking pace varies and the dropout rate is high. Personal chemistry is critical in such a stressful partnership.

Another surprise is how physically demanding a thru-hike is. "It's still, I think, the best physical-conditioning experience you can have," said Elmer Hall, proprietor of The Inn at Hot Springs. "You don't have to pay one hundred dollars a week to do aerobics. You just walk ten miles a day. You'll get in shape."

After four to six weeks of steady backpacking, most people are in the best shape of their lives; still, aches and pains are a regular feature of trail life.

Your body takes a pounding day after day. "I had a different ache or pain every day," said Phil Pepin. "Always something hurt. I would walk like an old man for a couple hundred yards coming out of a shelter," he said. He'd be better after he got warmed up.

Bob "Sweet Pea La Foot" Hill counted fourteen blisters during his first few weeks on the trail. "It was slow going. I had heavy German boots. I'd thought they were broken in properly, but apparently they weren't." In New England, he had dysentery for three days. In Massachusetts, he had to rest for a month with a hairline fracture of his foot.

Bob's other surprises were more pleasant. Also a PCT end-to-ender, he said, "The A.T. is a botanical paradise. There's nothing like the Smokies in the spring or New England in the fall."

"It was more painful than I expected," said Marilyn Pasanen. "I thought it would be a nice walk through the country." But, she added, "It was great having that time living away from civilization. It's more work than you ever do otherwise, but it's real work. You're close to the land, close to nature.

"I got discouraged a lot just like you do in real life. But you have to pick yourself up and keep going. The most discouraging thing was in Pennsylvania when we saw two rattlesnakes. We were inches away from the first. The biggest fear for a woman is rattlesnakes. I was going crazy."

But she and her husband, John, completed the trail. "Now I think everything's possible," she said. "With a little money and imagination you can do a lot. I'm not afraid to do things like home school for my children and other unconventional things."

"You always want to see a romance to it, but it is a job," said Rick Hancock.

In some ways, it's easier to prepare for a thru-hike than it's ever been. Detailed planning guides and videos have been produced in the past five years. More and more experienced hikers are willing to provide information. ALDHA's fall gathering of long-distance hikers is a prime resource for prospective thru-hikers.

Most veteran hikers advocate some physical preparation for the trail, such as running or climbing stairs. But as Jim "Jimmy Bee" Bodmer, a 1990 hiker, put it, "I thought I was in good condition, and I was in good shape for what I was doing before the trail. I just wasn't in good condition for backpacking. It was much harder than I expected."

Of course, there's no way to fully prepare for the exertion of hiking ten hours a day up and down mountains carrying a forty- or fifty-pound backpack. By starting slowly on a long trek, you can work into shape. But on shorter hikes, you may never get into top-notch shape.

One way to mentally prepare is by expecting misery much of the time and realizing that other parts of trail life compensate for the suffering. Expecting to escape unscathed is a sure path to disillusionment.

New backpackers, worried about their time, tend to start too fast at Springer. They don't realize that although an eight-mile day in the Georgia mountains might seem tough in April, a twenty-mile day in Virginia two months later might seem easy. Hikers who start fast risk becoming injured or discouraged. Greg "Pooh" Knoettner began a northbound hike at the end of April. "I was haunted by this feeling that I had to hurry the whole trail because I was a late starter," he said.

Money can be another surprise. Most middle-aged or retired people find backpacking the A.T. for six months a cheap way to live. But many students and younger people have their trail experience diminished or even ended because they run out of money. The current rule of thumb, at least for long hikes, is that you'll spend $1 to $1.50 per mile. But Warren Doyle spends perhaps a tenth of that, and other hikers spend two or three times as much. The easiest places to spend money are restaurants, hotels, and grocery stores. Some hikers, repelled by civilization after living in the woods, keep their town breaks brief. Others find a renewed appreciation for such luxuries as refrigerators, garbage cans, and running water, and stay for days. One trend that's become more common in recent years has been younger hikers, with no deadlines, backpacking as far as their cash carries them, then finding odd jobs to replenish their finances before moving on.

New hikers can take inspiration from Bob "Rerun" Sparkes and Leonard "Habitual Hiker" Adkins. Both came to the A.T. in 1980, and neither covered even half the trail that year. Both have gone on to finish the A.T. three times. Bob lacks only a few sections for five completions, and although he's in his seventies, he's eager to return to the trail.

He began with a six-mile walk near Harpers Ferry in September 1979. His reaction was, "This is easy. I can do this." The following April, Bob was back on the trail. He does not consider that incomplete 1980 trip a failure, but a learning experience.

Leonard found that he was not serious about thru-hiking in 1980, but took side trips and partied and generally enjoyed himself. Since then, backpacking and hiking have become a way of life. He met his wife, Laurie "the Umbrella Lady," on the trail, and they married at Peaks of Otter, a picturesque setting of mountains and a lake along the Blue Ridge Parkway, which was formerly part of the A.T. Leonard, who has hiked all over the country, has authored four hiking guidebooks, including one on hikes along the Blue Ridge Parkway.

"On my first trip, not knowing what to expect, I was frustrated," Leonard said. "I'm in North Carolina. Maine is still way up there. I was not accepting the way the trail went. I was fighting the trail. The second year, I looked at every day as a day hike."

In 1989, two hikers used "I.O.W.A.—Idiots Out Walking Around," for their trail names. As the slower of the two, Harry "H. B." Fisher one day put fifteen pounds of rocks into partner John "J. B." Brau's pack. When they reached the shelter at the end of the day, John said, "Man, my pack feels so heavy," and found the rocks. It's a trick that more than one backpacker has suffered. On her 1976 thru-hike, Susan Gail Arey didn't find the rocks for five or six miles. She retaliated by putting a frog in the culprit's water bottle.

Harry and John walked forty miles one day into Damascus, Virginia. On the same day, Bill "Stats Godric" Gunderson did thirty-three miles, earning his honorary "idiot" status for doing such a grueling hike.

Few people came to the A.T. with less hiking knowledge than John "Indiana John" Stephenson. "If there was every any greenhorn that went out there it was me," he said. "I didn't get the right pronunciation of Katahdin till I was in Maine. My first time up Katahdin I didn't even know where the top was. I went to the tablelands and thought that was the top. I met someone at Abol Bridge and he said he was going to climb Katahdin. I said 'I'm sore' but I went anyway.

"I was planning on doing Maine maybe and then going back home. I'd never realized there was a world like that that I could aspire to. By the Maine–New Hampshire border I had decided to do the whole trail. I came across another hiker with the guides and maps. The guy had planned for fifteen years to do the trail, but he hurt his knee crossing a creek and that was it. It was ironic that I finished and he didn't."

Luke "the Journeyman" Wiaczek

*I*t takes a serious person to keep at the trail, mile after mile and day after day, accumulating those five million steps. But it's refreshing to come upon someone like Luke who laughs easily about his adventures. His thirst for travel not yet quenched, he has bicycled cross-country and plans to do the Alaska Highway. We talked over dinner; as Luke says, with thru-hikers, "It always comes back to food."

Luke "the Journeyman" Wiaczek had a five-year-plan to propel himself across the United States. He would hike the A.T. from Georgia to Maine and spend the winter in Maine; cycle to California and winter there; hike the PCT and winter in Washington State; cycle to Alaska; and sail in the spring from Alaska to Greenland by way of Cape Horn.

Asked if he were a sailor, he replied, "No, but I wasn't a hiker, either." He's made adjustments along the way, but he's completed a remarkable amount of his plan. In 1990, with partner Kristin "the Journalist" Guter, he bicycled from Key West, Florida, to Springer in seventeen days, then hiked the A.T. The next year, he bicycled cross-country. The year after that, he bicycled from Katahdin to the northernmost point in Maine.

"It's called wanderlust," he said. "I can't get it out of my blood. I like the natural ways of traveling, seeing things at a slow pace, not zipping down a road. The more you do, the more you want to do."

From his A.T. hike, Luke has gained the confidence to tackle other adventures. As he prepared to cycle the Alaska Highway, he said, "I don't have any worries about this trip. I know I'm going to be wet and cold. The bike's going to break. The pack's going to break. I don't even consider it any more. I just know the experience, the scenery, is definitely worth it."

On Luke's first day on the approach trail to Springer, he ran into Joe "the Italian Scallion" Barella. "I see this old guy in a rain poncho and shorts and lightweight hiking shoes. He starts walking across this wooden bridge, saying, 'You know, you have to watch out for this stuff. It's slippery and you could fall.' I'm thinking, 'This guy has no idea what he's talking about.'" That night at the Stover Creek Shelter, Luke found out it was Joe's second thru-hike. "I started to learn right away that you can't judge people by their looks out there."

That first night, while everyone was lying in sleeping bags in the shelter, Joe said, "The elements are no big deal. The walking's no big deal. But you have to get used to the mice. You'll by lying there sometimes and the mice'll run right across your sleeping bag or right across your forehead." Luke looked over at Kristin, and she looked at him. "She had this 'Oh-my-God look,'" Luke recalled. "The next time I looked over, she had her sleeping bag pulled up with just her nose sticking out. She was scared that the mice were going to carry her away or something like that."

Joe Barella also told them, "You'll get your trail legs after about the second week. You'll know you're a thru-hiker when you find yourself walking and doing nothing but talking about food."

"We said, 'Sure, sure. Yeah, yeah. Crazy old man, what's he know?'" Luke said. "But in a couple of weeks, we were coming down this hillside, a nice gradual descent, nice cool area, and I said, 'If there was a Burger King around the next corner, what would you order?' I started it. We just got going and spent the entire day talking food. Strictly food."

Another time, Luke and Kristin were with a group camped just outside of Hot Springs. They made careful plans to "do the food thing right."

"We would go in first thing in the morning and catch the AYCE (all you can eat) breakfast and then go to the AYCE lunch and do the AYCE dinner. So we all stopped early. We were in the shelter and done eating our measly portions by six o'clock. It was three hours till it got dark, and it was a little chilly. There were six of us in this shelter, lying there with nothing to do but dream out loud about what town was going to hold as far as food. And we spent five hours just lying there talking about food.

"The next morning it wasn't the usual 'Oh, boy, we've got to get up and put the pack on.' It was 'All right. Town's right around the corner.' We went running down the hill. It was fantastic."

Like pregnant women, thru-hikers get strong cravings for special foods. "I remember the fried-chicken craving hit when I was five days out," Luke said. "It's in your dreams. You're lying there, and pieces of fried chicken are dancing before your eyes.

"I remember walking into Dot's in Damascus, sitting down at the table, getting a menu, reading it. The waitress came over. I said, 'Two fried chicken dinners, might as well just bring out the desserts with it, large Cokes, and some extra rolls.' She said thank you and started to walk away. I said, 'Wait a minute, the lady would like to order, too.'

"Before my hike I ran into a thru-hiker at Sunfish Pond, in New Jersey. He said, 'One day, when you're on the trail you'll go into a town, have a whole large pizza, then go get a pint of Ben and Jerry's [ice cream], finish that, and then figure out where you're going to eat next.'

"One time in town, I had a large pizza and was just scraping out the Ben and Jerry's when it dawned on me. That guy was right."

Thru-hikers typically eat foods that provide a lot of carbohydrates, are easy and quick to cook, require little water, and are lightweight. For many, that means Ramen noodles, macaroni and cheese, peanut butter, and instant oatmeal. By the time a hiker finishes the trail, he's usually willing to part company with those foods for a long time. "Oatmeal," said Luke with unconcealed scorn. "I would sooner plaster the walls with it than eat it. I'll eat cold, stale bagels before I'll eat oatmeal in the morning."

Luke recalls a visit in southern Pennsylvania from a trail angel, Rex "the Keystone Kop" Looney. Rex showed up at the shelter with three large, hot pizzas and a backpack full of beer on ice. Luke thought, "Man, I can't believe it. This guy's carrying pizza. Who is he, and where are his wings?"

In New Jersey Luke and Kristin took a break to visit their families. "People said, 'If you get off in your hometown midway through the trail, you'll never want to get back on,' but I was ready. The whole time I was off, I had that itch to get back on again."

When Luke returned to the trail, his father walked with Luke and Kristin as far as Sunfish Pond. It was a walk they'd done many times before. "But this time it was different. I had my pack on and I knew that I was going to continue walking," Luke said. At the pond they talked for quite a while. "At some point we both realized it was time for Kristin and me to go. We stood up, I gave him a hug and said 'We're going.' He turned south, back to the car and the 'normal life' and we turned north and started walking back into the outdoor world. It was a strange feeling, like a parting of the ways."

Luke had originally planned to do the trip solo. On a group bike ride, he explained his plans to Kristin, casually mentioning that she was welcome to come. He didn't expect her to take the idea seriously, but she did. He found the partnership quite beneficial. A female partner provided a different perspective. And people were friendlier and more trusting than they would have been with a lone man. "A couple of guys—solo hikers—in the South had bottles thrown at them," said Luke. "They mentioned they were jealous of us. Seeing a woman along, people were more apt to be respectful. And getting a ride into town was easier." Women hikers can benefit, too, since some are reluctant to hitchhike alone.

The year Luke and Kristin were on the trail, two thru-hikers were murdered at the Thelma Marks Shelter near Harrisburg, Pennsylvania. A few weeks later, a man was arrested when walking into Harpers Ferry, West Virginia, and later convicted of the crime. While hiking in northern New England, Luke heard about the murders. Most hikers remained on the trail but became more cautious.

"You naturally become family with the people you're hiking with," Luke said. "We found that when news of the murders spread up and down the trail, the bonding became a lot tighter. Trust in strangers just walking down the trail became a lot less. Everybody knew that the guy who did it was still out there. Normally, you'd come up to a shelter, automatically drop your pack, and start talking to the people. A lot of us were more inclined to keep the pack on and evaluate who was sitting there. It took a while for everybody to start talking about it. It was just like the death of a family member."

The same year in Tennessee, fishhooks were strung up along the trail at eye level, and the Don Nelan Shelter was burned down. "It was weird to go from a carefree manner—where all you're concerned about is, Do we have water? Do I have any cookies left? Where are we going to sleep tonight?—to, Is somebody going to bother us? Are there going to be real problems?"

"In the Whites [in New Hampshire], Kristin and I both started realizing that it was going to come to an end too soon. The hundred-mile wilderness was not long enough. By that time, the temperatures were nice, the scenery was nice."

Near the end, Luke still didn't take finishing for granted. "I remember thinking to myself that the only way I'm going to say I'm going to finish the trail is when I'm about ten yards from the sign. Because I know if I trip and fall and break a leg, I could still crawl and touch it."

Walking the Appalachian Trail

And then they reached Katahdin and the end of the trail. "We were sitting at Katahdin Stream the day before summit day," Luke remembered. "I said to everybody, 'If you could have anything you wanted, what would it be?' It's funny how your ideas change. I'm sure if I were to do it now, I could list things that cost tens of thousands of dollars. But I remember at the top of my list were dry socks and a new pair of boots. Those are the biggest things I really wanted."

Adjusting to society after the trail was difficult for Luke. "When you get down to the basics, spend six months out there, you find out what really matters," he said. "The basic physical things—staying dry, warm, food, water. To go from that frame of mind to 'I make this much money, I drive this car, I'm going here, I'm getting this, I'm doing that.' That's a real adjustment.

"Another adjustment was sleeping in the same place more than two nights in a row. Thinking I'm going to be in this exact same position, this exact same location, every night for x number of months or years. That was a big adjustment.

"I don't sleep on a bed. I'm still in a sleeping bag on a Therm-A-Rest. There's always that feeling in the back of my mind that I still want to go, and I know the more you have, the harder it is to go.

"I don't think I've adapted yet. If you enjoyed the trail, it stays in your mind, in memories, in pictures. It stays with me in the sense that I appreciate the simple things; I understand what the basics mean. I'm like everybody else. I get caught up in the wants and the haves. But I still know I can revert to staring into a candle or a fire and going back to any given point on the trail and refocus on what it meant. I still think about the trail every day, 365 days a year."

Ways to Hike the A.T.

*I think I laughed and cried more in those six and one-half months than
I have in the rest of my life.*

Connor "Carolina Cookers" Coward
1990 trail report to ATC

M OST YEARS FOR MORE THAN A DECADE, STARTING IN 1973,
Mary Jo "the Tortoise" Callan would take the bus east from San
Diego and hike north from Springer Mountain. The farthest
she ever got was Waynesboro, Virginia. A cheerful grandmother who backpacked into her seventies, Mary Jo felt comfortable with the section of trail
she knew and didn't harbor any desire to complete the whole thing.

One year, Charlie Trivett of Damascus, Virginia, had heard Mary Jo was
coming. On a rainy day when she hadn't made it in, he went to Abingdon
Gap Shelter with Warren Doyle to check on her. He found her at the shelter, and he introduced himself and said, "I've come to get you."

She said, "Come to get me?"

He said, "Yes. I'll take you in, let you shower and spend the night, then
I'll bring you back tomorrow and let you hike on in."

She said, "Young man, you can take me in, but you won't bring me back.
I've been trying for three days to get off this mountain and I couldn't."

She ended that year's hike there.

On her last trip, Mary Jo found the trail increasingly difficult. "She'd
leave notes at the bottom of a hill, tell her age, and leave her pack, asking
someone to carry it up for her," Charlie said. The last year she came through

Damascus, Charlie missed her, and he's always regretted it. She died in 1989 at age eighty-one.

"There are two A.T.'s," one speaker told the 1993 ATC meeting. "One, an App-a-latch-i-an Trail, runs from Georgia to Maine. Another, the App-a-lay-shun Trail, runs from Maine to Georgia." In truth, there are dozens of Appalachian Trails, each what a hiker wants to make of it. The physical trail—the 265 mountain climbs, 255 shelters, and thousands of two-by-six-inch white blazes that mark the narrow footway—is in many ways the least important of the trails. The trail is also an abstract concept, a path to a hiker's dreams and aspirations. After all, what separates the A.T. from other trails is not something tangible, but rather its mystique, its history, its trail community. More than seventy years after Benton MacKaye proposed the trail, his idea resonates as powerfully as ever.

It's difficult to find agreement even on relatively simple notions about the physical trail. For instance, just how much trail is there? In 1993, the ATC listed the length as 2,146.7 miles. But only three years ago, Warren Doyle and two members of his expedition, Steve Rarity and Ken Miller, rolled a measuring wheel, dubbed Mr. Yuk, from Springer to Katahdin. This was the first time a wheel ever covered the trail in a continuous journey, and the verdict was 2,164.9 miles. ATC attributed part of the difference to the difficulty of correctly calibrating the wheel. Also, as my two young sons frequently point out, a thru-hiker has to walk hundreds of extra miles to shelters, water sources, and resupply points.

Debates rage over which trail to hike. To a nonhiker, the debate may seem to be about subtle points, but it proceeds with great passion and occasionally venom wherever hikers gather. The question is this: Should one stick to the white blazes—the official trail route—no matter what? Veteran hikers know that in many places, side trails—blue blazes—are available. Sometimes the blue-blazed trails are shortcuts or easier routes; other times they are harder, more scenic, or avoid a hitchhike into town. A third option—called "yellow blazing" since the mid-eighties—is to skip trail sections entirely, perhaps by hitchhiking or taking a bus. A fourth alternative is to hike some days without a full backpack (known as "slackpacking").

Slackpacking is one of the least controversial ways to hike the A.T. Often when a hiker is staying at a town or a hostel, someone will keep his pack and shuttle him to a trailhead, so he can hike for a day without a pack. Some hikers are reluctant, having become quite attached to their packs; a pack is a hiker's closest companion for four to six months. Some even carry their packs up Katahdin instead of leaving them at the ranger station. Also, packs occasionally get stolen, and hikers like to keep a close eye on them to prevent a spoiled journey.

Purists insist on following the white blazes. They argue that you have not hiked the whole trail unless you stick to the designated route. Mark "Second Wind" Di Miceli, a five-time thru-hiker, believes the danger is that once you deviate from the white blazes, it's difficult to stop. Before you know it, you skip big sections of the trail and lose your desire to finish. You end up with a much less satisfying trail experience. He also feels every section of trail offers something. By hiking the trail continuously, your journey is more than the sum of the parts. The contrast between the sections helps you appreciate the truly outstanding areas.

Pieter "the Cheshire Cat" Van Why notes that some purists are so pure they will take big risks to stick to the white blazes. "If they were going over the balds in bad weather, and there was a bad-weather route going around it, they'd stick to the white blazes. But people who take convenience [and choose shorter routes] tend to lose their drive."

The purist question has been around almost as long as thru-hikers. Earl Shaffer had no doubt that he wanted to follow the white blazes. But sometimes, particularly in southwestern Virginia, there were no white blazes and the footway was indistinct for miles. Gene Espy, the second thru-hiker, made a point of retracing his steps after side trips so he'd return to his original spot on the trail.

Dick Jones has hiked sections of the trail for fifteen years and has no intention of finishing. He says some parts of the trail are inferior, and he has no desire to hike them. "The trail, just because of the very nature of it has an awful lot of what I call 'fillers' [sections of the trail that act only as links]." Yet he returns to other places again and again to see them in winter or in peak foliage season. "To me, that's much more rewarding than bragging that I went from Oglethorpe to Katahdin."

Another view comes from Bob "O. D. Coyote" Pierson, who hiked the A.T. in 1980 after having done the PCT. A strong, opinionated hiker, he reported to ATC that his objective was not to hike the entire A.T. but to hike a continuous route from Springer to Katahdin. And that is what he did. He said, "I was not a rigorous A.T. follower, for sometimes it went where I did not want to go, and sometimes I wanted to go where it did not." He did such things as walk along the Blue Ridge Parkway to have a meal at Peaks of Otter because he'd heard the restaurant was good. His aim was to be the first northbound thru-hiker to start at Springer and the last to finish at Katahdin, and to enjoy himself along the way. And he did all those things.

Arthur "A. B. Positive" Batchelder met two women who'd hike a few days, go into town, and hitchhike ahead. "This is how they were doing their vacation. They'd say, 'We'll do it our way.' We do get tied in too much to this," Arthur added. "Oh, you're a purist? You're a thru-hiker? Are you having fun? If you're not having fun, what are you doing out here?

"You should be able to say, 'I took this trail and I saw fourteen moose.' Sometimes those side trails have more views, more flowers, something you wouldn't find on the regular trail. Let's face it, how much wildlife did you see on the regular A.T.?"

Keep in mind that the A.T. is not cast in stone (though sometimes *on* stone). Rarely, if ever, is the trail the same for two straight years. Sections of the trail are constantly relocated to improve routes and to avoid eroded spots, encroaching developments, or heavily logged areas.

For many years, following the white blazes would not have gotten a hiker from Georgia to Maine. It was not until the mid-1930s that Egbert Walker, an internationally known Smithsonian botanist, and the PATC developed standards for white paint blazing.

Dr. Harry F. Rentschler, a founder of the Blue Mountain Club, resisted ATC's efforts to standardize white blazes, saying the paint detracted from the trail's natural quality. Mary Dorsey, a friend of Myron Avery, found a way to change his mind, according to an account by Maurice J. Forrester, Jr., in the *A.T. News.* Mary convinced Dr. Rentschler that she was worried about getting lost when she did trail work alone. She claimed she had trouble spotting the old ax marks. He permitted her to put paint blazes where she felt it necessary. She decided it was necessary to paint blazes frequently and spent a summer putting the first paint blazes on a 100-mile stretch.

Another issue is whether to thru-hike or section-hike the trail. People with limited vacation time must do the trail in short sections or wait for retirement. Hiking the trail over many years has its advantages: It gives one something to savor in the off-season. Many section-hikers study the guidebooks thoroughly, learning more about the trail and surrounding areas than most thru-hikers. Ken Scott, who did the trail in twenty-five separate trips from 1972 to 1985, deciphered dozens of bus and train lines all along the East Coast because that's how he got to the trail nearly every time. For thru-hikers, the trail can be a tunnel—a long, wonderful tunnel—but a tunnel nevertheless. Something a hundred yards off trail might as well be in China.

Those who piece the trail together are among the most dogmatic in sticking to white blazes. Each time O. W. "Red Owl" Lacy completed a section he would cross the road and touch the first blaze on the other side, assuring that he wouldn't miss any of the trail. For section hikers it's perhaps more difficult to assure themselves that they have hiked the entire trail.

Ned Greist, a former ATC vice chair, claimed a section-hikers' record. Forty-six years elapsed between the time he first set foot on the trail (hiking from Franconia Notch to Mount Lafayette, New Hampshire) and when he completed it (at Spivey Gap, Tennessee, in 1975, at age sixty-six).

Ray Hunt earned a special distinction among section-hikers. He was the first ATC chair to complete the trail while serving in that capacity. (Myron Avery completed the trail in 1936 while chair, but the trail was not officially completed until the following year. As a lawyer, Avery surely would have understood such a fine distinction.) Never a long distance backpacker, Ray has been, though, an avid hiker for a long time. He spent from 1967 to 1989 piecing together sections of the trail, always less than ten days at a time. "It took me fifty trips over twenty-two years to finish the trail," Ray said.

"When I started, I had no intention of doing it all. I was just hiking with friends. At about five hundred miles, they told me I was going to do it all. I said that's ridiculous. At one thousand miles I realized they were right. I started to do it more intently. I was doing fifty miles a year. At that rate I figured I wouldn't finish until age eighty-five. I felt compelled to finish."

Jim "Pony" Adams has been hiking the trail in sections since 1987. After retiring from the Air Force, he found he missed the discipline of doing something every day. Now, he's addicted to the trail. Hiking in bits and pieces, he's not in as big a hurry as thru-hikers. "They have to be on the move all the time," he said. He also likes that he can get charged up again each year and choose when to return to the trail. "I wouldn't do it any other way," he said.

O. W. "Red Owl" Lacy did the trail in "dribs and drabs" from 1970 to 1980. As a sign of his determination, he vowed not to cut his hair until he finished the trail. By the end, he had a waist-long ponytail tied with a rubber band, an unusual style for a college dean. (Surprisingly, no one ever asked why he was letting his hair grow.)

O. W.'s motives for doing the trail, like those of most 2,000-milers, were never clear. "They were vague and broad-based and poorly articulated," he said.

He first heard of the trail in 1936 when President Franklin D. Roosevelt dedicated Shenandoah National Park. His family listened to the ceremony on their first radio. As the speakers explained that the park protected ninety miles of the A.T., O. W.'s older brother said, "Let's do that sometime." O. W. thought the idea intriguing.

His brother died in World War II, though, and the idea of hiking the trail got pushed to the far back burner. Then in the mid-sixties, as dean of students at Franklin and Marshall College in Pennsylvania, "I was getting pretty wiped out." That turbulent era "was one of the stupidest times to be a dean of students."

O. W. was looking for an outlet, and one day a colleague said, "Come along with us, we're going to hike some of the A.T." O. W. became interested. "The old dreams came back and I got hooked."

"The thing that really guided me was a talk with an early A.T. hiker who also worked at Franklin and Marshall." Montgomery Lampe had walked from Maine to Georgia; he also maintained some twenty miles of the A.T. in Pennsylvania and was active in several hiking clubs.

O. W. asked him how to backpack the A.T.

"Don't," Montgomery said.

"What do you mean, don't?"

"Don't carry your kitchen and bedroom on your back when you can sleep between clean sheets each night and have somebody cook your meals for you."

He continued with more counsel: "The Appalachians are made up of a series of ridges. Every seven or ten miles there are usually gaps and transmontane roads. Often, there are little camps or small hotels where you can stay near the trail. Walk from gap to gap rather than shelter to shelter.

"Don't walk uphill if you can walk downhill. Walk from high gap to low gap.

"Anything else I should know?" O. W. asked.

"You'll never do it if you don't take the next step."

O. W. took Montgomery's advice. "Instead of following the long green tunnel, I saw the trail in every one of the fifty-two weeks of the year," he said. "I remember floundering in snow up to my armpits. I didn't make many miles that day, but it was glorious."

"Thru-hikers tend to think of themselves as the elite," he said. "But there's a certain elitism to taking ten years. The beauty of the trail is that it's there for each person to discover in his own way."

Other decisions await prospective A.T. hikers. Should one hike north to south, south to north (as most do) or a little of both ("flip-flop")? Hike alone, with a single partner, or in a group? Hike quickly or slowly? Bring a dog along? Take side trips? Complete the thru-hike, then turn around and go back ("yo-yo")?

Most thru-hikers start in Georgia mid-March to mid-April and hike north. That way, you follow spring north and have a longer time to complete the trail before harsh weather sets in. The advantage for sociable hikers is that they have plenty of company; on the other hand, there may be too much company. As for weather, most people prefer either cold- or warm-weather hiking—but not both. Adjusting your starting date by even a few weeks to suit this preference can greatly enhance your enjoyment of the A.T.

Hiking southbound, most people wait until late May or June, when the worst of Maine's blackfly season is over. Except for a few weeks when northbounders are passing by, the southbounders don't have much company. In the South, they hit hunting season and maybe some early winter storms.

Rod Kinley hiked southbound from June 27 to December 1, 1973. "We were still hiking in shorts in December, we were so toughened by then," he said. In North Carolina, it was eighteen degrees on his eighteenth birthday, and he walked in shorts. Kinley and his three hiking partners had most of the trail to themselves. "After New England, we never shared a shelter with anyone," he said.

Because of the lonely stretches, southbounders often crave company. Rod remembers meeting a group at a cave near Erwin, Tennessee. "They had filled the cave with dry leaves two or three feet deep. We saw their packs on shelves inside, and we asked if we could join them. They used a forked stick to cook meat for stew over a fire, making it warm in the cave. They were from a church college nearby, and they did this often."

Some people compromise by flip-flopping, hiking the trail in several sections and different directions in one year. They can start later in the South, hike perhaps half the trail to Harpers Ferry, then take a bus or hitch-hike to Katahdin and start south. On their southbound leg, flip-floppers may meet hikers they met in the South. Flip-flopping makes it easier to handle the weather, especially for older hikers who average fewer miles per day. It diminishes the crowds but interrupts the continuity of the trek. Some flip-floppers regret not having a climb of Katahdin to mark the end of the trail.

Paul "Bigfoot" Tourigny hiked south from Katahdin to Lonesome Lake, New Hampshire, in several trips in 1974 and 1975. In 1976, he hiked north from Springer, finishing at Lonesome Lake. "When I got to Lonesome

Lake I had finished it, but I wasn't elated about it, because I wasn't on top of Katahdin. It left me with an ambivalent feeling." He went back to Springer in 1978 to do the trail again. At the end, "I experienced this euphoria. It really meant something to me to complete it end-to-end, uninterrupted. My first completion was anticlimactic. I don't recommend anyone do it that way."

The first yo-yo occurred in 1982–83, when Steve "Yo-Yo" Nuckolls hiked from Georgia to Maine, climbed Katahdin, turned around, and returned to Georgia, then turned around again, three thru-hikes in all. In 1984, Phil Goad did three thru-hikes in one calendar year. Ward Leonard in some years hikes the trail almost continuously, and at last report he'd completed the trail ten times, including once in 60 days and twice in 150 days. The first woman to do a yo-yo hike was Bonita Heeton in 1990–91.

Speed-hiking has been around for a long time, even though ATC discourages it and many thru-hikers frown on the practice. In an echo of a question often heard about every thru-hike, people ask "If someone hikes so many miles a day at such a fast pace, how can they enjoy the woods and mountains?" Record holder David "the Runner" Horton points out that his average pace was under four miles an hour. He claims he appreciated the views and remembers what he saw as well as most thru-hikers. What he missed were the social parts of the trail. The average thru-hiker has six months to meet people and less pressure to get miles in. Horton did the whole trail in fifty-two days.

Benton MacKaye did not favor thru-hikes, and he especially frowned on speed-hikes. "Some people like to record how speedily they can traverse the length of the trail, but I would give a prize for the ones who took the longest time," he said.

Few organized groups have hiked the whole trail. Except for Warren Doyle's four expeditions and one by Kirk Sinclair, most thru-groups have been loose collections of hikers who met along the way and stuck more or less together for large sections of the trail. Albie Pokrob, who hiked the trail alone in 1978, with Warren's 1980 expedition, and with the informal "Last Wave" in 1984, found that he preferred the freedom of going at his own pace. "It's nice to have the feeling that you have everything you need on your back, and you can stop wherever you want to. With a group stopping at road crossings, it took away a lot of the spontaneity." But Albie realized that many people wouldn't go except with a formal group.

Leave your dog at home. Listen to thru-hiker Henry Phillips, who has such a love for dogs that he keeps fifteen at home. He says that he detests dogs running around a shelter on a rainy day, shaking themselves dry over his sleeping bag. Dogs can foul water sources, get in fights, and frighten hikers. And extended hikes can injure some dogs. They are not permitted in Great Smoky Mountains and Baxter Parks.

For all that, certainly many people would not go anywhere without their dogs. Jerry Harper, who was on the trail in 1993, said his dog, George, could find water many times when he could not. "He takes off and I know there's water. A thirsty dog will find water." The only times Jerry got lost were when he didn't trust George's sense of direction. Many dogs are well mannered and a joy for other hikers to be around.

Side trips and hobbies can also make the thru-hike more enjoyable. Sonie "Light Eagle" Shames decided partway through her trip that this was likely a one-time adventure and she was going to make the most of it. She hitchhiked off the trail to Hershey Park, county fairs, and music festivals. She found they added an extra dimension to her thru-hike. Such natural features as Old Rag-Whiteoak Canyon in Shenandoah, Anthony's Nose in New York, and Gulf Hagas in Maine make for interesting side trips.

Others like to pursue their hobbies. Collins Chew, a 2,000-miler and ATC vice-chair who wrote a book on A.T. geology, studied the rocks along the trail. Joe "Cool Breeze" Fennelly liked to drop in on bluegrass festivals. Jim "Jimmy Bee" Bodmer raced through 1,400 miles of the A.T. so he could walk to an orienteering meet in Connecticut. Syd "Not That Vicious" Nisbet liked to measure the temperature of springs. (The coldest: Edmands Col in New Hampshire at thirty-five degrees Fahrenheit in August 1990.) Mark "Second Wind" Di Miceli, amassed an impressive collection of Indian arrowheads and artifacts. Ken Miller, on his 1989 thru-hike, periodically hitchhiked off the trail as far as Florida to do contra dancing.

David "the Runner" Horton
and Scott "Maineak" Grierson

*I*n 1991, David Horton and Scott Grierson decided, independently of each other, to break the A.T. speed record. Each set his target at fifty-six days, an astounding average of almost forty miles a day. They both started in Georgia, two days apart in mid-May. "What are the odds that in the same year two people would independently decide on fifty-six days and start within two days of each other?" David said.

A few months before their start, they learned of each other's plans and talked on the telephone. At first, each was skeptical of the other's abilities. "I dismissed him at first," said David, who was forty-one then. "I thought a hiker can't beat me, and he thought the same of me. But the more we found out about each other, the more we developed a sense of respect."

Scott, twenty-four, had thru-hiked in 1988. Along the way, he'd learned about speed-hiking from Greg "the Traveler" Key. "I was astounded he could run uphill with a full pack," Scott said. Greg taught him which packs and hiking shoes were best, how to lengthen his stride, and how to use his arms to help propel himself forward, as one does in cross-country skiing. He also shifted to an internal-frame pack, which permitted greater freedom of movement. Later that trip, he hiked the length of the A.T. in Connecticut in a single day. It was his first big mileage day, and it took him a few days to recover. "But I realized I could walk fifty miles in a day," Scott said.

David Horton is a world-class ultramarathoner. A regular marathon is twenty-six miles. Ultras are commonly fifty or one hundred miles and may take up to four days to complete. David often races on mountain trails, enduring dramatic elevation changes. Some races offer more elevation change than one would get by running from sea level to the top of Mount Everest in a day.

Although he hadn't hiked much, David, who lives near the A.T. in Lynchburg, Virginia, had run races that included parts of the A.T. "I couldn't imagine going the whole way from Georgia to Maine," he said. Then in 1987, he read an article on the fiftieth anniversary of the A.T.'s completion and thought, "Man, I'd really like to do it some day." He had in mind a traditional thru-hike but figured he couldn't take enough time away from his family and job as chairman of the physical education department at Liberty College.

Finally, in July 1990, he decided to do the trail—and to do it fast. He learned from Warren Doyle that Ward Leonard, with a full pack and no support crew, had hiked the trail in 60⅔ days. The prior record was 65 days, 21 hours, and 15 minutes by John Avery in 1978. Warren had done the trail in 66⅓ days in 1973.

David calculated that he needed to do thirty-six miles a day to finish in fifty-six days. But he also figured he'd have to take some days off. Initially, he planned on carrying a fifteen- to twenty-pound pack. But that was before help arrived.

David advertised in *Ultramarathon* magazine for runners who lived along the trail and would be willing to support his trip. Thirty responded. They met him at road crossings with food and Conquest, the sports drink he drank each day. At night they took him home or to a motel. Thanks to the support crew, he needed only a light day pack while hiking.

Since David is always in training for ultramarathons, he didn't do much physical preparation for the trip. He runs 70 miles a week routinely, and 90 to 100 when he's training hard—about 3,600 miles a year. Nearly every Saturday he'll run 25 to 30 miles in the mountains. Before he did the A.T., he took a two-day backpacking trip of about 80 miles and another of three days and 120 miles, both with a fifteen- to twenty-pound pack. "It was a struggle. It liked to have killed me," he said. He realized he would have a tough time setting the record with a full pack.

One thru-hiker David talked to told him he thought David could make the record-breaking trip. "It gave me a lot of confidence, but I still didn't think I could do it," said David. "I expected it to be an exercise in futility."

Scott started from Springer on May 7, and David started two days later. Their crews kept them apprised of each other's progress. David credited

Scott's competition with helping him go faster. He finally caught Scott in southern New England, and they leapfrogged for a few days before David went ahead for good.

"I don't like to say this, but I really struggled the first thousand miles," David said. Days six to nine were especially hard. Coming out of the Smokies, running long downhills caused shinsplints. On one memorable day near Hot Springs, his right leg was badly swollen, and he had to carry his heavy pack. He was urinating blood, his fingers were swollen, and it was pouring rain. In an article for *Runner's World*, he wrote, "With every step, I had to tell myself not to wince. I'd try to block out the pain and, in spite of it, stay on schedule."

Three things helped him get through this period: packing the leg in ice at the end of each day, anti-inflammatory drugs, and prayer. In Shenandoah, David developed a problem with his quadriceps. But soon thereafter, his physical problems began to diminish and he speeded up. Near Harpers Ferry, he had what he figured was his fastest mile of the trip. Checking the markers along the C&O Canal towpath, he ran a mile in eight minutes and fifty-seven seconds at the end of a day.

During this stage, he was pleased with his good health. "The level of fitness I reached on the trail surprised me," David said. "Warren Doyle said that in two to three weeks, you develop a much higher level of conditioning. It sounded logical, but the average person's not in real good shape when he starts the trail. I found there's a higher level of conditioning even for someone in very good shape. The body is remarkable in how well it adapts to stress. In the evening, as the hours passed, I could feel my body recovering. Until the last ten days, I woke up refreshed and ready to go."

After Harpers Ferry, David continued to feel better. He was right on schedule, averaging 38.6 miles per day. From there to Mount Moosilauke in New Hampshire, he picked up the pace, averaging 44.4 miles a day. "I felt fantastic," he said. He ended up spending twenty-seven days on the first half of the trail and twenty-five on the second. In Pennsylvania, he had two straight days of fifty-two and fifty-three miles. The weather was cool and the terrain moderate.

Coming into Boiling Springs, Pennsylvania, he read a register entry by someone hiking with Maineak saying that he'd done a fifty-mile day. "I thought if he went fifty miles here, I could, too," David said. "It turned out that he didn't."

From Moosilauke north, it was again a struggle for David. Until that point, he'd spent eleven hours a day on the trail. From Moosilauke to Katahdin, he spent thirteen and a half hours a day. One of his problems was that it was hard to meet his support crew in the White Mountains, where a day's hike of thirty-eight miles "usually left you in the middle of nowhere."

Before the White Mountains, David ran the flats and downhills and walked the uphills. He usually tried to stop before a climb, so he could start slowly in the morning by walking the uphill. "I'd do an easy fifteen to twenty minutes to wake up." His 6:54 A.M. start at Springer was his latest of the entire trip. During the last few weeks, when he had to put in longer days because of the more difficult trail, his average start was 4:54. "I liked the mornings and hated the afternoons," David said. "I was the reverse of Maineak. He didn't get as much sleep as I did. He'd hike till midnight, one, two in the morning every day. It took him time to wake up."

In the Whites, David had trouble keeping to his regimen. "The pace was unbelievably slow there," he said. "I didn't get enough sleep. I didn't eat enough. I got tired of eating to eat. I went physically downhill and hit roots and rocks more. I was emotionally breaking down. I was beating myself to death. Those last two states, I was near total destruction." In the last week he'd fall a half dozen times a day, too tired to pick his feet up. A fall near Katahdin left a six-inch cut in his arm.

"Eating enough is the key," he said. "I had been eating five thousand to six thousand calories a day. In New Hampshire and Maine, I didn't eat that much. From Massachusetts on, they don't have buffets in restaurants."

Still, he kept going and never really considered taking a day off. "I can't say that it would have helped," he said. "One of my crew members in New England said, 'You're ahead of the pace you need to set a record, why don't you take a day off.' It was like asking a miler on world-record pace to slow down. I felt like it was a personal insult. One day off wouldn't have helped. I needed weeks off, months off."

A born-again Christian, David depended heavily on the power of God, the power of prayer. "I realized how fortunate I was. Not many people really get to chase their dreams. Not many people get to do something no one else has done. Not many get to do an unbelievably challenging experience. There were days when I felt tired and didn't think I could do it. Somehow, some way, He'd give me the energy."

At Katahdin, he felt only pain and relief. He hadn't enjoyed the last ten days. "It didn't feel real until the day before," he said. "I felt I was on a perpetual A.T. treadmill. It seemed like it was going to go on forever."

The first week back he had the worst nights' sleep of his life. "I'd have nightmares. I'd be dreaming I was going uphill, and I'd never get to the top of the mountain. I'd wake up and think, 'Where am I? What am I doing in a house?' Four days later, on July 4, I ran two miles. It hurt so much. In September, I ran a fifty-mile race and placed third, and I felt I wasn't recovered. In October, I ran a hundred-mile race and won, and I felt recovered.

"Mentally, it took a few weeks—physically, three months—to recover. I'd lie on the couch and watch TV because I didn't have the energy to get up. I hated going to the basement because I didn't want to climb back up the stairs." His mental recovery was shorter than that of most thru-hikers, perhaps because his trip was more compressed. Still, he went through many of the same experiences. "It seemed really strange, the traffic, cars, noise. I didn't feel like I belonged. It was hard to feel motivated to catch up at work."

Like many other hikers, David said the A.T. taught him patience, adaptability, and how to make the best of circumstances. "The A.T., it's a part of me," he said. "I really feel at home on the A.T. I love talking to thru-hikers. There's a special bond, like among people who go to war. We shared so much together. Maineak and I became great friends. We went through rain, pain, heat, uphills, and downhills. There's a real camaraderie."

Both David and Maineak endured a certain amount of ridicule from other hikers. But David points out that an average hiker walks two miles per hour, and he averaged 3.54 miles per hour. "How much more can you see at two miles per hour than at 3.54?" he asked. "Very, very little. I can talk about all the beautiful and spectacular places along the trail and all the horrible places. The horrible places, I got through quicker. And in the good places they'd see one spectacular overlook a day and I'd see three or four." He hiked only short stretches in the dark, usually the first fifteen minutes in the morning. He never hiked in the dark at night. "I wanted to see the trail, too," he said. "The only thing I missed was the social experience."

Scott, too had to deal with flak about the speed-hike. But he counters, "Anyone who is trying to do the trail in one year is under time constraints," Scott said. "You're not out there counting the rings on a fungus and covering fifteen miles in a day."

Of course, Scott covered a good deal more than fifteen miles a day. He averaged 2.3 miles an hour for sixteen hours a day. He'd start out slowly, then hike long into the night. "Most people go out too fast in the morning," he said. "Go slow until your body warms up."

Scott came to the A.T. in 1988 as a novice hiker and has hardly left since. He didn't get off to an auspicious start, however. He was at Springer one month after he decided to hike the first time. He'd bought a huge pack and stuffed it with seventy-five pounds of gear including forty pounds of food, enough to last until Hot Springs, North Carolina. He was planning to resupply only four times on the whole trail.

"I've made quite a transition," Scott said. Quickly he learned to shed weight and the other tricks of the trade. He didn't have any synthetic clothing, now a staple of hikers, until he was three-quarters finished with the trail. He took six and a half months and "it was a wonderful experience. I came from a simple background. People go to the woods to get away from the pressures of everyday life. I had it different. I had a magical childhood and a magical little world in Maine. For me it was meeting America head on."

For Scott, the speed-hike was the ultimate test. "This is what I'm made of, can I handle it? My mental state was, 'I will do this, no matter what. Quitting was not an option. I didn't consider it. The trail was the perfect place to do that [test]. I felt at home on the A.T."

David knows that eventually his record will be broken. "But I'd like it not to be for a long time," he said. "I thought sixty and a half days was soft, but fifty-two days and nine hours is not soft. I had no major injuries, no horrible weather. In fact, I had spectacular days on Katahdin and in the Presidentials. I had rain nine of the first twelve days, but it wasn't bad. It kept me relatively cool.

"The real threat is, will Maineak decide to break the record? Sometimes he talks about doing it in under fifty days. I think that would be real tough.

"I would like for people to have tried it and failed. I'd help them, though. I'd give them advice, and when they got to my area, I'd go out and help them. But I don't think it's going to be broken for a while."

Repeat Hikers

The thing that shines through the most this time is the peace I learned. I found a peace within myself that I always knew or felt was there but did not know or understand how to get it out . . . The A.T. has really changed my life forever. I am a more loving person because of it . . . No matter where my life takes me I'll always be waiting to hike the A.T. again.

John Hess, 1984 trail report to ATC
after his second thru-hike

A FTER THRU-HIKING THE A.T., HIKERS USED TO TUCK THEIR backpacks away in a closet and get on with their lives. No longer. Of the three thousand listed thru-hikers, more than one hundred have done the trail twice, and probably two dozen have done it four times or more. One man, Ward Leonard, has hiked the A.T. ten times since 1980. Warren Doyle has completed the trail nine times, and both he and Leonard were still hiking on the A.T. in the summer of 1993.

Isn't one time enough? After all, it's a difficult journey, and the spirit of adventure can't be as strong the second time. Can it?

Three pioneer thru-hikers repeated the trail: Earl Shaffer, Grandma Gatewood, and Dorothy Laker, and each had different reasons. But mostly it came to this: They had all enjoyed their time on the trail and wanted to revisit places and people they'd seen the first time.

Jan "Sacajawea" Collins hiked the trail in 1982 and 1985. By the time she reached Virginia, Jan had already decided to hike the A.T. again. Why the second time? "If you have a chocolate ice cream cone and you think it's the greatest thing in the world, you don't think you'll never have one again."

Pete "Woulda, Coulda, Shoulda" Suscy, who thru-hiked in 1984 and 1991, said he'd had it in the back of his mind since the first trip that if the opportunity arose, he'd like to do it a second time. "Thru-hiking is such a total lifestyle," he said. "If someone enjoyed living in Paris, he might get a yearning to live back in Paris."

Ginny "Spiritwalker" Frost hiked the trail in 1988 and again in 1992. "There were some things I really missed," she said. "I wanted to see if the reality was as good as the memories." But the second time she had more fears. "I knew about the pain and the rain."

Joe "Cool Breeze" Fennelly has spent fifteen years hiking more often than not since his first thru-hike in 1978. "My true vocation is hiking," he said. "I don't fit into civilization any more. At forty-four, I'm not going to change. I enjoy friends and I need civilization for certain things, but every spring and fall I go hiking for two to three months. It's a way of life for me. I define myself by it, not by my work."

Robin Phillips, who hiked the trail in 1979, wrote to the *A.T. News* several years later about his reasons for returning to the trail. "Even a thru-hiker has barely scratched the surface of what the trail offers. The change of seasons, direction of travel, and time of day all affect perceptions of any area. Wildlife, flowers, berries, and other hikers are all variable. There is simply too much to see for one trip to suffice. A lifetime supply of adventure, scenic splendor, and wonderful people is available to the hiker, and that's the real beauty of the Appalachian Trail."

Leonard "Habitual Hiker" Adkins, who has done the A.T. three times, says he's found that he's happiest in the woods. "If I had my way, I'd be hiking 365 days a year. I'm a happier, better person out on the trail." Adkins has organized his life around hiking and backpacking, supporting himself by writing guidebooks and with seasonal ranger jobs. He now has backpacked fourteen thousand miles.

In 1980, his first year on the A.T., Adkins hiked nine hundred miles and then returned to his job. "In my mind's eye, I kept seeing the places I'd been and thinking about the people I'd met. I wanted to finish what I'd started." The next year, he took another leave from his job and did the remaining twelve hundred miles. "Afterwards, I was thinking it's time to get serious about my job and career. I was okay until March 1982. Then I started thinking about the people who would be starting the trail and the grand adventures they would be having. I asked my boss for a third leave. My boss said no way. I quit and went to Georgia and did the whole A.T."

Twelve days into the trip, he met Laurie "the Umbrella Lady" at Muskrat Creek Shelter, near the Georgia–North Carolina line. He kept meeting up with her, and they finished together. Later, he and Laurie were married at Peaks of Otter. For a honeymoon stroll, they hiked the Continental Divide Trail in the Rockies.

"When you have a backpack on, no matter where you are, you're home," said Leonard.

Alf Loidl was the first Australian to hike the A.T., in 1982. A resident of Tasmania for much of his adult life, Alf grew up in New York City (a few blocks from Roger Brickner) but moved to Australia as a young man. A magazine article rekindled youthful memories and brought him back to the A.T. He attempted his third thru-hike in 1993. In Pennsylvania, however, a mysterious illness drove him off the trail. He enjoys the changing of the seasons, seeing the animals early and late in the day, and swimming in the lakes in Maine with the loons singing. Since Alf started, other Australians have followed in his footsteps.

Most repeat hikers find that at some point they burn out or lose their desire to do a thru-hike. Mark "Second Wind" Di Miceli did the trail five times. But several other times he has returned to Springer and dropped off the trail within a few days. Paul "Bigfoot" Tourigny went to Springer in 1983 for what would have been his third thru-hike. Out on the trail, "I said, 'I'm not going to do it. I came home.'"

Arthur "A. B. Postive" Batchelder thru-hiked in 1990 and has done stretches since, but he doesn't plan to do another thru-hike. "The A.T. has got something that catches you, that rivets you," Arthur said. "I don't know how to describe it. For some people that's enough. I know for myself I'm at that point where I know it's time for me to move on to something else."

Wanda "the Breeze" Kurdziel

*I*f you see a five-foot-four-inch blur on the trail with a ski pole or two, it could
be Wanda. On the Pacific Crest Trail, legend has it that she must be eight feet
tall to hike the way she does. In the course of her backcountry travels, Wanda
has endured tremendous pain and learned to appreciate the joys of the wilderness.
"We thru-hikers have to like it all," she said.

It's no wonder that Wanda "the Breeze" Kurdziel has backpacked more
than any other woman ever has. Few people sound more excited than Wanda
talking about hiking. And few people shrug off pain and misfortune as well.
Other experienced hikers are in awe of her feats, of her facility with maps,
of her ability to hike alone.

"I'm quite a rarity," she said. "I've never really hiked with someone. Of
my sixteen thousand miles of backpacking, only a couple hundred miles have
I kept hiking with someone for even a few days. Mostly, I've wanted to do
more miles than they did."

She's lucky to be hiking at all. In 1975, she was thrown through the
windshield of a car in an accident on Interstate 95 in Connecticut. "I came
within a half inch of being killed," she said. As it was, she fractured her spine.
Although she is proud of overcoming her disability, she still cannot do certain things, like standing in one place for long. "When I'm hiking, I don't
stop and talk," she said. "As long as I keep walking, I'm okay. And I can't
carry as much weight as some people." Weighing 120 pounds, she tries to
keep her pack under 40 pounds. But she's carried more than 50 pounds in the
High Sierra of California, where resupply points might be one hundred
miles off the trail.

After the accident, her doctor told her she wouldn't walk again. "Walking with a pack was the last thing I had on my mind," she said. "But walk she has. Starting in 1983, Wanda has hiked all of the A.T. three times; she's working on her third hike of the PCT; and she has done many shorter trails, such as the Wonderland Trail in Washington State, the Long Path and Finger Lakes Trails in New York, the Colorado Trail, and Ozark Highlands Trail in Arkansas. "I wanted to hike every single trail I could find, and I enjoyed them all," she said. In one "peak experience," on the Wonderland Trail, she saw a whole field of purple lupines in bloom surrounded by snow. "I live for those special moments. Of course, there's some drudgery in it, but the special moments make it all worthwhile. I like the simple lifestyle."

She began hiking as a teenager at summer camp, when she took a day trip to Mount Moosilauke. "It made such a big impression," Wanda said. "It was my first time out in the woods, smelling the pines. It's still one of my favorite mountains."

After finishing graduate school in 1982, Wanda hiked from Monson to Katahdin. "I ate nothing but peanut butter and jelly sandwiches for six days," she said.

From the beginning, she fast-hiked. "This was before speed-hiking was common," she said. "Back then, it was a big deal."

One time, she did three straight weeks of twenty-five-plus-mile days. "I was on a roll. I don't know why I did it. People would say, 'Wow, a woman doing that.' I don't know why. I just could do it. I did aerobics, and I was in generally good shape, but it's mental more than anything. A lot of times I'd just ignore the pain."

She believes that a hike should reflect a hiker's capabilities and inclinations. "I want the individual experience to be right for them," she said.

Wanda is also an avid student. "I collect college credits like I collect hiking trails. I have four hundred credits from twelve colleges."

A linguist who speaks a dozen languages, she went to an Army language school in Monterey, California, in 1974 and was the first woman there to get the top award for language skill. She's continued studying Slavic languages, including Russian, Serbo-Croatian, and Polish. "During a hike I always carry a book in a foreign language and make time each day to read a chapter. I would not go to a grocery store without a book. You never know when you're going to have time to read." Mostly, she prefers good classical fiction.

Her 1975 car wreck destroyed her "worldly ambition. I've had little jobs since then, but the pursuit of money or career does not interest me. I'm cursed with a high I.Q. but not the ability to do much with it."

Why spend so much time in the woods? "The gentler lifestyle," she said. "I turned down a Fulbright scholarship to Russia for the A.T. the year after I got my master's. I didn't stop backpacking, as some people do after they accomplish their goal. I somehow kept going.

"On my hikes, I'd get enough confidence and strength to come back to society. I love the simplicity. You have just what you need. I don't need a lot of money. It's unusual for a woman to get into this lifestyle, where you're at a different place every night.

"After I got off the trail in 1983, it was a failure to find a place in society and a desire to see the western trails that brought me back out. I had sent my name to a dozen colleges to teach Russian, without success. If I had gotten a position, it might have changed my life. Instead I thought, 'Spring's here and I don't have a commitment.' I was a substitute teacher and could leave when I wanted. Sometimes I hiked till November. Now I take classes from September to May, so it limits my season.

"In 1986, I did my second A.T. I wanted to see it without the standard crowds, see things at different seasons, see the relocations, see the views that had been socked in." She flip-flopped to avoid crowds. "There weren't too many backpackers. I liked it," she said.

Throughout her hiking career, Wanda has had to deal with adversity. "On my first A.T. hike, my toes got infected just outside of Damascus. My toenails got ingrown. I had to have surgery that winter. I did half the Pacific Crest Trail to Canada, but I had to go out late in the season because I waited for my toes to heal. Then all of my gear was stolen. I just wouldn't give up. In Southern California, they called me 'the stubborn one.'

"In 1986, I had Lyme disease and liver disease. I had to come back for my liver scans every few months. I hiked through a lot. I also had major depression. But as long as I was in motion, I felt better. Pumping out endorphins while walking made me feel better."

Is she afraid of hiking alone? "I like the night noises. I haven't been afraid of animals, just strange people. A man came to a shelter with a gun on my third A.T. hike in 1987. He left and came back several hours later. Meanwhile, three guys had showed up. I probably wouldn't have stayed if the other hikers hadn't come so soon.

"I met other weird guys. I found talking firmly kept them in check. I'm shy, but I've come out of my shell in the last few years. One time on the trail, I met a guy who growled, and I growled right back.

"I'd hiked on the A.T. and then on the PCT with a guy I had trusted. But once he was smoking dope and tried to choke me. It hurt enough that I had to go to the hospital. I got some therapy and did the same stretch of the PCT again to overcome it. He was a Vietnam veteran suffering post-traumatic stress disorder. I feel for him."

Wanda believes that hiking is therapeutic for some people with serious mental problems. "Hiking helps them in some way," she said. "But the trail can't heal everybody. There's a point of diminishing returns. I might have reached that, too. Now I have a balance in my life."

In her first relationship after so many miles, her boyfriend put a lot of pressure on her to stop hiking. "For one year, I was in bad shape," she said.

"In 1991, I came within a week of being married. I ended up going into the Grand Canyon on what would have been my wedding day. A part of me was relieved. I had lost who I was."

Then she met and married another man. He day-hikes but doesn't back-pack. "My husband got me back into hiking," Wanda said. "He got out the maps and encouraged me to hike."

In the summer of 1993, she was planning to do the rest of the Finger Lakes Trail, then go to Russia to study language for a month (her master's degree is in Russian), followed by a month hiking the Colorado Trail. She's also working on her third PCT trek and is planning to hike in Oregon and the High Sierra. "Now, I'm hiking a month at a time, not all summer," she said.

Like most backpackers, Wanda has difficulty describing what she thinks about during those long hours alone on the trail. "I spend time to acknowl-edge God. I'm not a terribly religious person, but I'm very spiritual. On the trail, you can be at the mercy of the elements. It humbles me and uplifts me at the same time. I also think a lot of mundane thoughts. Can I afford a little, itty bitty snack now? I play word games."

She's had good luck and some unique encounters with animals. Once, she woke up nose to nose with a bear. "I've had deer walk right along with me. I walked with a mountain lion. He could sense I wouldn't harm him. Another time, I awoke where elk were mating."

The trail and hikers have changed in the years Wanda has been hiking. "Now, so much money is being spent along the trail," she said. "I never went to any motels or ate in restaurants. I believed that if you go there with any money, you're not accessing the complete wilderness experience. That's not what I wanted. I didn't care what I ate.

"I did lose a lot of weight my first hike. I got down to 112 pounds. I carry more food now and treat myself better.

"I have a great metabolism. My mind retains calories. Guys get ravenously hungry. I have even seen someone on the PCT eat a quart of mayonnaise. He was a skeleton. Women have an advantage over men in retaining calories."

Despite her vast backpacking experience, Wanda still finds it difficult to adjust to the trail each year. "It doesn't get easier the more you've done. I still feel it. The first week is the worst. You feel better by your third week. If you don't stay out for more than a week, you never get to the point of enjoying it or being in shape. My knees hurt when I go down hills. I realize other people's don't. It's more difficult now than when I was in my heyday. I take it a little easier. Now I'm carrying more food, more warm clothes, a Therm-A-Rest. I'm not as willing to suffer as much any more."

As with many strong hikers, Wanda never hits the trail early. "I'd start at eight or eight-thirty and do ten miles by noon," she said. "I'd have my big meal at lunch. You need calories more to hike in the afternoon than you do to sleep at night. A lot of times I'd eat my main meal when I got to water."

Wanda sees backpackers as a breed apart. "There's something poetic about them. They're more sensitive than most people. Even the ones who joke around, deep down they're poetic." She added, "We're all searching for something. Some of us are striving for what Thoreau called living authentically.

"I've never thought of backpacking as a perpetual vacation. I have thought of it at times as a perpetual punishment. You see teenage delinquents sentenced to backpacking, and sometimes I wonder, did I get a life sentence? But more than anything, I've enjoyed it."

Food and Lots of It

Mary Mungummory shook her head . . . "I wonder again what I wonder nightly as I watch the circus in my wagon: is man a savage at heart, skinned o'er with Manners? Or is savagery but a faint taint in the natural man's gentility, which erupts now and again . . . ?"

The Sot-Weed Factor by John Barth

IN 1990, MARY ANN MILLER WAS A MEMBER OF WARREN DOYLE'S group of thru-hikers. When they reached New England, the mother of one of the support-van drivers, Diane Watts, invited the group to her house for dinner. She asked Diane how much to prepare. Since there were twenty people, Diane suggested twenty pounds of spaghetti.

Her mother said, "That's funny, hon. Now how much do we really need to buy?" Diane said, "Twenty pounds of spaghetti, Mom."

As Mary Ann tells it, "Being polite hikers that we were, we ate dinner first before we went. And then she fed us. They had lots of spaghetti and salad and bread. I don't know if she cooked twenty pounds, but there was a lot. Enough for one helping each. So we ate, and she said to her daughter, 'See, that was enough.' After we had already eaten our dinner."

Sooner rather than later, every hiker's conversation turns to food, and hikers' thoughts rarely stray far from food. The U.S. Department of Agriculture calculates that a typical woman consumes sixteen hundred calories a day and a man twenty-four hundred. A typical A.T. hiker burns four thousand to six thousand calories a day, two to three times what a normal person does. A winter hiker needs even more, as he burns fuel just to keep up his body temperature.

One study postulated a "vicious cycle" in which hikers couldn't carry enough food to replace what they burned. In her master's thesis, Karen Lutz, a 1978 thru-hiker and currently ATC's Mid-Atlantic representative, calculated that the energy expended carrying more food would be greater than the value of the extra food. She did find that despite the caloric shortfall, hikers' general nutrition was adequate. What they lack are calcium and vitamin A. For calcium she suggests carrying powdered milk, cheese, and sardines packed in oil. Dried fruits, such as dates, figs, and raisins, are high in vitamin A. Her study was based on a small sample of one year's thru-hikers.

Hikers may counteract the "vicious cycle" during their stops in towns to resupply. Most hikers spend one day each week laying over in a town. During town stops, most eat prodigious amounts of food. Nevertheless, a typical thru-hiker loses ten to twenty-five pounds, and some lose up to fifty pounds. A small percentage of hikers do manage to gain weight, with some picking up as much as twenty pounds. Folk wisdom along the trail has it that those who need to lose weight do and those who need to gain weight do, too. That tendency may be correct but hikers need to plan their diet with care. As Lutz says in her thesis, many people may leave the trail because they lack energy—an early symptom of a poor diet.

Rod Kinley, a southbound hiker in 1973, started at Katahdin weighing 125 pounds, was down to 112 pounds by Monson, Maine, and finished the trail at 145 pounds. "We became so efficient at our pace that I was able to gain weight despite not eating too much," he said.

David Denton, a 1992 winter hiker, has become an avid student of nutrition. He also believes that many hikers drop off the trail because of poor nutrition. He thinks thru-hikers rely too much on foods that are quick and easy to prepare but barren of nutrition.

In *Walking with Spring*, a book about his first thru-hike, Earl Shaffer wrote that near the Georgia–North Carolina line, he stopped to cook lunch. Feeling weary, he was considering dropping off the trail. Since he'd skipped some meals because of bad weather, he cooked a double portion, figuring to save the rest for later. He wrote, "To my amazement the entire kettleful of 'sawdust pudding' disappeared like magic, along with a half a pound of brown sugar, a can of milk, and some raisins. Almost instantly my legs lost that leaden feeling and I felt like hiking again. It had been a case of starvation pure and simple, despite no unusual sensation of hunger. From that time on my strength increased and so did my food bill."

One remedy is to prepare much of your food before you start. Dan Nellis and his wife, Kathy "Backpacker" McClelland, both 2,000-milers, use a simple, homemade dehydrator to prepare all types of nutritious meals and stockpile them for the trail. Dan also uses a lot of dehydrated milk, which helps avoid calcium deficiency.

Most thru-hikers will eat just about anything. Dave Marshall survived a thru-hike in 1980 eating only macaroni and cheese every day for lunch and dinner. By the time the hike's over, though, many blanch at the thought of one more portion of macaroni and cheese or oatmeal or peanut butter.

"It seemed like a long day to get to Springer on the approach trail," said Pete "Woulda, Coulda, Shoulda" Suscy. "It was a big, big climb, and we had heavy packs. We stopped halfway up for a meal, and we had a can of sardines. Those sardines tasted great for some reason. At Neels Gap, I bought one can of sardines for every day until our next resupply point at Wesser. We got tired of sardines and at Wesser fed the rest to the cats there. I never have eaten a sardine again."

Most A.T. hikers resupply about once a week. It can be tempting when one is always hungry to eat extra the first few days and be left short by the end of the week.

Every thru-hiker has a favorite story about huge feasts along the trail. Mary Ann Miller recalls with gusto a trip to the restaurant at Big Meadows in Shenandoah National Park. "The waitress brought us a basket of bread, and we ate all the bread and were drinking water and Cokes, and we ordered lasagna. They brought us the lasagna and a basket of garlic bread. Then more Cokes. Then she came back and said, 'Can we get you anything else?' We each ordered a half chicken and mashed potatoes and vegetables and another basket of bread. I had eight Cokes and several glasses of water, too. When she came back over, we ordered dessert."

Noel "the Singing Horseman" DeCavalcante wrote about an incident in which two short-term hikers gave him two pieces of oatmeal bread to feed Canadian Jays near their campsite. After they left, Noel gave the jays a few crumbs and ate the bread. He chuckled as he thought to himself, "Imagine giving this wonderful bread to the birds."

Eateries along the way are a constant source of speculation on the highly efficient trail grapevine. One place that hikers consistently rate highly is The

Inn at Hot Springs, North Carolina. It is the first real town that many north-bound hikers visit and as such a welcome sight after perhaps three weeks in the woods. Elmer Hall hiked most of the trail in 1976 and has run The Inn since 1977. Once a chaplain at Duke University, he has been a professional vegetarian cook for almost thirty years. When he's cooking, he displays the concentration of a great artist. So great is the respect with which his food is regarded that hikers even observe table manners there. They know that The Inn is more than just a place to grab a bite. Known also as Sunnybank, this 1875 inn is on the National Register of Historic Places. Hikers have been staying in the rambling Victorian house since 1890. Jane Gentry, a longtime proprietor, was a noted folk singer. Elmer has kept up the tradition of mountain hospitality, making sure that guests mingle. He's adept at helping the motley crew that flows through The Inn. Many people can point to an idea or a book that he's introduced them to, or some help he gave them finding a job.

Ranking with The Inn in most hikers' minds would be Shaw's in Monson, Maine. Shaw's is a boarding house run by Pat and Keith Shaw. They started out taking in mental-health patients, but since June 1977, they've catered to hikers and other outdoor people.

"I was born on Labor Day, and I just kept on working," Keith said. He grew up on a farm near Patten, Maine, northeast of Katahdin. At age eight his folks gave him eight cows to milk. Each year on his birthday they'd add another cow. When he left home at sixteen he was caring for sixteen cows. He got married at sixteen and had three daughters by nineteen.

He's a walking testament to the miracles of modern medicine as well as to the virtue of hard work. He's overcome injuries received during World War II and recovered from several operations, including quadruple bypass surgery. He said he gets to meet some of the nicest and most interesting people in the world by staying right at home.

At the opposite end of the culinary spectrum from The Inn, Shaw's features traditional, hardy Maine logging camp fare. It's hard to find a hiker who is not delighted by Pat's creations or Keith's huge breakfasts. He offers three breakfasts—a Shaw's, a hiker's special, and one for normal people.

Pancakes are a much-prized item along the trail. Some believe the Mount Cube Sugar House in New Hampshire serves the best pancakes on the A.T. The trail used to run right through this historic farm, owned by former governor and Mrs. Meldrim Thomson, Jr., since they moved to New

Hampshire in 1954. Now, the trail crossing is two miles away, but many hikers still find their way to the farm at the northern base of Mount Cube. It has been called the Mount Cube Sugar House since at least 1840. Mrs. Thomson has been doing most of the cooking herself since she opened the restaurant in 1970. She is known along the trail for her pancakes. "The hikers are starved for fats," she said. "They eat lots of butter and mountains of ice cream." Her hiker's special breakfast is six pancakes and four sausages. "They can eat that in the blink of an eye," she said. "Sometimes they get a second one."

The Thomsons put up hikers in a barn that features an exquisite view of Mount Moosilauke. Thanks to the birds in the barn, there are no insects. Both hikers themselves, the Thomsons have climbed all of the New Hampshire peaks over four thousand feet. "A day doesn't go by that I don't appreciate it here," Mrs. Thomson said.

Her first contact with a thru-hiker was when Grandma Gatewood stopped by on her first thru-hike. "We knew about the A.T., but we didn't realize then that anyone actually hiked the whole trail," Mrs. Thomson said. "Grandma Gatewood came after the kids had gone to school. There was a knock on the door. It was a little old lady, almost frail looking. She had a pack like a laundry bag, slung over her shoulder. She had a couple of news clippings by then, and she said, 'You've probably heard of me' but I hadn't. When I asked if she'd like something to eat, she got enthusiastic. She stayed on and did her laundry. She came two years later. By then, we were fast friends, and she was a celebrity, and she stayed over."

The Carrying Place near the Kennebec River in Maine rated near the top of the list when Dorie and Bud Williams were the proprietors. While they properly prided themselves on the quality of the food, hikers used to gorge on the breakfast. Bud would say it wasn't an all-you-could eat pig-out place, but he wouldn't let anyone leave hungry. The standard order of pancakes was twelve, the average was in the twenties, and one hiker supposedly ate seventy. The story goes that the hiker went back to the nearby Pierce Pond Lean-to and rested there till the following day.

The magic letters along the A.T. are AYCE—all you can eat. Hikers flock to these places, but they in turn are not prized customers, as they have been known to practically set down roots in the throes of a gorge cycle.

Another treasured commodity among hikers has always been ice cream. Most noted along the trail was the store at Pine Grove Furnace, Pennsylvania, where many hikers have tried to enter the "Half-Gallon Club" by eating a half gallon by themselves at a single sitting. The store was closed for renovations in the summer of 1993 but was expected to reopen in 1994.

"I remember craving ice cream so much when I got to one trail town in the South. It was so cold, I was shaking. But I ate my ice cream," said Rick Hancock.

Those who know ice cream favor the Vermonster, a huge assortment of Ben and Jerry's ice cream, toppings, and fillings. Manchester, Vermont, is a good place to try this creation, but bring some friends along to help. In ten minutes, Bill "Stats Godric" Gunderson and three other hikers polished off an entire Vermonster—twenty scoops of ice cream, strawberries, four bananas, crumbled brownies, a pint of whipped cream, hot fudge, and butterscotch, served in a big metal bowl. "It's the only time I've had an exclusive ice cream lunch," Bill said.

Rick Hancock and John Kuzniak did a twenty-five-mile day to reach Abol Bridge in Maine. Rick recalls, "Some campers who were going home had some extra food, and they gave us a whole canned ham. We squatted in the road, right in the dirt, started at either end, and met in the middle. We were like two cannibals."

David Denton

I had to be threatened with death before I took an interest in eating right,"
David Denton says. It's hard to listen to him for long without reconsidering
what you put in your stomach. He learned the hard way that poor diet has
a direct impact on your health and well-being. Thru-hikers put a lot of stress on
their bodies, but if they don't take care of their feet and stomachs they won't make it
to Maine.

David Denton's 1992 thru-hike was the happiest time of his life, but the
aftermath was a nightmare. Several weeks after completing his hike, he was
still suffering from fatigue. A doctor diagnosed his problem as a rare, fatal
genetic disease, called PFK, which causes muscles to degenerate. For nearly
two months at age twenty-five, he believed he had a terminal illness that
would kill him within two years. It was not until seven months after his initial complaint that he learned the truth: He had simply been undernourished
during his trip.

Every hiker has problems getting proper nutrition and sufficient quanti-
ties of food. David had two complicating factors: He has an unusually fast
metabolism, and he did half of his hike in winter, starting at Springer in
January and finishing at Katahdin in July. Winter hikers must consume food
at a furious rate to stay warm.

His condition baffled a string of doctors. "I was confused and misled," he
said. "Doctors don't see too many specimens who walk in the door in as good
shape as someone who just walked from Georgia to Maine. A thru-hiker's
physical condition is so out of the ordinary that if he has any kind of health

problems, he needs to have the doctor understand what he's just gone through.

It took two months to decide it was PFK," David said. "Then two months to decide it wasn't. For two months, I was pretty depressed about my life being over.

David started to get better on his own, which baffled the doctors too. A specialist repeated earlier tests and did a muscle biopsy, finally proving it wasn't the rare disease.

The problem, in simple terms, was that his body ran out of fuel and began eating muscle. It's not unlike an Olympic marathoner, who experiences a severe fuel deficit during his race. "He doesn't just get up the next day like nothing happened," David said. "He takes a little time to recuperate."

In retrospect, David believes he couldn't have hiked in winter without doing some muscle damage, though he could have minimized the problem by eating more complex carbohydrates, such as whole-grain rice. His experience has made him a student and passionate advocate of proper nutrition.

"It probably wouldn't have affected me if I hadn't started in winter," David said. "If five thousand to six thousand calories is enough in summer, you might need ten thousand to twelve thousand calories in winter. You use the same amount of vitamins and minerals. The only thing you need more of is carbohydrates."

His biggest mistake, he says, was using commercial processed foods from which much of the nutritional value had been removed.

When David backpacks now, he eats beans and whole-grain rice. He soaks the mixture all day in a pint container in his pack. This cuts the cooking time to within a few minutes of the processed foods most thru-hikers use.

He now believes that many thru-hikers quit the trail, often unknowingly, because of poor nutrition. "If you cut carbohydrates out of your diet for even two days, you feel bad. Food really does play a big role in your well-being," he said.

A number of common hiker foods are without nutritional value. "It might fill you up, but it's not doing you any good. It's like putting water in your gas tank. The gauge will say full, but it won't get you anywhere.

"On the trail, your body is functioning on such a high level you could probably digest anything short of nails. It's what you don't get that's a problem.

"You're already eating all your fat. You're dipping into your body's reserves. Cravings are not craziness. When I got to town, my body wanted the fat meat. My body wanted pure fat. I would eat a gallon of ice cream during my stay in a town. It's a standing joke, everyone wants ice cream. It's the body telling them they want fats."

Most thru-hikers start in Georgia in late spring. Starting at Springer in late January, David had some unique experiences. "I enjoyed starting in the winter," he said. "Solitude can teach you a lot.

"A couple of times I came close to hypothermia. I would try to write in registers and would have a tough time. If you're hiking solo in the winter, you have to pay attention to your body. There's no one to tell you if your speech is slurred."

The difference in his pack weight between winter and summer was forty pounds. In the winter he carried four sets of insulated underwear. Yet, "there were times when I had every stitch of clothes on and I was still chilly. I'd be in my tent inside a shelter, in a sleeping bag rated for zero degrees. I didn't have any body fat left. That gets you cold in a hurry."

One of his worst times on the trip occurred just south of Mount Rogers, Virginia, on Whitetop Mountain. "I crisscrossed the open summit and finally saw the blazes go into the woods. There was a big drop-off from the snowbank. I went face in with my pack on top of me. I couldn't get out. It was like being in an ice bath. It took me twenty seconds to know I would be able to get out. By then I was able to wriggle out of my pack. But I was six feet deep, face down. It was a little scary, a minute's worth of fright."

A highlight of the trail for him was meeting the people in towns. "It took me three towns to realize that I wasn't dreaming, that the people really were that nice. I've never been around that many nice people. It's more so in winter. People were just shocked when they found out I was a thru-hiker. First, they thought I was crazy, then they'd feel sorry for me, then they'd take me home."

Problems with his feet drove David off the trail for a week in Hot Springs. His feet had stretched from a size ten to a twelve and he had to get new boots. "By fifty miles before Hot Springs my feet were really bad," he said. "Most of my toenails were gone. A podiatrist told me that everybody's feet would stretch widthwise but the shoes will, too. You can predict whose feet will stretch lengthwise and cause problems. If the little toes are longer than the big one, even if they are curled under, the feet stretch out."

Later, in Pennsylvania, fifteen miles north of Duncannon, he stopped at the Peters Mountain Shelter. "I was sleeping away and at 11:30 there was a loud crash. I could see two of my silvery metallic food bags and the dim outline of a bear. He just stood there, then sauntered off. I put my boots on and went after him. I tried to make noise and scare him, hoping that he'd drop some of my food so I'd have some the next day. Then I got my camera because I'd heard that sometimes that scares them. That didn't work, but I got some good bear shots. The next day I got to thinking, what if he'd been really hungry and snacked on me? But all in all, it was pretty neat having that experience. I wasn't hurt. He just wanted my food."

Like many hikers, David was flooded with conflicting emotions when he climbed Katahdin. "I definitely didn't want to finish the trail." David, who lives in Atlanta, said, "If I'd had the money, I'd have turned around and walked back to Georgia. There's a drop in spirits when your trip is over. I stayed with another thru-hiker for three days and eased back into civilization. It's good to share that time with someone who understands your experience instead of someone who has no clue about what you've just gone through."

Despite the traumatic physical problems in the aftermath of his hike, David has fond memories of the A.T. "Hiking the trail was the happiest time in my entire life," he said. "I learned more about myself. I don't think a thru-hike could be overrated if you're having a good time. I was tired, but I was always in hog heaven hiking the A.T."

Harpers Ferry and Bear Mountain: The Middle Miles

Little did I dream more than fifty years ago when I sat down with two men in the New Jersey Highlands and outlined to them my idea of a footway through the Appalachians, that such plans would be translated into the institution that has now come to pass. I did little more than suggest the notion: I set the match to the fuse and set the chain reaction that has come about.

Benton MacKaye, statement read to ATC meeting
in Boone, North Carolina, 1975

B Y THE TIME A THRU-HIKER HAS COVERED A THOUSAND MILES with a thousand left to go, spirits often flag. After two or three months, the novelty has worn off. Many hikers say that by then, it's become a job more than a vacation. Most of them consider the high points of the trail to be at either end, with the middle something to be endured rather than savored.

Hikers especially dread Pennsylvania because of its fearsome stretches of rocks. Robie "Jumpstart" Hensley was told at the Port Clinton Hotel that "the trail workers get out here every spring and file those rocks to nice sharp points." Although it is paradise for geologists, it can make mincemeat out of hikers' soles. Like a used car on a long journey, a thru-hiker's body and equipment often begin to break down during the middle miles.

Sharon "April Fool" Rise, who hiked in 1989, felt ambivalent about the trail by the time she reached Pennsylvania. After hiking twenty-eight miles one day from Eckville to Lehigh Gap, Pennsylvania, she felt burned out. She went home to New Jersey for an event, traveled back to the trail, then went home again. She returned and hiked from the Delaware Water Gap to Tiorati Circle in Harriman Park, New York, then went home a third time. She waffled for a month and a half, undecided whether to quit or continue. While she was home, she missed the trail; while she was hiking, she longed for her friends and family back home. Finally, she returned to the trail for good, pleased with her decision to continue. Now, she works in a county park, sharing her love of the outdoors with youngsters.

Ralph Leuken hiked half the trail in 1990 and then bicycled parallel to the trail the rest of the way. He had intended to hike the whole way, "but I got to the point where I wasn't enjoying it. The weather was getting hotter, and in Pennsylvania there was less water. I had a bout with diarrhea and giardia for a couple of weeks."

Ralph found the trail more crowded than he expected. "I was expecting to be out on my own and secluded. I only spent one night alone in a shelter. I'm not antisocial, but I didn't expect to need to interact so much."

People drop off the trail every stretch of the way, from the parking lot at Amicalola Falls State Park to the Katahdin Stream Campground, the base of the final climb. But along the way people offer encouragement, and hikers look forward to seeing special sights. An unselfish gesture or a kind word can make the difference to a hiker who's discouraged by sore feet or a long spell of rain. Early in the trip, a hiker can anticipate the high mountains and botanical wonderland of Great Smoky Mountains National Park or the balds of Tennessee. Susan Gail Arey would look forward to the next town or national park. "It's the old saying," she said. "If something seems impossible, try to divide it into little pieces."

For Barb Briggs, two of the highlights of the trail were getting into Virginia—and getting out. After more than five hundred miles in the state, "I just wanted to be somewhere else," she said. "Before the hike, I had been willing to consider dropping out in Virginia, but I was surer than hell going to get to Damascus. Then Harpers Ferry was a big milestone. I was incredibly stubborn. I didn't want to have to go back and say I couldn't do it. Early on the trail my feet were killing me, but some other hikers got me back out there."

Rusty, whose Hard Times Hollow is for many hikers the favorite refuge along the whole trail, said he grew tired of seeing so many hikers drop out at Waynesboro, Virginia. He decided that if they had a place for rest and recreation, many would continue. But he's made his hollow, tucked in along the Blue Ridge Parkway, so pleasant for hikers that many find it hard to leave, and some stay for weeks.

A welder, Rusty moved to the hollow in 1980 and began fixing up an abandoned shack that was surrounded on three sides by national park land. The place had been farmed fifty years earlier but had been unoccupied for the past twenty.

Rusty's generous spirit has made the place a must-visit for thru-hikers, who started coming in late 1982. He's had almost forty thru-hikers at a time, and he is continually adding new bunkhouses and storage sheds as time and money permit. It may be the only place along the trail with both indoor and outdoor dartboards, as well as a ping-pong table. With the help of hikers who stay for a while, Rusty keeps chickens, turkeys, ducks, and other animals, and grows vegetables. He hunts and fishes, too. People pitch in with the cooking, and everyone eats together. A few years ago, he put in a wood-fired sauna fed by a pipe from a spring. He heats his house with wood and goes through eleven cords a year. For light, he relies on kerosene.

Be advised that rest here is not synonymous with sleep. Rusty wants hikers to have a place "to cut back and stay loose," and people party long into the night. Even in the winter, people stop by all the time. During the last few years, there haven't been forty-eight hours go by without someone staying at the hollow.

Not far up the road, a week to a week and a half for most hikers, is Harpers Ferry, West Virginia, the symbolic midpoint of the trail. There are many pretty mountain towns along the A.T. route, but none can match Harpers Ferry's combination of dramatic scenery and compelling history. Here, in a prelude to the Civil War in October 1859, John Brown led a raid on the armory and briefly controlled much of the town. The raid quickly failed and Brown was hanged, but it helped to galvanize the nation and set the course for war. During the war itself, Harpers Ferry was badly damaged as it changed hands eleven times between Union and Confederate forces.

In Harpers Ferry, the Shenandoah and Potomac Rivers cut dramatic gorges, which occasionally lead to massive flooding. One flood in 1936 destroyed the bridges across both rivers, and A.T. hikers had to rely on ferries until the late forties. Somewhat earlier, Thomas Jefferson wrote that "The passage of the Patowmac [sic] through the Blue Ridge is perhaps one of the most stupendous scenes in Nature." He added, "This scene is worth a voyage across the Atlantic."

High on a hillside, out of the river's way, sits the ATC headquarters. For the past quarter century, Harpers Ferry has been identified with the ATC. No one personifies the ATC more than Jean Cashin, who's been on staff since 1972. Jean was the second person hired after ATC switched from all-volunteer to some permanent staff. From her front desk, she greets most entering hikers, earning the nickname "Trail Mother" for her extensive knowledge and sympathetic ear. Said one hiker who spent a lot of time as an ATC volunteer, "She is the Appalachian Trail."

Cashin joined ATC shortly after Lester Holmes, the first executive director, moved the office from Washington, D.C., to Harpers Ferry. A casual day-hiker back then, Jean knew little about the A.T. Now, after talking to thousands of hikers, she is the court of last resort for questions about the A.T. It's been a ritual since 1979 to have Jean take pictures of all thru-hikers in front of the ATC office. While visiting ATC headquarters in early March 1993 I overheard Jean fielding calls from students planning to spend spring break in the Smokies. She patiently warned them that there could be a lot of snow. A little over a week later, the great blizzard of '93 stranded dozens of people in the Smokies.

By the time hikers get to Harpers Ferry, many are so acclimated to the woods that they have difficulty adjusting to town. Jean says that when she gives a hiker a ride she tries to drive slowly and keep them talking as a distraction. She remembers one hiker who couldn't drive when he got home; at first, he couldn't even cross the street.

Laurie "Mountain Laurel" Potteiger has seen Harpers Ferry from both sides. She thru-hiked the trail in 1986 and later joined the ATC staff. As a hiker, she found Harpers Ferry an unfriendly trail town. On staff, she at first found it difficult to be in an office while hikers downstairs chatted about their adventures. Now, she sometimes finds herself a little embarrassed by the hikers' lack of consideration, though as a thru-hiker herself, she understands their attitude. For months, they have been celebrities; many have looked forward that whole time to walking into ATC headquarters. The reality is that a lot of busy staffers have other things on their minds besides thru-hikers. "It's funny how my opinion of thru-hikers has changed," Laurie said. "Before I hiked the trail, I would rather have met a thru-hiker than a president. Now their character seems to impress me less than the average visitor."

A recent development makes the middle section more pleasant for many northbound hikers. Since 1987, Damascus has held a Trail Days celebration in mid-May at the peak of the thru-hiker wave. Many current hikers hitchhike to be there for the party, which also attracts hundreds of former hikers. The festival culminates in a hikers' talent show, high-spirited and imaginative. In 1993, entrants included women hikers in a skit about eating bugs, a harmonica-playing contortionist, and a song about trail miseries.

Often what pushes hikers through the middle miles is plain good company. In 1977, Bob Hill met Charlie Gilbert near Damascus. Soon, Phil Pepin joined them. At first the three weren't close, but as they continued hiking together, their friendship strengthened. Sixteen years later, they are like blood brothers. "We don't see each other often now, but when we do, it's like no time has elapsed. We have a real bond, like I have with few other friends," Bob said.

For Jim "Jimmy Bee" Bodmer, there was nothing to ease the pain of the middle miles. He stubbed his toes in Tennessee and then immediately put pressure on them on a long downhill. "They were hurting real bad," he said. "I was afraid to take off my shoe because of what I'd find. I had a blood blister on top of the toe, and it was black and blue."

Jimmy finally went to a doctor, who told him he had a hairline fracture. The doctor advised him to rest completely for a few days and then to cut off the top of the boot to relieve the pressure. Instead, he did eighteen miles that day trying to catch his friends, and sixteen the next. "Those that are stupid and stubborn keep going," he said. "I don't quit. After I got going in the morning, the pain in the toe would stop. But afterwards, on rainy days and when it got cold, the toe would hurt again until it warmed up. Also, I had shin splints, an Achilles tendon pull, and a back problem."

The middle section was a blur of pain and drudgery, and in retrospect, Jimmy wishes he had eased up. "I burnt out both physically and mentally. I called up my wife and said, 'What do you think if I drop off the trail?' She said, 'You've come so far. You'll never forgive yourself if you quit.'"

For several of Jimmy Bee's 1990 hiking companions, the middle section was also grueling. Nine hikers got together near Damascus, including one who'd been married at Trail Days under a canopy of hiking sticks. The nine friends had several weeks of enjoyable hiking together—one called it the highlight of his trail experience—but then, one by one, five came down with serious cases of giardia. End of fun.

John and Marilyn Pasanen had enjoyed the trail in the South but were growing weary in the middle states. They dropped off to attend a wedding and considered not coming back. But going through their packs back home, they found a pink slipper. Hikers that year had been passing it back and forth, slipping it into one another's packs. That tipped their decision to go back to the trail. Later, they got a postcard from a friend farther north on the trail, whose glowing praise of the White Mountains and Maine provided further incentive to continue.

The middle of the A.T. takes on special meaning, because historically it was the beginning of the trail. It was here that Benton MacKaye hatched his notion of an Appalachian Trail. And it was here that the actual building of the trail began.

In an article, entitled "An Appalachian Trail—A Project in Regional Planning," which appeared in the *American Institute of Architects Journal* in October 1921, MacKaye proposed a ridgetop trail from Mount Washington, New Hampshire, to Mount Mitchell, North Carolina. He also proposed a series of shelter camps (lodges), community camps, and farm camps along the way to serve as refuges for "the toilers in the beehive cities along the Atlantic seaboard and elsewhere."

On October 7, 1923, the first sixteen-mile stretch of trail was dedicated at Bear Mountain. On October 26–28, 1924, a meeting at Bear Mountain Inn with MacKaye, Raymond Torrey, Major William A. Welch, and others was the first major meeting devoted to the A.T. At that time, Welch's diamond A.T. symbol became the official trail marker.

The Bear Mountain Bridge, which the A.T. crosses, opened in 1924. Before that there were no bridges south of Albany except a railroad bridge at Poughkeepsie. Traffic had to cross the river on overcrowded ferries. Until the Bear Mountain Bridge was built, it appeared that hikers might have to cross the river farther north, at the Newburgh-Beacon Ferry. At the time, the Bear Mountain Bridge had the longest central span of any suspension bridge in the world—1,632 feet. For many years, hikers had to pay a dime to cross it, the only toll ever on the A.T.

On the east side of the bridge, the trail used to go straight up the face of Anthony's Nose, one of the best viewpoints along the Hudson Gorge. During World War II the military closed the trail for fear saboteurs would use it. After the war the trail on Anthony's Nose reopened for a few years; more recently it has run along the side of Anthony's Nose because the top came under the possession of Camp Smith National Guard base in the 1950s.

Heading west from Bear Mountain Bridge, the A.T.'s first route followed the old Queensboro Trail above Popolopen Brook. A quarter mile from the bridge, the trail followed a steep ridge up the north side of Bear Mountain. In 1927 construction of the Popolopen Drive (now the route of the Palisades Parkway) forced a relocation to the south of the road. In 1931 the trail was relocated around Hessian Lake and the Inn and past the ski jump, close to the trail's current location. Part of the A.T. is now known as the Major Welch Trail.

The area between Bear Mountain Inn and the bridge is an area of historic significance and of two trail distinctions. Near the Bear Mountain Nature Museum, which opened in 1927, the elevation of 124 feet is the lowest along the entire A.T. The zoo and museum complex, which is locked at 5 P.M., is the only place along the trail that is shut at night. It's also the best place along the trail to see a bear.

The whole middle area echoes with Revolutionary War history. The Hudson River Gorge, ringed with mountains as high as sixteen hundred feet above river level (from Storm King and Beacon in the north to Hook Mountain at the Tappan Zee), was a key military objective during the war. In an attempt to divide the colonies, British forces repeatedly tried to take control of the river there. At the mouth of Popolopen Creek were two forts, Clinton and Montgomery, which militias from Orange and Putnam Counties defended against British attack in 1777. In 1779, General Mad Anthony Wayne led an attack around Bear Mountain to Stony Point. The A.T. crosses both the 1777 and 1779 trails.

Because the Bear Mountain Bridge spans the narrowest part of the Hudson, revolutionary forces strung a chain across the river there to prevent the passage of British ships. A short distance to the north is the site at which Benedict Arnold, commander of West Point, plotted to turn over his post to the British.

East of the Hudson River, the middle section of the trail ends when the A.T. crosses into Connecticut. Many thru-hikers find their most luxurious A.T. accommodations just before the border, at Graymoor Monastery in New York. For more than twenty years, the center has provided long-distance hikers with a night's lodging in a private room, shower, laundry room, and dinner and breakfast. The rooms in the old friary would not strike most people as plush, but they are ideal for hikers. Brother Jerry Dalton, who now takes care of the hikers, dates the practice to the early seventies, when an animal ate an A.T. hiker's food. The hiker kept heading north. He came across the field and saw the monastery, he figured that if anyone would help him, someone there would. Now almost four hundred long-distance hikers a year stop at Graymoor. The monastery doesn't charge, but hikers' donations nearly cover costs.

Earl Shaffer

*E*arl Shaffer's name is magic to hikers. Friends and neighbors told me he's hard to track down but still enjoys talking about the trail. They were right on both counts. On a hot August Saturday I visited Earl at his home near the trail in Pennsylvania. We stood in the sunshine talking about his hikes, his Army service, and his other wide-ranging interests as his cats darted around. Earl appeared suddenly and left suddenly, melting away into his house, leaving a three-hour trail of stories, facts and figures, prophesies and philosophy, plans and regrets. No one better epitomizes the thru-hiker than this trail pioneer. "I'm a loner, but I've been in the swim of things," he said.*

Earl Shaffer's life is a throwback to an earlier, simpler age, when people enjoyed the mountains unencumbered by bureaucracies and other modern trappings. A man of contradictions, Earl shuns attention but sometimes rues being left out of the limelight. A sensitive, artistic soul, he seems incapable of understanding duplicity or guile and nurses the slights of too many losing battles. Something of a loner, Earl has maintained his love of the trail for more than half a century and has generally retained close ties to the hiking community. Even now, in his seventies, he talks of making a third A.T. thru-hike, while his physical condition permits.

Wanda "the Breeze" Kurdziel claims all hikers are poets at heart. Well, Earl actually writes poetry. His account of his 1948 thru-hike, *Walking with Spring,* is a classic trail diary. He is a good enough guitar player that his neighbors say he could be a professional.

For most of his life, he has supported himself refurbishing antiques. Now he lives a basic but active lifestyle, what he calls "camping out," on a homestead of a few acres. He raises some of his food, keeps bees, and works hard to fix up the property, which he acquired a few years ago. Although he usually keeps to himself, neighbors occasionally find a bag of his home-grown lettuce or strawberries on their doorsteps. And when they get him talking, the conversations can stretch far into the night, ranging from history to current events to biblical prophecy, and a host of other topics.

During his boyhood in York, Pennsylvania, and on a farm outside of town, Earl loved to roam the mountains and read about adventures and Indian lore. By age twelve, he was doing a man's work all day on the farm. In World War II, both Earl and his hunting and fishing buddy, Walter Wine-miller, served in the Pacific campaign. Earl and Walter had already talked about hiking the A.T. But Walter was killed in the first wave of the invasion of Iwo Jima. Earl worked on radio and radar. In an age before miniatur-ization, that meant lugging heavy equipment to perilous locations in the Pacific, where he served for three and a half years. Having studied German in high school, Earl thinks he could have made a good scout in Europe, but the Army had other plans for him. Before he shipped out for the Pacific, Earl was bivouacked in San Francisco's Cow Palace. Back then, cattle were still shown there, and Earl spent several rainy, muddy weeks, bedding down with his mates in a cramped stall. It was no doubt good preparation for backpacking.

After he returned from the war, Earl's interest in the A.T. was rekindled by an article on the trail in *Outdoor Life* magazine. He decided to walk the trail and clear his head of wartime traumas. He wrote that he was "confused and depressed."

The trail then was rough and difficult to follow. Earl found it heavily overgrown, with thousands of downed trees blocking the route. He was able to pick up the trail at intervals but frequently had to content himself with paralleling the A.T. as closely as possible. Sometimes, he wouldn't see a trace of the trail all day. His report to the ATC, in which he describes the diffi-culties finding the trail, is in sharp contrast to the current debate among hik-ers over whether to follow every white blaze.

South of the Smokies, Earl came across two hikers, one of whom had started a week before Earl, intending to hike the whole trail. After Fontana Dam in North Carolina, he never saw them again, nor did he see many other hikers.

Using mostly military surplus gear, Earl traveled light, putting up with a lot of discomfort to do so. He mailed his tent home near the start of the hike, finding it heavy and ineffective. By the time he reached the Smokies, he'd figured out what gear he needed for the rest of the trip. His pack, a mountain-troop rucksack from a surplus store, put weight on his shoulders and hips, unusual for packs of the time. To save weight, he removed most of the straps and a large outside pocket. For sleeping, he had a medium-weight blanket with a zipper. He used a single pair of moccasin boots, which he twice had resoled. Near Tapoco, North Carolina, he stashed his pack in the woods and walked to a country store. The owner gave him a burlap sack in which to carry his supplies back. Many times, especially in the White Mountains, he'd wrap his feet in the sack at night to keep warm.

Earl was a strong hiker, keeping up a steady pace that averaged seventeen miles a day. During a nighttime rain, he'd huddle under his Marine Corps poncho and cheer for an early dawn. He especially remembers spending two cold, rainy nights under his poncho in southern Virginia. "I just put up with it," he said. That year, it rained so much that his feet were rarely dry. He'd keep walking until he found a place where he could make a fire. The trail then went over the Pinnacles of the Dan in Virginia, which he considered one of the hardest parts of the trail. "It was somebody's idea of a joke," he said. Earl hurried to climb this steep, rocky stretch, using narrow ledges with precipitous drops to the Dan River, before rain would make it even more treacherous. In places, he had to descend facing the mountain.

Near the midpoint of his journey, at Holmes, New York, he wrote a poem on a postcard and sent it to the ATC meeting at Fontana Dam.

> The flowers bloom, the songbirds sing
> And though it sun or rain
> I walk the mountain tops with Spring
> From Georgia north to Maine.

This was his first contact with ATC during the trip.

When Earl finished, the ATC greeted his claim with skepticism until he showed his hundreds of slides and gave detailed descriptions of the trail. The first notice of his trip in the *A.T. News* was a four-inch blurb entitled "Continuous Trip over Trail" on the back page of the September 1948 issue.

After his thru-hike, Earl wrote an account of his trip for the *A.T. News* and the AMC's *Appalachia*. *National Geographic* reported on his hike in an August 1949 article on the trail. The publicity inspired many future thru-hikers.

Earl has stayed involved with the trail. He relocated sixty miles of the trail in Pennsylvania. He served as ATC corresponding secretary for five years. Hikers looking for information about the trail would write to him. He even hiked a few days with various thru-hikers in the fifties. While rehiking a stretch, he spent a week with Dorothy Laker on her second thru-hike. They hiked together from Curley Maple Gap Shelter near Erwin, Tennessee, to Damascus, Virginia. He was supposed to rejoin her in Pennsylvania, but they didn't connect. He still enjoys talking to hikers and often visits the trail near his home.

Jim "Pony" Adams speaks of the time he was returning to the A.T., walking along a Pennsylvania highway, when an old van passed him. The driver suddenly slammed on the brakes, swung around, and came back. Alone and apprehensive, Jim hurried into the woods. A man ran a hundred yards along the trail to catch him. It was Earl Shaffer, just wanting to talk about the trail.

In 1965, Earl hiked the A.T. southbound, becoming the first person to thru-hike the trail in both directions. Describing the trip in an article for the *A.T. News* entitled "Chasing Autumn," he said one third of the trail was new and much improved. He hiked the trail in ninety-nine days, an average of twenty miles per day, partly because he hurried to escape bad weather near the end of the trip. He started on July 19, finished on October 25, and found water scarce along the way. Because of the dry weather, he seldom made cooking fires. Instead, he ate a lot of peanut butter sandwiches. He used much of his original equipment, including his pack. He did carry a lighter load, about thirty pounds, compared to forty on his first trip.

In Georgia Earl endured much misery with cold rain nearly every day; he even considered abandoning his trip. For warmth at night, he'd pile leaves on the ground, wrap himself in his plastic tarp, and cover that with leaves, leaving only his head sticking out. At times, he thought he was "a goner."

Desperate to finish, Earl descended into Unicol Gap, Georgia, where he saw a man with his family. He recognized Gene Espy, the second person to hike the A.T. By chance, Gene had brought his two daughters to see the fall leaves.

"I had no idea he was on the trail," said Gene. "Five minutes earlier or later and we wouldn't have met." Gene took Earl into town and helped him replace some of his worn clothing and his depleted food supply, and revived his spirits. "He gave me the boost to finish," Earl said.

Throughout the eighties, Earl tried to relocate to a cabin near the Pennsylvania A.T., but plans fell through, disappointing him greatly. He figured living near the trail would have gotten him involved again, and given him a chance to help hikers. He pictured himself roaming the trail on sleepless nights under a full moon.

Difficulties and Dangers along the Trail

There's a race of men that don't fit in,
A race that can't stand still;
So they break the hearts of kith and kin,
And they roam the world at will.
They range the field and they rove the flood,
And they climb the mountain's crest;
Theirs is the curse of the gypsy blood,
And they don't know how to rest.

Robert Service, Poet of the Yukon, from
"The Men that Don't Fit In"

THE A.T. IS NOT COMPLETELY SAFE, BUT DON'T BRING A GUN. Mosquitoes are too small to shoot, and mice are too elusive. People worry about snakes and bears, but they shouldn't. It's possible to get mauled by a bear or bitten by a poisonous snake, but the odds of having a traffic accident on the way to the trailhead are much greater.

One likely will encounter other miseries or dangers on the trail. Possibilities include heat and cold, snow and rain, malnutrition, hypothermia, giardia, diarrhea, drowning, lightning, and pack snatching. Serious crime, while rare, has happened. There have been murders, rapes, and less serious assaults.

Cataloguing the physical challenges he overcame, Noel "the Singing

Horseman" DeCavalcante wrote, "I lost forty pounds. I pulled knee ligaments, got blisters, shinsplints, twisted ankles, and a stress fracture. I hurt my Achilles, and lost my toenails. I pinched a nerve in my neck and got poison ivy and a million cuts, scratches, and lacerations. I had hurts I can't even remember."

Hypothermia, a potentially fatal drop in body temperature, is a common problem along the A.T., particularly for lone hikers. One is susceptible on rainy, blustery days when the temperature is above freezing. Those are precisely the conditions one frequently encounters in spring in the southern Appalachians. Actually, dangerous conditions can occur in any month, at any point along the trail. Keep in mind, also, that fatigue and hunger can aggravate the symptoms of hypothermia, which include shivering, lethargy, and confusion.

Sonie "Light Eagle" Shames recalls being on the verge of hypothermia when she arrived at a Georgia road crossing on her 1988 hike. Her teeth were chattering so hard, she could barely talk. Fortunately, a woman came to her aid, offering her hot tea and warm clothes.

Paul "Bigfoot" Tourigny found himself approaching hypothermia at Walnut Mountain Shelter in North Carolina. "I'd been wet, I'd been cold, and I kept plugging on. I was just wiped out. I still had my senses, but I was shivering. I wasn't hungry. Who comes to the rescue? Albie Pokrob." Albie arrived at the shelter soon after Paul got into trouble. He thawed him out with warm soup and drinks.

Defend against hypothermia by carrying enough warm clothes. Wool and synthetics are better than cotton at retaining body heat when wet. Leave the blue jeans at home.

Another defense is knowledge. Keep in mind that the weather can change quickly in the mountains. Most hikers who start in Georgia in March or April go through at least one big snowstorm. In the north, particularly in the Whites and the higher mountains of Maine, cold weather, including snow, is possible even in July and August. Hikers have made the mistake of mailing warm clothes home after a seventy-degree day, only to find it in the thirties a few days later. Syd "Not That Vicious" Nisbet, on his fourth thru-hike in 1990, made that mistake again. He, like other thru-hikers, mailed his warm clothes home after crossing the Smokies, but before climbing 6,200-foot Roan Mountain and the range beyond. Severe snowstorms can hit that area quite late in the spring.

Walking the Appalachian Trail

One time, Ray Hunt got a personal lesson in why one shouldn't rely too heavily on weather forecasts. Holed up overnight in a Georgia shelter in heavy rains, Hunt's companions were four men from the long-range weather-forecasting bureau in Atlanta. They'd picked that weekend for a hike because the weather was supposed to be fine.

One part of the A.T. experience that Ray thought was among the most dangerous was crossing the bridge over the Susquehanna River at Duncannon, Pennsylvania. He had to walk on a narrow sidewalk next to a two-lane highway with 32-wheelers roaring past. When trucks went by with big mirrors, he had to lean away to avoid being hit. About ten years ago, a new bridge opened up with a wider, more protected walkway.

Giardia has become more common in the last decade. This waterborne parasite can cause intestinal problems for a long time, particularly if not properly diagnosed. Symptoms of giardia include diarrhea, nausea, and extreme fatigue. Generally picked up in drinking water, giardia was originally spread by animals; at one-time it was called "beaver fever." Roly Mueser believes that in the backcountry people spread it with poor hygiene. Roly found that, contrary to expectations, people who treated water were statistically as likely to get sick from water-borne illnesses as people who don't. But he, like most people, recommends treating suspect water. Hikers should treat at least some of their drinking water by filtering, boiling, or adding chemicals. Most hikers do not treat water that comes directly from an underground spring. Other than that, views vary, but most hikers treat at least some of their water and few treat all of it.

In 1990, five hikers traveling in a group in southern Virginia contracted giardia. They spent time in emergency rooms or clinics, and most spent at least a week convalescing before they could return to the trail. It's not always easy to diagnose giardia, but those who have it must receive medical treatment. If you experience lingering diarrhea, see a doctor.

Lightning is a real problem along the trail. Although reportedly no A.T. hikers have ever been killed by lightning, many have had close calls. Each year, lightning kills about one hundred people in the United States. On his 1977 hike, Phil Pepin had brushes with lightning in New York and the White Mountains. As he was walking along a road in New York, he saw a flash that seemed to come out of the ground a few feet from him. It sounded like jumper cables shorting out. He could feel the hair standing up on the back of his neck. Suddenly lightning struck thirty feet ahead of him. Then another bolt hit nearby. He raced ahead, found a building, and huddled out of the storm. "The lightning was like a shotgun blast," he said. "I have a healthy respect for lightning."

Paul Tourigny has developed a strategy that minimizes his exposure to lightning. He starts hiking early in the day and tries to be in a shelter by four P.M. He finds that most mountain storms hit later than that. Getting in early gives him more time to recuperate, wash, and hang up his sweat-drenched clothes to dry. It also improves his chances of finding space in crowded shelters.

Roger Brickner, the A.T.'s weather expert, confirms that in the summer, three quarters of mountain thunderstorms hit after late afternoon.

Open country and exposed places above treeline are the most hazardous for hikers caught in thunderstorms. Many hikers have felt vulnerable in the open stretch north of Roan Mountain. Roly Mueser, who is a physicist and was the Bell System's lightning expert for part of his career, says during a lightning storm, hikers should avoid the highest part of the landscape. Hair is raised by the electrical field preceding a lightning bolt. That's a sign—albeit a late one—to get off the mountaintop. Lying in a ditch is safer than standing, especially if you're the tallest object around. One also should avoid isolated targets like lone trees and mountaintop shelters.

Mary Jo Callan, the grandmother who repeatedly hiked the southern A.T., was on her first A.T. backpacking trip when lightning came calling. According to Jean Cashin, Mary Jo and her hiking companion were knocked across their tent by a lightning bolt. Mary Jo's companion decided she had better things to do with her time, but Mary Jo continued hiking.

A far more common danger for hikers is falling. Hardly anyone covers the whole A.T. without at least a few falls. Some cause broken bones or even death. Bill "the Orient Express" Irwin, the blind thru-hiker, must have the record with an estimated five thousand falls.

Mitch "Breeze" Keiler had one close call going up Kinsman Mountain in New Hampshire. "I didn't read how tough it was going to be. The guidebook said grab hold of any roots or rocks you can. Coming down, I did a complete somersault and landed in a fir tree on my pack." Luckily, he escaped serious injury. "In the Whites I fell every day," he said.

Foot, knee, and leg problems are among the most common hiker ailments. Dan Nellis, an outdoor-education instructor, stresses that you should wash your feet and socks often. He washes a pair of socks every day and hangs them on his pack to dry. He also suggests inspecting your feet every few days to see if serious problems are developing. He notes that it's human nature to hope that problems will go away. But if we treat minor problems before they fester, major problems can often be avoided. It's not uncommon for hikers to be driven off the trail because of, say, infected blisters, which could have been averted.

The most common cause of foot problems is boots that fit poorly or are not properly broken in. Some boots, especially lightweight models, are easier to break in than others. But bear in mind that just because boots feel good walking around your house doesn't mean they will hold up for full days of hiking steep, rocky trails with a heavy pack. If you have a problem, try to rectify it before it knocks you off the trail for good.

"I never really believed I'd make it," said Laurie "A Traveling Wilbury" Mack. "I'd had knee problems since I was young. I met a neuromuscular therapist at Trail Days in Damascus. Before we'd hardly said hello, he asked if I was having problems with my knees. He said, 'Your ankles are swollen.' I hadn't noticed. He did massage therapy on my legs several times, and it was incredible. I had one thousand miles pain free."

A less obvious source of danger is the confidence, almost hubris, that thru-hikers acquire. "I felt I was nothing but hard muscle and spring steel," said Dan Nellis. "It was exhilarating." But he believes that sometimes this attitude can lead to trouble. One instance he cited was sprinting down the trail, catching a foot on a rock, skinning a knee and denting a pack frame. "With my outdoor experience, I know that when we're real confident, the accidents happen," he said.

For the most part, following the trail now is not hard, but few hikers escape without getting lost at least once. Jean and Mortimer Weiser did the trail in sections, day-hiking as much as possible. They got through Mahoosuc Notch in Maine by noon. Because Jean was the slower hiker, she decided to get a head start on the steep climb up Mahoosuc Arm. Meanwhile, Mortimer became disoriented and went partway back through the notch, a narrow jumble of boulders that is the slowest, toughest mile of the trail. They were eventually reunited, but then it started to rain, and they still had the steep descent of Old Speck to do in the dark. They borrowed a flashlight and headed down, spotting only one blaze at a time. Sometimes, they had to sit down and feel their way. "Things kept going from bad to worse," Jean said. They finally emerged at 10 P.M.

It's not unusual to get disoriented on the trail, particularly starting in the morning from a shelter. Bill Irwin, the blind hiker, would always sleep pointed toward the next day's travel.

An unusual but painful problem struck Pete "Woulda, Coulda, Shoulda" Suscy and his partner at the start of the trail. Pete started in mid-May, and for eight straight days, it was bright and sunny without a cloud. Most hikers start earlier in the spring, when it's usually cloudy and rainy. The leaves still weren't out, and Pete had just gotten a short haircut. "My ears got really sunburned," Pete said. "I wore a baseball cap, but it didn't cover my ears."

Insects are often the biggest annoyance on the trail. Several hikers, including Grandma Gatewood and Paul "Lucky, Lucky, Lucky" Holabaugh, reported that wearing sassafras leaves in a band on their heads kept most bugs away.

In North Adams, Massachusetts, Dick "Lo-Tec" Cieslik found he had trickles of blood on his stomach from blackfly bites. He'd been wearing a net shirt. The bites eventually swelled to the size of half-dollars, lasting a month.

Another growing concern is Lyme disease. It is spread primarily by tiny deer ticks. The symptoms of the disease include a red, inflamed circle around the bite; fatigue; joint pain; and nausea. Since these symptoms are common in other afflictions, Lyme disease is difficult to identify without a blood test. If a doctor can't identify your illness, inquire about Lyme, reminding him that you've spent a lot of time in the woods. It can be effectively treated with antibiotics if caught early.

An unexpected, but nonetheless real, danger for hikers is their own equipment. They can impale themselves on their walking sticks, break their packs, and turn their stoves into fireballs. Frank "Red Blaze" Shea had been fiddling with his white-gas stove the whole trip. Every few weeks, it would clog up and stop working. He cleaned it and usually got it to work, but this time was different. He was sitting at the picnic table in front of the Rausch Gap Shelter, (also known as the "Halfway Hilton") in Pennsylvania. The stove wouldn't work. He cleaned it, tried again, then walked away to calm down. When he returned and lit it again, a flame shot eight feet into the air. "I jumped halfway across the valley in a second," he said. The fuel can, which had been full with thirty-two ounces of white gas, burned for ten minutes.

In the A.T.'s seventy-year history, seven hikers have been murdered, five since 1981. There is some debate about the efficacy of firearms for personal defense, but the ATC and most hikers discourage their use. Noel "the Singing Horseman" DeCavalcante wrote a letter to the *A.T. News* saying that

Above: Shadbush and clouds are visible from the summit of Blood Mountain, highest point on the A.T. in Georgia and an early landmark for northbound hikers.

Left: Peaceful and flower-filled in summer, these fields north of Roan Mountain in North Carolina are the site of severe storms that catch many hikers by surprise. Elevation here is over five thousand feet.

Above: Hump Mountain, along the
Tennessee–North Carolina border, is one of the
unique southern balds.

Top right: Upon descending into Spivey Gap, the
thru-hiker has come more than three hundred miles
from Springer Mountain. The trail signs along
the way are both encouraging and daunting. Here,
in 1975, Ned Greist completed the A.T.; it had
taken him forty-five years to hike the two
thousand miles.

Right: Wooden ladders, known as stiles, help hikers
cross pasture fences without letting the livestock
out. This farm, in Virginia's Sinking Creek Valley,
is near the ATC regional office in Newport.

APPALACHIAN TRAIL

SPIVEY GAP – 3252

HIGH ROCKS – 4280	→	1·1
WHISTLING GAP	→	1·8
LITTLE BALD – 5185	→	3·5
BIG STAMP	→	5·5
BIG BALD – 5516	→	5·7
STREET GAP	→	9·5
SAMS GAP – U.S. 23 HWY.	→	11·3
LOCUST RIDGE LEAN-TO	→	20·5
HOT SPRINGS, N.C.	→	49·5
GREAT SMOKY MTNS. NAT'L PARK	→	°81·3
SPRINGER MTN. GEORGIA (TRAIL TERMINUS)	→	307·1

U.S
NATIONAL
SCENIC
TRAIL

SOUTH

Right: Trillium and mayapple flourish on Thunder Ridge, near the Peaks of Otter in Virginia. Thru-hikers enjoy a profusion of spring wildflowers as they head north through the Blue Ridge.

Below: The pond at Punch Bowl Shelter, in Virginia, makes a scenic campsite.

Crabtree Falls, Virginia, on a side trail of the A.T., is one of the highest cascades in the eastern United States.

Above: At Humpback Rocks, south of Shenandoah National Park, Harry "the Indian" Thomas tied up a rattlesnake to guard his pack.

Top right: Maryland Heights offers a fine view of Harpers Ferry, West Virginia. The A.T. Conference headquarters is located here.

Right: Pennsylvania's Rausch Gap Shelter, in St. Anthony's wilderness, is known as the Halfway Hilton because of the beautiful setting. Here, in 1990, Frank "Red Blaze" Shea's backpacking stove exploded, sending up a geyser of flames.

Left: The A.T. descends from the Appalachian ridges to cross Kittatinny Valley in New Jersey, one of the low sections hikers cross in the middle miles of the trail.

Below left: Laurel blooms near Cat Rocks in New York, north of Roger's Appalachia Cottage at Greenwood Lake.

Below: Island Pond is in Harriman State Park, New York.

*Above: The Lemon Squeezer, a tight path
between jumbles of rocks, is another landmark
in Harriman State Park, a short distance
north of Island Pond.*

*Top right: Bright fall foliage quickens hikers'
pace as they overlook Tyringham Valley in the
Berkshires of Massachusetts.*

*Right: Cheshire, Massachusetts, is a classic
New England village that can be appreciated
from the Cobbles.*

Above: Little Rock Pond is one of the many scenic gems along the A.T. in Vermont.

Right: After leaving the Green Mountains, the A.T. passes through Vermont's lowlands as it heads toward the White Mountains. This field is between Thistle and Bunker Hills.

Left: At the base of Mount Cube, New Hampshire, blueberries are put to good use in pancakes served by the Mount Cube Sugarhouse.

Below: As the hiker looks south from Mount Lafayette, Mounts Flume and Lincoln loom ahead. Ridgewalking in the White Mountains of New Hampshire is one of the highlights of the A.T.

Left: Surplus Pond is one of dozens along the A.T. in Maine. For most hikers, the ponds, blueberries, moose, and wilderness character of the state make Maine their most memorable section.

Below left: Bear Pond Ledges, north of Monson, forms part of a 100-mile remote stretch through the Maine wilderness.

Below: This area near Katahdin Stream Falls, looking toward the Katahdinough, was a favorite of A.T. visionary Myron Avery.

*In Daicey Pond hikers see the reflection of what
has been their goal through many long and weary
days: Mount Katahdin.*

as a former career military officer and lifelong hunter, he does not object to guns in general but feels they have no place on the trail. Others point out that four of the murder victims were attacked in their sleep, so what good would it have done to carry a gun?

As Maurice Forrester, Jr., put it in the *A.T. News,* the age of innocence on the trail is gone for good. The idea that the trail is a sort of haven, immune from the ills of society, is out of date. Still, the A.T. remains remarkably safe. "The Appalachian Trail may not be the paradise our fancies would like, but it is still a far better place than most others," Forrester concluded.

Every year, at least a few packs are stolen. Rape is a continual concern, particularly on the section of trail north of Elk Park, North Carolina, a high-crime area. Although many women do hike alone safely, they need to observe proper precautions, as do male hikers.

"It was brought home to me by Andy Coone, when his pack was stolen," said Jan "Sacajawea" Collins. "I came across his things on the trail. It was 1982, the year after the murders [of a young couple at Wapiti Shelter, Virginia]. I found Andy's sleeping bag and tent scattered in the bushes, but no pack. That's all I could picture—a copycat crime. We booked it [walked fast] to the road and tried to flag down a car. It was ninety degrees, and we looked like slimeballs. We were so distressed. Finally, I decided to stand in the middle of the road and get somebody to stop. I needed to know where Andy was. A nice couple stopped and rolled down their window a crack, just enough to hear what I had to say. I told them my friend was missing. They had a tremendous amount of trust to take us to the police. The police couldn't find his name because they had it spelled wrong. Finally, they told us he was okay. The couple drove us to his hotel, and there was Andy. He was so scared. He had been there a few days. He didn't want the incident to end his trip, and he asked us to go back with him to get his remaining things." Andy had been beaten up and had thought his arm was broken. No one would stop for him or let him into a house to make a phone call. Later, describing the attack in a shelter register, Andy wrote a courageous and humorous entry that closed with "People shouldn't pick on short people." He's continued to hike the A.T., completing five thru-hikes and working as a hostel or shelter caretaker other summers.

Even veteran hikers are careful whom they tell about their travel plans or where they'll be staying. Women, especially, need to be attentive when crossing roads. Many pretend that they are with a group by using the plural ("we're going to do this"), and by looking down the trail as if they're expecting someone. Most advise that if you pick up "bad vibes" about a person or a situation, it's best to move on. "If somebody gives you the creeps, get away," said Susan Gail Arey. Often a person's senses pick up subliminal cues about a situation that are on target but don't readily translate to the conscious mind. Always be prepared to move on if you don't feel comfortable at a shelter. Some hikers try to avoid camping near a road or at an easily accessible shelter.

Still, the risks, while real, need to be kept in perspective. "I've done most of my 5,600 miles of backpacking alone," Susan Gail said. "If I didn't go alone, I wouldn't go at all. There are things that are a whole lot scarier than backpacking alone."

"Walkin'" Jim Stoltz

*A*mong thru-hikers, "Walkin'" Jim Stoltz stands out in many ways. One in
particular is that he has continued to hike, largely off major trails, for the
last twenty years. A singer, guitar player, and photographer, he's also
become an influential advocate for the preservation of wilderness lands in the West.
I spoke to him at the 1993 ALDHA Gathering in Athens, West Virginia, where he
has given concerts for many years.

"Walkin'" Jim Stoltz thru-hiked the A.T. in 1974 and ever since has
continued to take long hikes through the wilderness. "It was one of the turning points in my life, although I didn't realize it at the time," he said. In
between long hikes, he tours the country giving concerts and slide shows
about his trips. He carries a guitar on his pack and writes songs. Of his hiking, he said, "It's a rich man's life without the money."

He got his start, in both hiking and music, in the Boy Scouts. When his
scoutmaster took the troop camping, he would bring his guitar, sing folk
songs, and dispense bits of wisdom. That's when Jim first picked up the guitar. A few years ago, he gave a concert at Bowdoin College in Maine and
invited his old scoutmaster, who now lives nearby. "It was exciting for me,"
Jim said. "I wanted him to see what I've done with my life." Jim dedicated
one of his songs to the scoutmaster—"Searching for the Road Not Taken,"
based on the well-known Robert Frost poem. "I was really proud he could
see it," Jim said.

In 1973, after dropping out of college, Stoltz was hiking in Shenandoah
National Park when he ran into a thru-hiker. "I had no direction and was

pretty insecure," Jim said. "I was captivated by this grand adventure. I questioned him for an hour. The next year I did the A.T.

"The A.T. changed me in a lot of ways," he said. "It made me more social and helped me blossom as a human being. The kindnesses I received all the way restored a faith in humanity that I'd lost."

He took six and a half months—from March to mid-October—to complete the trail. His father kept track of his progress by sticking pins in a huge wall map. Along the way, Jim stopped and did some short side trails, to such places as Gulf Hagas in Maine and Crabtree Falls and Whiteoak Canyon in Virginia. When he reached Maine, he slowed down. "I didn't want it to end," he said. Already he was planning his next walk: a five-thousand-mile coast-to-coast trip.

Jim admits his A.T. thru-hike didn't get off to a promising start. He had heavy hiking boots, and after a couple of days, he also had big blisters on both heels. "I was limping along. It was the most painful situation ever for walking," Jim said. "What kept me going was that I wanted to be there. It added some adventure in my life. Even though I was hurting, I was enjoying it.

"I have a song that goes 'It's funny how the spirit will see you through the hard times.' The spirit, the will to be out there, keeps you going. After eighteen thousand miles, the hard times are just part of it. You just accept it after a while. The real steep climbs are a part of it—like the flat trail."

There were plenty of hard times. Three days out from Springer, he ran into tornadoes and rainstorms. He didn't have a tent and was totally soaked. He hitchhiked into Dahlonega and threw his clothes into the dryer.

After nearly twenty years, he still has vivid memories of the A.T. "For about five years, I could tell you the name of every place I stayed," Jim said. A lot of his memories are of people, often fellow hikers in trail shelters. He recalls taking refuge in the Standing Indian Shelter in North Carolina during a big ice storm. There were eleven long-distance hikers crammed like sardines into a shelter for two nights. "All we did was talk about food, snakes, and bears," he said.

He was on the southern A.T. one windy night. A shelter was in bad shape, so he and some other hikers set up their tents. They were standing around one tent talking when they heard a loud noise. A tree had crashed down on an empty tent. "We were all in shock," Jim said. "It was a close call. If the hiker had been in his tent, he would have been killed. It was a real lesson. Now, I'm always aware of where I set my tent up."

Jim also had a brush with hypothermia. He had done his longest day on the trail, thirty-one miles, trying to get to the post office in Port Clinton, Pennsylvania, on a Saturday morning before it closed. As it turned out, the post office was closed all day, and his big hiking day was for nothing. It rained all day, and he grew wetter and colder. He made it to the shelter before Port Clinton, but his hands were so numb he couldn't use them. With his teeth, he pulled his sleeping bag open and crawled inside. He was scared but thinking clearly, indicating the hypothermia was not advanced.

He had mixed feelings when he reached Katahdin in mid-October. "It was exciting to be finally up there and say I really did this, but I was sad to be finished. If I'd had enough money, I'd have turned around and kept going. It was a mixture of sadness in the ending and joy in realizing I had done it."

Because of the harsh weather that late in the season, he had to wait four days to climb Katahdin. When he finally did, it was a perfect day with fall colors down below, ice and snow on top, and views far across the Maine wilderness.

When Jim finished the trail, he had one penny left and two weeks's worth of food that other hikers had given him. He hitchhiked around for a while and finally got a job.

The next year, 1975, Jim set out on a five-thousand-mile, eighteen-month cross-country walk that confirmed his life as a wilderness hiker. He started at West Quoddy Head, Maine, the easternmost part of the forty-eight contiguous states. From there, Jim walked to Katahdin and followed the A.T. to Clarendon Gorge, Vermont, before heading across the Adirondacks. He followed abandoned railroad grades in western New York, then crossed into Canada and hiked the Bruce Trail. He returned to the United States via the upper peninsula of Michigan.

Across the upper Midwest, he took two breaks of six weeks each. In between, he snowshoed for three months. On the frigid night of November 10, 1975, when the ore boat *Edmund Fitzgerald* went down in Lake Superior with no survivors, Jim was camped by the lake. "It was the most miserable night I've ever had," Jim said. The falling wet snow would pile up on his tent roof, and then the high winds would knock the tent down. Every few hours, he'd have to crawl out, remove the snow from the roof, and put the tent up again. "I was totally soaked," he said. He had lingering ill effects from that night for weeks.

Once he fell through ice into chest-deep slushy water. The air temperature was about ten degrees, and when he managed to climb out, everything quickly started to freeze. Although he didn't usually have a campfire, he had gathered some wood before he fell in. He was able to build a big fire and warm himself and dry everything.

He ended his coast-to-coast walk in Cape Alava, Washington, the westernmost part of the forty-eight contiguous states.

During that trip he used a walking stick that was a piece of driftwood he'd picked up on the Atlantic coast. "The plan was to drop it in the Pacific. When I got there I couldn't let go of it."

In 1979, Jim walked the Continental Divide Trail from Mexico to Canada. Since then, he's taken many other long walks through Arizona, Utah, Wyoming, Oregon, Idaho, and Montana. In 1988, after he was married, he and his wife, Leslie, took a three-week honeymoon hike in the Grand Canyon. They intended to hike the length of the canyon, but Leslie hurt her leg. Jim has taken three long hikes with Leslie. "As much as I love hiking with her, it's different from hiking alone," he said. "It's a barrier to nature. Often we're talking. I'm aware of the other person rather than what's going on around me."

He writes most of his songs while he's hiking. "It's re-creation," he said. "I need a spark of creativity." Now, he's doing shorter hikes of two to three months because his music has become so popular. Having turned forty, he finds that he's slowing down a bit. "If I do a twenty-mile day, I really feel it," he said.

He also finds that he is satisfied now with less food on the trail. "Before, I could never get enough." He normally carries a two-week supply of food and has carried up to twenty-two days' worth of provisions.

He began carrying a guitar on his Continental Divide hike in 1979, and now he carries one all the time. It weighs two pounds. He carried his old guitar for eight thousand miles with no case, just lashing it to the back of his pack with the neck down. The rain drenched it and the sun burned it, but it still worked. He even credits it with saving his life.

While hiking through Utah, he spent a night on top of a steep mountain. When he woke up, he saw that the mountain was icy. Trying to skirt a cliff, Jim slipped, falling toward the edge. He kicked his feet in and clawed with his hands, but nothing worked. Realizing he was going over the edge, he rolled onto his back to see where he was headed. As he did, the neck of his guitar jammed into the ice, stopping him. Now, he says, "My advice to hikers is, if they're ever crossing an ice field, carry a guitar."

"My life is so blessed. I've seen so many special things. I'm lucky enough to make my living doing what I want to do.

"The more I'm out there, the more I'm convinced it's the time, not the miles. It's not the eighteen thousand miles, it's the twenty years. I'd much rather take my time."

Mental Challenges and the Importance of Attitude

Keep on going, and the chances are that you will stumble on some-thing, perhaps when you are least expecting it. I never heard of any-one ever stumbling on something sitting down.

Charles F. Kettering

O NE "LUCKY" IS FOR LIFE, ONE FOR BEING ON THE TRAIL, THE third for good fortune along the way. Maybe no one has ever brought a better attitude to the trail than Paul "Lucky, Lucky, Lucky" Holabaugh. Where others saw problems, he saw opportunities. Where others merely complained of the blackflies, he arranged sassafras leaves in a bandanna and shooed them away. Others saw rainy days; he saw the sunshine in between.

It's nice to have good equipment, be in superb shape, and have pleasant companions. But what's really critical for a 2,000-miler is attitude. You could hike the whole trail with a rotten attitude, but you wouldn't enjoy it and probably wouldn't make it very far. Successful hikers are fiercely determined; they say things like, "It'll take more than one broken bone to stop me."

The successful hikers are the ones who find goodness and joy even in the difficult times, who see beyond the misery to the beauty of nature and the comforts of trail society. They're the ones who know that the rain turns the forest into a magical wonderland and provides the rainbow that caps the day.

Warren Doyle's well-known A.T. weather forecast is one nice day for hiking out of five. But Jan "Sacajawea" Collins would wake up every day and say, "This is beautiful." Even if it were raining, she'd say, "This is the best day of my life."

"Any day I'm outdoors is a good day," said Laurie "A Traveling Wilbury" Mack. "There's always something different on the trail."

Veteran hikers advise rookies not to fight the trail, to accept it for what it is. The trail's not going to change, the argument goes, so you'd better change. "The ones who don't survive are the ones who can't change the way the trail demands," said Jim "Bald Eagle" Owen.

Wanda "the Breeze" Kurdziel says she doesn't want to look at maps that show how steep the day's hike is. "I take it as if I'm discovering it. If it's there, I'm going to do it, no matter what." It's easy to fall into the trap of criticizing the route the trail takes, or to question why it was relocated to a particular spot, but such thinking only frustrates a hiker. Often, the reason for the trail's location is not readily apparent. Perhaps the land isn't in public hands or there has been a compromise between competing interests.

"The trail taught me about patience," said Dick "Lo-Tec" Cieslik. "I was edgy and nervous and short-tempered before the trail. You can't push the mountains around. You have to learn to adjust to them."

Hikers say that it's easier to enjoy yourself on the trail if you have firm goals in mind, whether it's hiking the trail end to end, making friends, or learning wildflowers. If you have goals, they say, you won't be persuaded to do things you don't want to do. Many hikers walk too fast to keep up with friends, which makes them more prone to injury, frustration, and defeat. Jim "Jimmy Bee" Bodmer hiked with serious injuries to keep up with others, and he regretted it.

What goes through a hiker's mind on the trail? Even if a hiker has a partner, he typically walks many miles alone, perhaps joining others at breaks and mealtimes. Few hikers will actually say they get bored on the trail, although some admit that the miles can get monotonous. A hiker's senses can become saturated by the beauty continually surrounding him.

Most hikers think about food, then they think about it some more: What to have for dinner tonight? What's the heaviest food left in my pack? Should I eat it now? Am I due a snack? What should I eat when I hit town?

Other details of daily life get some attention, too. Where should I sleep tonight? Am I going to make the mileage I figured on? What's the trail like up ahead? Where should I put my foot? Where can I find water?

Dan Nellis liked to focus on different interests as he walked; sometimes he played mind games. He tried to inject humor into his journey by celebrating each month on the trail with an anniversary cake. Some hikers like to invent word games, such as figuring out different phrases that A.T. could stand for: Addictive Torture, for example.

Others have creative daydreams. Wayne Sellman once wrote in the *A.T. News*, "I am a dreamer. Hiking on the trail I forget the worries, the cares, the problems of the world. My main concern is for food to eat, water to drink, and a place to sleep. On the Trail, I have written several books. I have started numerous businesses, sold some, and made millions. I have sailed the seven seas, traveled the whole world. I have courted the beautiful, the rich, from all corners of the globe (though my wife is still number one). I have owned everything from mopeds and limousines to airplanes and yachts. I have been counsel to foreign governments and have helped make laws in our own land. I have eaten the best cuisine in all countries. Again, of course, all of this has happened in my dream world while hiking the Trail."

Many hikers, especially the young, think about what they want to do with their lives after the hike. It's not often that one has five months away from the distractions and pressures of the daily grind to take stock of one's life.

Jeff Hansen finds that many people come to the trail after some emotional distress. "We've had people who've lost family members in accidents, and the trail becomes their family," he said. "I think it's a great idea, to use this to sort things out." He believes the trail simplifies a person's life and lets him get closer to his innermost thoughts. "A simple walk in the woods for the afternoon does that. Six months of it has to be that much better," he said.

Hikers sometimes wonder whether it's self-indulgent to hike the trail. Many have worked hard all their lives and find it odd to be without a job.

"Sometimes I questioned myself, is this being responsible?" said Laurie Mack. "I was talking to the postmaster in Linden, Virginia, and I said, 'Are there a lot of hikers going through?' He said, 'Too many. They should be out working like the rest of us.' A small part of me wondered whether I should be working or in school."

"It's not self-indulgent, unless you want to say that living life is self-indulgent," said Mike "Hago" Harrington.

What motivates thru-hikers to keep going in the face of misery, pain, and exhaustion? After thirty days on the trail, Keith "Wolf" Kimball had endured twenty-six days of rain. He'd severely injured his ankle. He'd had almost no company. The blackflies were terrible. Why didn't he drop off the trail? Despite the problems, he enjoyed being on his own in the wilderness. He could sense that he was growing up and that this was where he should be. And, like many other hikers, he didn't want to face the embarrassment of going home after failing to achieve what he set out to do.

"Almost every day, I thought of dropping off," said Holly "Doc" Leeds, a 1990 thru-hiker. "I wasn't even on the trail for ten days when I wrote home that this was like a job. I get up every day, pack my gear, hike from nine to five, make dinner, go to sleep. And then the whole thing starts again. The pain never ends, it was just in a different place every day. But I hate quitting. I just couldn't conceive of the words 'I quit.'

"When I started I didn't legitimately think I was going to be able to finish the trail. I hoped I could, and I planned to finish, but I didn't think I could. I was surprised to learn that my body had limits far beyond what I'd imagined. I could walk all day in the rain and cold and not be miserable. It taught me that limits are most often what's between my ears and nothing more."

"It gets in your blood," said Reese "the Sagwagon" Lukei, Jr., who hiked the trail in sections over thirteen years. "It becomes such an integral part of you like eating, sleeping, breathing. You just don't separate the trail from the rest of your being.

"It's an opportunity to clean out the cobwebs. I had an intense experience as a C.P.A. I had to find an escape. Piecing the trail together was part of the challenge." By chance, he finished the trail at Sugarloaf Mountain in Maine on August 14, 1987, the same day a ceremony was being held there to mark the golden anniversary of the trail's completion.

Initially, the idea of doing the whole trail motivated Greg "Pooh" Knoettner. "To keep myself going, I'd tell myself I have to finish this thing, but that wore off quickly. I discovered I love hiking and that's what kept me going. It's hard to hike the whole trail if your only motivation is that you want to finish."

Others do enjoy the challenge of trying to meet the goal for its own sake. Difficulties encountered along the way simply make reaching the goal more rewarding.

"It takes a willingness to endure," said Mike "Hago" Harrington. "People expect a feeling of total freedom and the chance to be goofing off and frolicking in the wilderness, but you've got to hike from early morning till late in the day, or you're not going to do it in one year. The weather window is not that wide. It's a job, in a way. You're going to have bad days and good days. It's part of life."

Many hikers set intermediate goals to make the distance seem less forbidding. It can be overwhelming to set foot on Springer Mountain and know that you are five million steps away from Katahdin. When you're in Georgia, Maine may seem about as far away as China, but the Smokies seem like a short hop away, and that's someplace you've always wanted to go. After that, Hot Springs, Roan Mountain, and later Damascus creep into range. Then there's Shenandoah, Harpers Ferry, the Hudson River, and New England.

In the South, thru-hikers seem a little nervous, a little flabby. By the time they've been on the trail a month or two, they're calmer and leaner. There's not much left besides muscle. As their bodies and packs have slimmed down, their minds have changed, too. Warren Doyle likes to say they've shed their "emotional fat." They've learned patience and fortitude, and had their faith in the essential goodness of mankind restored. They've learned that every time they see a new hiker coming down the trail, it's a new friend. They've learned that the barriers of age, occupation, and geography mean nothing here. Moreover, they've learned new diversions: climbing firetowers, jumping in swimming holes, studying nature.

Thru-hikers are often the only ones in their families who are serious hikers. It's sometimes difficult for their family and friends to understand what they are doing. "My family definitely thought I was nuts," said Bob "Sweet Pea La Foot" Hill. "I don't know how I turned out this way. None of my relatives are backpackers. After the trail, they met some of my friends and heard my stories, and they realized I'm not the only crazy person. Now they appreciate what I did in my youth."

Warren Doyle

O ne weekend I stayed at Hemlock Overlook Center for Outdoor Education, which Warren runs. I told him I'd like to talk when it was convenient. He said "Let's make it four A.M. so we won't be disturbed." I thought he was joking, but Ron Keal assured me he was serious. At exactly 4:00 A.M. I heard Warren's voice across the bunk room; we proceeded to talk in the cramped office off the dining hall kitchen. At 5:30 Indiana John stuck his head in the door and I joked, "I thought there wouldn't be any interruptions." By 6:50 Warren rested his head on the desk, weary after three hours of nonstop conversation.

Warren Doyle is a familiar figure to nearly everyone who's come close to the Appalachian Trail in the last twenty years. He's hiked the complete trail nine times, and he's not finished yet. He's continually hiking sections, attending meetings of hikers, showing his slides. His friendships and influence extend the length of the trail. It is not easy to be neutral about Warren, for he can be a devoted friend or a determined adversary.

His appearance is deceiving. He does not have the lean, hungry—almost emaciated—look that one comes to expect in a long-distance backpacker. Nor does he have the detached manner of an academic, even though he is a professor of Appalachian studies at George Mason University in Virginia. He has more the fiery mien of a rebel leader preparing to man the ramparts, or a dissident tweaking the KGB. At forty-three, however, he is mellowing somewhat, sidestepping some of the battles he would have waged only a few years ago.

People question nearly everything about Warren: his beliefs, his sanity, his motives. But no one questions his love for the A.T. He has a family and many friends and interests, but his devotion to the A.T. is boundless. "When I like something, I approach it with intensity," he said.

A testimony to Warren's gifts as an organizer, his energy, and his strong personality is that he was able to form and keep together ALDHA, the largest group in the country devoted to long-distance backpacking. It's hard to organize a bunch of antisocial individualists who have little patience for the paperwork and meetings that groups require. Many are cavalier about answering mail and telephones, and some don't even have permanent addresses.

His slide show, polished over the years, displays his intensity, commitment, and showmanship. He runs around, he sings, he recites poetry, he exhorts. It is a unique performance, for most thru-hikers could no more sing before a large group than fly under their own power.

Hemlock Overlook has sprouted practically from scratch since he went there eight years ago. Now nearly thirty thousand students each year attend programs, making it one of the largest outdoor-education centers in the country. Warren also runs a canoeing concession on Bull Run, near the Civil War battlefield. Hemlock is no doubt the largest single employer of 2,000-milers, with a dozen on staff at any one time. At Hemlock, every incoming group hears "the speech," often given by Warren, which stresses the need for cooperation over competition.

His introduction to hiking did not suggest a long-term interest. After his freshman year of college, he went climbing in the White Mountains carrying a duffel bag loaded with cans of food and soda. Despite his poor preparations, he was "amazed at the grandeur of everything, the indescribable feeling." From then on, he would go camping whenever he could. As a graduate student in 1972, he hiked on the Long Trail in Vermont. He learned a lot by suffering. In his cheap boots, he developed blisters the size of half-dollars. He became dehydrated. Because it was mid-May, he encountered swarms of blackflies. Later that summer, he ventured into the Maine wilderness, climbing Katahdin. At the Hurd Brook lean-to he met a 2,000-miler nearing the finish. "That sparked the idea of a thru-hike," he said.

Meanwhile, his social conscience had awakened. After his junior year, he worked in the mountains of Jamaica. Later, he worked for poet Don West, who founded the Appalachian South Folklife Center in Pipestem, West Virginia, to educate mountain people about their heritage. Warren found that in both places, good people worked hard but were mired in poverty. He started to question society. He also started to read about primitive societies, their rites of passage, and their trials of fire. "I found nature to be very neutral with no prejudices," he said. "It was my arena for personal growth."

When his older sister died suddenly at age fifteen, he felt he had to accomplish enough for two people. When he decided on the A.T. as his "rite of passage," he included the added challenge of walking the trail in the shortest time. In 1973, at age twenty-three, he set off on his first thru-hike. His father, Warren, Sr., met him in Cloverdale, in southern Virginia, and continued to meet him until he passed Gorham, New Hampshire. Warren, Sr., was concerned that his son had lost too much weight, and so he began to cook for him and help around camp. "It made a big psychological difference" having his father along, Warren said. He ended the hike in record time, sixty-six and a third days, averaging thirty miles a day.

Back at school, Warren organized a series of day-hikes to do the Connecticut A.T. over seven Sundays. A core group formed, including his future wife, Ginger. On the last hike, people decided to walk the whole distance—fifty-six miles—in one day. Twelve people prepared for this superhike for two months. Warren found "tremendous energy" in the group. "It was a valuable learning experience," he said, and he began wondering, "If all this can happen in one day, how much could a longer hike achieve?"

Two weeks later, he had a dream. He saw a group of hikers with headlights, walking from Georgia to Maine. "It felt so right," he said, "I couldn't get back to sleep." He had already started a doctoral dissertation on postsecondary aspirations of rural districts in Vermont. He dropped that topic and lost a grant. Instead, he began planning a group thru-hike. It would be the first group of more than two people to hike the A.T. As a practical afterthought, he decided, he would study the group dynamics for his new dissertation topic. He put his University of Connecticut students through two semesters of preparation and planning, complete with classroom discussions and practice hikes. Warren had acquired from Don West the belief that people could unite to achieve a common goal. One of the group's objectives was for all nineteen people to finish the trail together—and they did. For this hike, Warren developed the concept of having a support van meet the group nearly every day. That way, people could hike with day packs, walking more miles each day, and squeezing in the entire trail between the spring and fall semesters. "I had a vision of a new world where people walk together and leave no one behind," he said.

While many 2,000-milers give moving testimony to the profound positive effects of a thru-hike, these effects have proven difficult to measure. In

Warren's doctoral dissertation standard psychological tests were unable to measure changes in students resulting from the 1975 group thru-hike. But Warren could point to claims by participants that powerful changes had indeed taken place. They were more confident of their physical endurance, mental discipline, and tolerance of other people.

Before his second group thru-hike in 1977, he created an interdisciplinary course covering the Appalachians, flora and fauna, mental and physical preparations for the trail, and other topics. This was the only one of his four expeditions from which people dropped out, one each in Vermont and New Hampshire. He also led groups in 1980 and 1990. A member of his 1975 group, Kirk Sinclair, led another group hike in 1983. A group scheduled to hike in 1995 began forming in 1992.

Testaments to Warren's physical feats are a staple of trail legends. Albie Pokrob was hiking near Pearisburg, Virginia, when he ran into Warren. Warren asked if Albie wanted to drive to Connecticut for a slide show. Albie said he didn't want to be gone so long; his trail friends would hike ahead in the meantime. Warren promised to get him back by the next morning. Warren did all but one hour of the twenty-eight hours of driving, putting on a ninety-minute slide show in between.

Warren is known for being among the most frugal of hikers. Before his last thru-hike he went to the Salvation Army and bought six pairs of sneakers for one dollar a pair—and used only three.

"Katahdin is my holy mountain. I try to climb it at least twice a year," Warren said. He still does long day-hikes, including an annual "Damascus by Dawn" sixty-four-mile trip. Another of his trips was the "Winter Wipeout," in which he climbed the seven highest peaks in New England and New York in five days.

Warren has now completed the A.T. nine times, including his early speed-hike, four group hikes, and four section-hikes. Even still, "I always see new things on the trail. That's why I keep walking," he said. "It's healthy for me. It's a leisure activity that's also goal oriented. That's my religion, that's my faith." He loves swimming in the streams along the way, playing, having fun. "It's a giant playground," he said. "Every day I can pick out three or four wonderful things. I wouldn't want to hike the trail if it wasn't fun."

Spiritual Awakenings
and the Pull of Nature

*I never knew a man go for an honest day's walk for whatever
distance, great or small . . . and not have his reward in the
repossession of his own soul.*

G. M. Trevelyan

N OT EVERYONE COMES BACK FROM THE TRAIL MORE INCLINED TO
worship indoors. But many hikers do return with a greater sense of
divine presence and an increased faith in the essential goodness of
mankind.

Robie "Jumpstart" Hensley wrote in his journal about reaching the top
of Moose Mountain in New Hampshire. "I found a grassy place on the top
of a flat rock with a view to the west. I ate supper and watched the loveliest
sunset I've seen in a long time. How could anyone enjoy all this beauty and
not feel a reverence for its creator?" A few days later, he added, "Sunday
morning and I hear church bells. Somehow I feel God's presence more out
here on the trail than I ever did in a church."

The Appalachian Trail brings a hiker to the tops of hundreds of mountains in all kinds of weather. It's a hardy soul, indeed, who can stand on the
summit of Mount Washington or Katahdin in a thunderstorm and not make
at least preliminary inquiries about the availability of some form of outside
intervention.

Jan "Sacajawea" Collins remembers reading a story on bird migration.

"They think some birds navigate by hearing the low-frequency sounds from massive objects like mountains and the ocean. That said to me that the mountains sing, they speak to us."

People have long believed that mountains can inspire and heal us. Recently, a branch of psychology has sprung up called ecopsychology. It examines the ties between people and nature, and tries to use that to help people. To Benton MacKaye, this would have fit nicely with one of his original reasons why the A.T. should exist: to serve as a retreat for urban people caught up in the frenetic pace of daily life.

Living intimately with nature for five or six months, thru-hikers touch parts of their inner selves that they often didn't know existed. None of this is a new discovery. People have long treated the mountains with respect—the Abenaki Indians in Maine were watchful of Pamola; the Chinese greatly esteemed the magical landscapes of Guilin. Taoists encouraged their holy men to live among the mountains. Buddhists established monasteries on holy mountains in China. In Japan, there has long been a traditional mountain religion. In urban America, on the other hand, mountains are too often just something to admire on postcards or from car windows.

Alan Gussow, an artist and conservationist who was the keynote speaker at the 1983 ATC meeting, wrote several columns for the *A. T. News* trying to define his concept of "a sense of place." He believes that nature has healing powers and that certain places are special to us because of our past associations. He said that people need "rootedness," so that our special places can provide spiritual and health benefits. In modern America, however, people have too often lost their sense of community. He cited the A.T. as an example of what he hoped would become more common. He understood "that this mingling of private pleasures, each individual's own sense of place, coupled with the body memory of shared work of 'building and caring' together, has, in the end, led to the creation of something greater than any individual experience, greater than any part. What has been created in the truest sense is a spiritual path."

Not surprisingly, Gussow believes that nature is a tonic for harried people. "Given the costs of medical care, I wonder if a return to landscapes as healers might turn out to be more productive of bodily and spiritual improvement." Describing his family vacation retreat off the coast of Maine, he wrote, "I know of no drug, no hospital procedure, that produces the same deep euphoria as a week on this small Atlantic island. Nature is restorative precisely because it enlivens all of our senses, thereby reminding us what it means to be fully human."

Gussow believed in the importance of staying in touch with childhood innocence, vigor, and fantasy. "As adults, nature heals by reminding us in a bodily sense what it was like to be a child." He went on to say that nature heals because it slows us down and encourages us to use our bodies. Gussow quoted painter Thomas Cole's letter to Asher Durand: "You sit, I know you do, in a close, air-tight room, toiling, stagnating, and breeding dissatisfaction at all you do, when, if you had the untainted breeze to breathe, your body would be invigorated, your spirits buoyant, and your pictures would even charm yourself."

Reinforcing the appreciation of nature may be the body's basic circadian rhythms, which influence, among other things, sleep and energy levels. Civilized life, which is increasingly detached from the natural world, mutes these forces. Dr. William N. Gordge noted in a column in the *A.T. News* that "Good sleeping is encouraged by a day's (physical) work, and a relaxed mind and sound sleep promote good circadian rhythms. Most people undertaking a wilderness experience describe a gratifying sense of inner contentment and well-being, a sharpening of the senses and an improved outlook on life. Could it be that this sense of emotional and physical well-being is due, at least in part, to the inner harmony of our many biological rhythms with the natural rhythm of our world? I think so."

Bob "Sweet Pea La Foot" Hill, who hiked the trail in 1977 after leaving the Marines, said "Because of the trail, I'm more spiritual, more in tune with nature and my surroundings and other people. I have a greater awareness of the joys of the simple things in life. I can't imagine what my life would be like if I hadn't done the trail. Life would seem pretty empty without it. There's not a day that passes that I don't think of the trail."

He adds, "I'll never forget the quietness, the feeling of well-being physically and spiritually, the people who treat you with generosity.

"It's an adventure of the soul, something to nurture the soul," said Steve "Offshore Steve" Gomez, who hiked the trail in 1986. "The trail was the start of a big change in my life. It was the beginning of listening to my heart more than what other people's expectations of me were." For Steve, who was a commercial fisherman from ages nineteen to twenty-seven, the trail rejuvenated him. "I felt at home out there. Things were simple. It's a good medium to get one's head clear, to know oneself."

"It was an almost religious experience," said Pete "Woulda, Coulda, Shoulda" Suscy. "You feel like you really are a part of nature. I wouldn't have known I could have that deep an emotional feeling without having taken a long hike. I wouldn't have understood why it's important to preserve the wilderness."

"You don't have much to think about except what to eat and where to sleep," said Connor "Carolina Cookers" Coward. "You explore a lot about yourself. You sort out what's important and what's not. I'm twenty-eight now and I have less stuff now than when I moved away from home. There aren't a lot of people that can say that. It was just a really incredible experience in growing up."

Jim "Jimmy Bee" Bodmer was doing a 34-mile day into Damascus with two friends, Polyster and Archer. They stopped at a shelter at dusk for dinner and then did the last short stretch in the dark. "As we got to Damascus, I had been singing 'I See the Light,'" Jim said. "Up ahead we could just make out the lights in the valley where Damascus is and I said, 'I see the light.' Just then a bolt of lightning struck nearby. I could feel the electricity. Polyster turned to me and said, 'Jim, don't do that again.'"

Hiker after hiker says that on the trail, there are no coincidences. They point to Gene Espy running into Earl Shaffer on his 1965 thru-hike. Or Pete Suscy hurting his ankle, hiking slower, and then marrying his new trail companion, Eleta Vaughn. Trail magic, they would call it.

You're in trouble and help unexpectedly arrives. Or you run into a friend in the middle of nowhere. Or you're watching the evening news for the first time in months and there's a segment on the A.T., and you decide to hike the trail. Trail magic.

On Albie Pokrob's third thru-hike, Jean Cashin, Dave Sherman, Ron Tipton, and Ed Garvey surprised him with a formal birthday party at the Blackburn Center in northern Virginia. Albie's hiking partner, Pete Suscy, remembers, "It was a big spread, with long tables and really formal looking tablecloths and settings. Ron was standing in the trail with a napkin on his arm and menus, looking like a waiter." By sheer coincidence, Albie's parents and sister had dropped in at Harpers Ferry that day while driving home from Florida. "Jean said, 'Wow. We're having a party tonight,'" Albie recalled.

Frank "the Hawk" Logue had once talked to a college roommate's father about hiking the A.T. Then in February 1987, he ran into him again. In that very day's mail was a *National Geographic* with an article on the A.T. He talked it over with his wife, Victoria "the Dove," and they decided to do the trail the following year.

Coincidences frequently plant the idea of a thru-hike. Len "Gearhead" Olsen was a mechanic when he spotted an A.T. sticker on a car and asked the driver what it was for. The driver, Jim Pittilla, the father of a 2,000-miler, piqued Len's interest in the trail. Jean Cashin often hears people say they watched the evening news for the first time in months, caught a story on Bill Irwin hiking the trail, and decided to do it. Or they just happened to see an article in a newspaper, or an A.T. road sign.

Charlie "Glove Kid" Gilbert left for the trail in 1977, soon after his mother died of leukemia and his girlfriend dumped him. "I spent more than one night on the trail in tears as I fell to sleep," he said. "It was a spiritual and mental challenge, and intensely personal. It's like it all happened last year. It never goes away. It was a deeply spiritual experience for me. I got into poetry and reading more. I found if you put the past behind you, what's in front can be a lot richer.

"The A.T. really opened the door to me as a way out of mediocrity. It was a way to get out of my system some of the vinegar and pent-up frustrations that a young guy builds up. I was never typecast as being able to do anything like that. I wanted to stand out. And then when I was done, I didn't want to stand out." Afterwards, he decided to try out for the Olympic rowing team. Without coaching or technical training, he nearly qualified. "One thing that came to me through hiking: If you want something, you can go get it.

"It's a great place to go to find the meaning of life for yourself. The trail's great, but you're not going to get any great reward at the end. So you're going to walk two thousand miles. Big deal. It will just help settle something inside that's missing."

Sonie "Light Eagle" Shames

I *first saw Sonie, an interpretative ranger at Amicalola Falls, standing by her park pickup truck, and I recognized her immediately from the descriptions I'd gotten. A few days later I attended a unique show: a one-woman hour-long dramatization of her 1988 thru-hike. Maybe it was just a good audience at the Dahlonega ATC meeting, but most appeared spellbound by her accounts of how she learned which items to cull from a too-heavy pack and of a serious brush with hypothermia. Those few people tempted to doze off sprang to life when Sonie produced a snake and started waving it around. Wide awake myself, I chatted with her after the show.*

It's a unique combination for a thru-hiker: part actress, part ranger-naturalist, and part Indian-mountain philosopher. Whatever else she is, Sonie "Light Eagle" Shames stands out among introverted thru-hikers as a polished, engaging performer with a delightfully different way of looking at the world.

Like many thru-hikers, Sonie began her trip at a transition point in her life. After a decade as a hospital administrator in Atlanta, she quit to try to fill what was missing in her life. After finding several A.T. books at the library, she decided on a thru-hike. She spent several years researching and planning her 1988 trip. To accustom herself to hiking, she'd go to Amicalola on weekends and hike up Springer Mountain. On her first trip, she rested by a stream and thought that one day she would work there. On her thru-hike, she helped a ranger at Mount Greylock, Massachusetts, give a program. She thought it was "neat" that someone could actually do that for a living. After her thru-hike, she moved from Atlanta to the north Georgia mountains and quickly took a summer job as a naturalist at Amicalola and teaching environmental education at a nearby camp. She's been a part of the north Georgia mountains ever since.

When she climbed Springer to start her thru-hike, Sonie was full of excitement and doubts. "This is the day," she said. "Can I do this?" She had told everybody, "I'll hike as far as I can."

In the Great Smoky Mountains, Sonie came upon an old woman who, wearing a dress, seemed out of place. The woman asked Sonie if she had seen the flowers. Sonie said, no, she'd been looking at the hemlocks as she hurried along. The woman took her to see some beautiful flowers. Sonie looked into the woman's eyes and saw the sweet, gentle manner of her Cherokee grandmother. The lesson Sonie took from it was that she should slow down and learn to appreciate the natural world around her. From then on, her trek became a classic combination of thru-hiking, interesting side trips, and fascinating encounters with people.

By Virginia, the physical challenge was over. What remained was the mental challenge, mind over matter. "I sort of figured out life in general," she said. "The more that I carry in the backpack, the less I enjoy the trail."

By Shenandoah she was lonely, with few thru-hikers nearby. "I started to look at nature a little more closely," she said.

She arrived in New Hampshire at the peak of autumn. She walked slowly, absorbing everything. "The spirit's going to get me to Maine," she thought. "I get to see the seasons change, but I've changed, too. Nature has opened her heart to me. Time has passed ever so quickly since spring. I've been on the wings of an eagle that soared."

Her most memorable encounters on the trip started in Tennessee. At a road crossing one Sunday evening, she spotted a church. She dropped by to see if they were having services. She looked forward to the singing and companionship and the chance to meet mountain people. A deacon welcomed her, and the minister announced her presence. Afterwards, everyone greeted her and thanked her for coming. The organist, a woman named Jean, put her up for the night and made biscuits with fresh apple butter for breakfast.

Farther in Tennessee, Sonie descended the steep slope to Devil Fork Gap along the narrow path framed by two barbed-wire fences. Ignoring the safety warning to not loiter at road crossings, she sat under a big oak tree on a beautiful day—the Saturday before Mother's Day—eating a peanut butter sandwich for lunch. Several cars stopped nearby with seven young men and a lone woman. They were drinking. Quickly, Sonie had qualms about her choice of a rest stop. They asked Sonie what she was doing, and she asked them a few questions. Finally, she asked if there was a telephone nearby to call her mother for the holiday. They told her they'd take her to Aunt Minnie's house, right down the road. When they got to the house, Aunt Minnie, an old lady, was making peanut butter cookies. As Sonie made her Mother's Day telephone call, Aunt Minnie plied her with homemade cookies and cold fresh milk; the others went to a store and got beer and hot dogs and hamburgers for a barbecue. With her backpack loaded with beer and barbecued meat, Sonie hiked five more miles to the next shelter, where her trail friends were growing concerned about her. She finally arrived at the shelter at 10 P.M. "I'm going, 'Man, my backpack is so heavy. I need help,'" Sonie said. "So they came out of their sleeping bags, picked up the backpack, and out rolled all the beer." Sonie gave them the barbecued meat, too. "We had a great time at the shelter that night."

She met Trapper John in Monson, Maine. He showed her his trap line and took her on a bear hunt. It was moose-hunting season, and they went to a checking station. He took her in his Indian-made birch canoe down the Allagash River. "If I had a measurement of time saying I have to get back on the trail, I would have missed that," Sonie said. "When I started to hike on the trail, each day became longer and longer because there was no time element. So long as I get my food, so long as I have my necessities, that's all I need. And I've learned that here in life today, so long as I have the necessities of life, everything's fine."

Sonie said that as she went along she could feel personal growth. "I needed the sunlight to nurture me to grow. I needed the rain to grow. The cold, the heat to nurture me to grow. In the woods, I felt like a seedling nurtured by nature to grow."

Sonie, with a touch of wistfulness, passes on her ideas to the new crop of hikers traveling through Amicalola each spring. She sees them and thinks, "'I wish I could go with you. Maybe another time.' But with that flow of hikers, I also receive that energy and give out that energy. They're going on a journey, and I may sit and talk to them to say, 'Hey, take your time. There's a lot out there to see if you have no limitations on your time. The trail is what you make it. There's no right or wrong in doing the trail. People have a lot of impressions, like it's wrong if I go on a blue blaze. But if you go on a blue blaze, you'll see something that no one else will see. So blue-blazing, by all means, is not bad. Take the time to explore. What makes it so special is see-

Walking the Appalachian Trail

ing the people, the Appalachian people. Go a bit deeper. Go to the church on Sunday that's a little out of the way."

Now, as a ranger at Amicalola, Sonie herself can be a guardian angel for hikers. In 1992, on Springer Mountain, she met a hiker named Charles, who badly wanted to do the A.T. even though he'd never hiked before. On a cold February day, Sonie took Charles home, out of the severe weather. Charles, wearing blue jeans, was soaked.

In the car, Charles said, "Sonie, I want to hike the trail. Can you help me?"

"We'll go through your backpack and see what you have," she said.

It turned out that Charles was carrying thirty little Bibles; he was planning on leaving one at each shelter.

"Well, that's great, Charles," said Sonie. "That's very spiritual of you. But that's also a lot of weight." Next, they found that Charles had fifty beanie-weanie cans. Sonie said, "Charles, you know you can have mail drops and send these ahead. You don't need to carry all this weight."

Charles said, "Well, I didn't plan. I just wanted to hike the trail. I'd heard about the trail, and I came." He was also carrying a hammer, pliers, screwdriver, and a few nails. He was planning to build a travois and carry his backpack on it like a horse would.

Sonie took him to a store and helped him buy proper outdoor clothing. He took her advice and replaced his loafers with hiking boots. Five days later, she got a call from a ranger at Camp Merrill saying that Charles was hurt. She put him on a bus home. But his spirit was, "I'm going to hike the trail."

Sonie puts on dramatizations of a thru-hike for various groups, including Elderhostel. Her audience consists mostly of people who may have wanted to hike the A.T. but never did. "But when I'm interacting with those people," said Sonie, "I'm seeing inside their eyes that, yes, they're hiking this trail. Maybe their body no longer can walk, or they don't have the energy, but their spirit definitely has walked this trail when the program's finished. And I ask myself, 'Is that my purpose in being at the park? Is that my teaching?' Our life here on earth is what we make it to be. The backpack that I carry on my back, I can put sixty pounds in it. I can put ninety pounds if I wish to. But the more I put in, the more problems I'm going to have. Do I wish to have problems? Or do I wish to have it a little bit easier, so I can move around a little bit easier? All we need are the necessities in life—shelter, food, water. The programs that I put on are to remind people why they are here."

Trail Angels and Trail Magic

*I am not going to advocate . . . the abandoning of the improved
modes of travel; but I am going to brag as lustily as I can on behalf
of the pedestrian, and show how all the shining angels second and
accompany the man who goes afoot, while all the dark spirits are
ever looking out for a chance to ride.*

John Burroughs

I DON'T KNOW ANOTHER FACET OF LIFE WHERE PEOPLE GO OUT OF
their way to help other people almost for the sport of it," said Dick Potteiger, a 2,000-miler and former ATC controller. Dick should know. He
hiked Maine's 100-mile wilderness with his wife, Laurie, who was finishing
the A.T. Laurie had stocked candy and fresh fruit to give to the first thru-
hikers they met. "You should have seen the look on their faces when she gave
it to them," Dick said.

A.T. hospitality is quite a tradition, and generally A.T. hikers have been
well received. Exceptions are rare but understandable. In some isolated parts
of the Appalachians, before television and the interstate highway system,
strangers were often viewed with suspicion. More recently, occasional inci-
dents of rowdiness or vandalism near the trail, often instigated by non-
hikers, have dampened some people's enthusiasm for the trail and its
travelers.

"Trail magic" is the term for the aid that townspeople and other "trail
angels" lavish on backpackers. Of course, it is not magic at all but an expres-
sion of the goodness and generosity of so many people. Hikers derive

inspiration from these well-wishers, who offer everything from encouragement to meals, rides, and lodging. Nearly all hikers, particularly those who take their time and remain open to such offers, have stories of unexpected help. And the trail angels find that hikers, with their simple lifestyles, appreciate the smallest gesture.

Dorothy "the Ankle Express" Mauldin is a hiker who was injured in an industrial accident. Although she requires crutches, her pace, energy, and good cheer put to shame many younger, healthier people. Every year, she helps hikers with supplies and encouragement. A prolific correspondent, she provides encouragement to many of the other angels. Her exquisite calligraphy and poetry can be found all along the trail.

She defined trail magic in an issue of the *A.T. News*:

> Trail Magic . . . is just a kind, kind way,
> of helping another have a much better day!
> It happens when you least expect it,
> but when you need it so much.
> It's the Magic of the Trail," with an Angel's touch!
> Little acts of kindness; little deeds of cheer,
> extended by a stranger . . . a Trail Angel so dear.
> You will know when it happens.
> You will never forget;
> all thru life you will remember . . .
> this I will bet.
> Trail Magic, Angels, everywhere.
> (Or Trail Magic means there are those who care.)

Henry Phillips remembers walking along a road near Mount Weather, Virginia. "A woman drove by, rolled down her electric window and said, 'If I were walking along this road, I'd sure like an apple,' and she handed me a bunch of chocolate chip cookies and an apple."

A couple in Catawba, Virginia, who operated a grain store, offered Jim "Pony" Adams refuge from a thunderstorm in a new grain shed. "I never spent a more pleasant night in my life," he said. Listening to the rain on the metal roof and smelling the grain, he was reminded of his grandfather's farm fifty years before.

Judi "the Butterfly Lady" and Ralph "the Hobbit" Goodenough were caught in a blizzard on May 7, 1990, on Roan Mountain. Ralph went on to

Roan High Knob Shelter, dropped his pack, and went back to help Judi. Meanwhile, the snowstorm intensified, and Judi wandered off the trail. By the time Ralph helped Judi back to the shelter, she was nearly hypothermic. Ralph made some hot soup, and eventually Judi felt better. But she was still upset. "I'm never going to meet a trail angel," she said. Early the next morning, the door flung open, and in walked Carol "Lagunatic" Moore with bagels, orange juice, crackers, fruit, and other goodies. Judi cried, "A trail angel."

A handful of people have been helping hikers for thirty or forty years. Former governor and Mrs. Thomson, proprietors of the Mount Cube Sugar House, have been taking in hikers since the time of Grandma Gatewood. Kay Wood, in Dalton, Massachusetts, has taken in hikers just as long. The trail used to go right by her house. She has moved, but now the nearby Kay Wood Shelter is a substitute.

Among the most revered of trail angels is Sam "Habitual Maintainer" Waddle. When you say "trail angel," Sam Waddle is the first name that springs to many people's minds. Growing up in an east Tennessee valley, Sam could see where the A.T. crossed Cold Spring Mountain. As a child, he rode a horse onto that mountain. In the mid-seventies he began maintaining a stretch of the A.T. there that includes Jerry Cabin Shelter. Since then, he's come up from his farm as many as thirty times a year to work on the trail, and he hasn't slowed down, despite being in his seventies. He's worn out two or three chain saws and made hundreds of friends. He figures he's put in more than 2,800 hours of trail work. "It's not been easy," he said. "But I'm dedicated and stubborn and refuse to give up. I met a lot of lovely people. I'd help however I could. I like to help everyone."

When Dorothy Hansen was thru-hiking in 1979, she ran into Sam at the shelter. He shared a snack with her and her companions, and told them about the trail up ahead. He also sent a letter to her parents to let them know how she was doing. Later, she wrote to Sam, "You were one of the best things that happened to me on my entire trip." It's just one among dozens of letters thanking Sam for his kindnesses.

In the early seventies Ed Garvey described Jerry Cabin as the dirtiest shelter on the entire trail. Sam took over several years later and has made it one of the best. He's put in a new roof, wooden bunks and a bogus light switch and telephone, and he's boxed in the spring. After this turnabout, Ed has been campaigning to get the shelter renamed the "Sam Waddle Shelter."

Sam has often handed out food or rescued injured hikers. "About every hiker I meet says, 'You must be Sam,'" he said. At his home, he has one of the largest collections of A.T. memorabilia: twenty-two photo albums and scrapbooks. He has files of letters from around the world and many gifts from hikers. In 1988, Sam scattered the ashes of Howard Bassett, his close friend and a 1968 thru-hiker, along the trail about a mile from the shelter.

North of the North Carolina–Virginia border are two towns, Damascus and Pearisburg, that compete for the title of friendliest town on the trail. Damascus has a long tradition of helping hikers. When Gene Espy came through in 1951, police chief Orville "Corney" McNish chauffeured him around town, gave him comfortable lodging—in the jail—and plied him with food. Paschel Grindstaff, Damascus postmaster for twenty-eight years until he retired in 1985, was a legendary trail angel. Even after all these years, the town has not tired of the hikers.

With the start of the annual Trail Days festival in May 1987, the town is an even more notable landmark for thru-hikers. Hikers who are separated on the trail have a chance for a reunion at Trail Days. Charlie Trivett, one of the founders of Trail Days, has taken care of the hikers' hostel in Damascus, known as The Place, since its inception. Charlie, a lifelong resident of the area, says that more than thirty thousand hikers have stayed at The Place since it opened in 1976. David Lipski was thru-hiking in 1975, when the hostel was being readied, and he gave it its name. "There was an old board out there, and he carved out 'The Place' and hung it up," Charlie said.

The winter before the hostel opened, Charlie read a book about the A.T., and he and his wife decided to help hikers. He hadn't known much about the A.T., but he'd been hiking those mountains all his life, putting in enough miles to do the whole trail several times over. That first year, Charlie brought most of the thru-hikers over to his house for a barbecue. He was largely responsible for adding some attractive A.T. features to a park at the entrance to town. He's put up a welcoming arch through which hikers pass.

Charlie loves meeting new people from all over the world. "When you get on the trail, it's just people with people. There's no 'I'm better than you.' There's no caste system on the trail. It's just people helping people."

One of the special people Charlie remembers meeting was Evelyn Candle, a woman in her sixties making her first big hike in 1976. She fell near Roanoke, breaking an arm. A few days later, with her arm in a cast, she returned to the trail. In New England, she fell again, breaking her collarbone. "To her, everything was beautiful," Charlie said. "Everybody'd be talking about a hard climb down in the Stekoahs. It was rainy. She'd say, 'But the rain was so beautiful, I didn't notice the climbing.'"

Not far north of Damascus is Pearisburg, where Father Charles converted an old barn into a hostel in 1977. Bill Gautier, a native of Pearisburg, has been tending to the hostel since 1984. "I enjoy talking to them," he said of hikers. "I do everything I can to help them." Of this area in southwestern Virginia, he said, "These mountains grow on you. They call it Pearisburg. I call it Paradise."

A short distance south of Pearisburg is a unique trail refuge, a cabin called Woodshole. Because it's a half mile off the trail and so close to Pearisburg, many hikers pass by Woodshole. They shouldn't. Tillie Wood and her late husband, Roy, purchased the cabin in 1939, when he needed to live in the area to research the local elk herd's feeding habits. Along the trail at Big Horse Gap there's a grove of white pine he planted to keep elk from damaging local crops.

The cabin is an oasis of tranquility in a small, steep, clearing. A short distance away is a building for hikers with loft sleeping quarters. Behind it is Moonshadow's Monument, an outhouse built by an earlier hiker. Roy and Tillie started taking in hikers in 1986 at the suggestion of longtime friend, Dave Sherman, a 2,000-miler and A.T. activist. Since then, Tillie has maintained the hostel herself, with help in recent years from Hugh "High Pockets" Penn. A naturalist in her own right, Tillie has a master's degree in mycology (mushrooms). Roy had the distinction of being fired from two different government jobs by James Watt, former secretary of the interior. President Carter, whom Roy had served in Georgia, appointed Roy an assistant secretary of the interior, and he stayed on for part of the Reagan Administration.

Tillie said that when only a few hikers stop at the hostel, she gets to know them well. But if there are, say, a dozen, they talk among themselves. "If they're by themselves, they come sit on the porch, or I go out and talk to them. They have a lot in common. They want to talk about their packs and their tents and what they're eating and cooking, and I'm not interested in that. Last night, there were three, and all three came up on the porch, and we sat and talked. I thoroughly enjoyed it." Like everyone else, Tillie is impressed by the way information travels along the trail. "The gossip that goes up and down the trail amazes me. Everybody knows where everybody else is and what they're doing."

Tillie and Roy were among the early founders of the Nantahala Outdoor Center in Wesser, North Carolina. After the Walasi-Yi Center in Neels Gap, this is the first outpost of civilization that northbound hikers find right on the trail. The Georgia Canoe Association, to which Roy and Tillie belonged, used to have their races there. Roy was the announcer and Tillie was registrar. Two club members bought the motel there in 1972. It has expanded greatly over the years and remains owned by its 350 employees. Many A.T. hikers stay over before tackling the Stekoah section, one of the hardest parts of the trail.

Pennsylvania has long had an outstanding group of trail angels. Perhaps foremost was Bonnie "the Ice Cream Lady" Shipe, who would give hikers an ice cream cone, a cold drink, and lots of encouragement. A few years ago the trail across the Cumberland Valley was relocated onto ridges and farm fields, and it no longer passes Bonnie's house.

In Port Clinton, Pennsylvania, a longtime A.T. tradition will soon end. Many an A.T. hiker has taken a meal or stayed overnight at the Port Clinton Hotel. Helen Carabaugh, who has run the hotel since February 1965, has been trying to sell it, maybe because she's eighty and does most of the work herself. Meals were whatever she had on hand, and few people complained. Surrounded by steep climbs and rocky trails, the hotel and the next-door peanut store were bright spots along this stretch. Helen has traced the origin of the hotel, once a stagecoach stop, to at least 1847. At one time, there were five hotels in town, but Helen's is the only survivor. About hikers, she said, "Some schnooks, but 98 percent were terrific people." Sometimes, when there were supposed to be two in a room, she'd find six. Others would drive nails into the walls or do laundry in the bathroom, which was against the rules. She remembers four men passing a "little bitty cigarette" around at the bar. She thought they didn't have much money and were trying to economize on their cigarettes. When she got a terrible headache, she realized it was marijuana.

Some trail angels are hikers from previous years who return to the trail from Georgia to Maine offering buffets or barbecues for hungry hikers. Countless others simply pick up a hiker here, offer a cold drink there, or shout encouragement as they pass. For many hikers, these acts of generosity are the best part of their journey. After they complete the A.T., they often mail postcards to those who've helped them on the trail.

Nevertheless, Arthur "A. B. Positive" Batchelder worries that hikers aren't sufficiently considerate of the trail angels. "They're an endangered species, as much as a wildflower is. We talk about just taking photographs, just leaving footprints. Well, that should be said about all these people who are out there allowing us to have our fun. We should be just as kind and considerate to them as we are to the flowers. How many people could make it from Springer all the way to Katahdin without these people? Very few."

Roger Brickner

*R*oger is unique among trail angels in any number of ways. For one thing, he advertises. For another, even among dozens of generous souls, he stands out for his many kindnesses to hikers. He's also one of the few who've hiked the whole trail. He's had two locations, New York and New Hampshire. And in an A.T. community full of people with single-minded intensity, Roger's fifty-year study of weather stands out. Finally, he's brave. He gave my three young children chocolate ice cream in the living room of his beautiful old New Hampshire home. In 1979 thru-hikers got together and gave Roger an ATC life membership.

Roger Brickner has been a fixture on the A.T. for twenty years. For many of those years, his Appalachia Cottage at Greenwood Lake, New York, was a refuge that many 2,000-milers looked forward to for much of their journey. Here and there along the trail would be signs advising hikers to be on the lookout for Appalachia Cottage. Frank "the Merry Slav" Krajcovic recalls seeing a cardboard sign in Georgia that read, "Thru-hikers, are you cold, wet, hungry? Don't despair, Roger's Appalachia Cottage is only 1,275 miles away."

Roger was a longtime resident of Queens, New York. In the early seventies, he sought a refuge in the country. Once Roger moved in to Appalachia Cottage, he began wandering around on Bellvale Mountain. The A.T. runs along its crest for many miles. In August 1973, Roger cut a quarter-mile trail from his cottage to the A.T. That became one of the toughest blue blaze trails along the entire A.T. Soon after he cut the trail, some ill-equipped Boy Scouts, cold and wet, straggled down on a stormy night. Roger gave them lodging. The next summer, during a series of thunderstorms, Roger began to think again about hikers on the ridge. Eventually, he left a handwritten note at the intersection of the A.T. and his side trail, saying "Hikers Welcome." The very first day, someone showed up.

Ever since, hikers have kept coming. Over the years, Roger has sheltered nearly two thousand hikers, giving them meals and often rides to help them resupply or to hike without their packs for a day. He's developed a reputation among hikers as a fast and good cook. Eventually, he started "The Oasis," a clearing just off the trail for hikers who didn't want to make the steep descent to his cottage. He put up a small table and chairs, and each day he or some hiker returning to the trail would drop off a cooler of lemonade and a copy of *The New York Times*.

"One person that really sticks out in my mind was Roger of Appalachia Cottage," said Jan Skadberg, who hiked in 1980. "Go down there, wine, hors d'oeuvres, just eat, drink, be merry. After-dinner drinks. Movies. Slides. I mean, there were six of us that night, and he made a seven-course dinner. Such a gentleman and such a giver."

"I have a lot of interests," Roger said. "I can't say I'm obsessed with the A.T. I believe that you do what you can when you can and where you are. The more I got to know these people, the more I realized—especially after having done the trail myself—how nice it is to just have a night off and be able to talk. Most of them are talkers. Especially those that are early in the season and on their own. Boy, are they talkers!

"There's something monumental about what people are doing, especially when they hike in one season, from one end to another. I guess that's to be respected and appreciated. And it makes you a little part of what they're doing."

In 1984 Roger retired as a high-school history and government teacher. Another reason Roger likes taking in hikers is the similarity to teaching. "You get a group and you talk to them," he said. He does limit the size so that it's possible to have civilized conversations.

After retiring, Roger began spending more time at his new home, a historic house (built in 1810) in Haverhill, New Hampshire. Now, he lives a fifteen-minute drive from the trail. Because hikers can no longer walk to his home, he has devised a new system. During a six-week season, he has hikers call between three and four in the afternoon, and he or a friend picks them up. In the rear of his house is a loft in which hikers can sleep. Beneath it is the Samuel Adams Inn. Along the side of the inn's Pub Room is a mural-map of the A.T., painted by many hikers but principally Mark Carroll, who thru-hiked in 1977 and 1986.

Now, Roger takes in hikers five days a week, leaving Wednesdays and Saturdays open for other friends to visit or for him to hike the trail. Limiting his availability seems to have prevented burnout, which has happened to other trail angels.

"I get people saying, 'Why are you doing this anymore?' Because I still enjoy it. I still enjoy talking to people, and from a sociological point of view I find it fascinating to see the change in who is on the trail." In earlier years, he notes, there was a greater proportion of young hikers. Now there are more women and older people. Hikers thirty to fifty were almost nonexistent in the late seventies and early eighties. There were a lot of late teens and early twenties. He believes the current dearth of younger hikers may be because "we have this increasing perceived or misperceived notion that life is so much more dangerous today. I'm not convinced that it is."

Hikers who've been out on the trail a while stink, Roger noted. "I wouldn't say it bothered me, but I was amazed at what a stench the body could manage," Roger said. "And their look didn't bother me, because the minute I would talk to them I saw they were regular human beings. I could imagine what I would look like if I were out there a whole week without showering." When they arrive at his cottage, he usually suggests, "Why don't you run and get a shower first?" According to Roger, "Anyone who's not used to it will smell them immediately. Occasionally, if we had visitors, they'd say, 'Oh God.'"

Behind the house is Roger's Museum of American Weather, again featuring paintings by Mark Carroll. The museum includes historic weather instruments and exhibits on major storms, including the hurricane of 1938, the storm of the century in the Northeast. That storm, which devastated parts of coastal New Jersey, Long Island, and New England, ignited Roger's lifelong interest in weather. As a nine-year-old, he lived through it, and as an adult he wrote a book about it: *The Long Island Express: Tracking the Hurricane of 1938*. It killed hundreds of people, destroyed thousands of buildings in its path, and altered the course of A.T. history. The final section of the trail was blazed and opened on August 14, 1937. Thirteen months later, the trail was devastated, as thousands of trees were blown down by high winds.

A casual hiker for much of his life, in the late 1950s Roger went out West five straight summers and day-hiked or took overnight trips in the

Rockies. He also had done some day-hiking in the New York area and New England, totalling about two hundred miles of the A.T. Tackling the whole A.T., however, seemed a forbidding prospect. Even today he cannot conceive of being away from home for five or six months. "I didn't do it that way because I couldn't conceive of it. You can't do something you can't conceive of." He added, "I find that there's a degree of monotony in just the coverage of mile after mile for the sake of just getting these 2,100 miles done. The way I have made it interesting, because of my own way of looking at things, is to do it in two-week bits."

Listening to the hikers who stayed with him had prompted Roger to consider hiking the A.T. himself. In the early eighties, he met Ann and Al Weed, one of the most adventuresome retired couples ever to hike the A.T. Ann and Al believed that being retired meant you had more time to play. They went on canoe trips, hikes, and long rides on their motorcycles. They kept telling Roger he should do the trail. In 1982, the Weeds set up their recreational vehicle in the southern Appalachians and began helping hikers. They offered to help Roger. They put him on the trail each morning and gave him a place to stay at night.

Roger kept at the A.T., finally finishing in 1987 at Mount Rogers, Virginia. There he was met by his own trail angel, Mike Patch, a 1983 thru-hiker. Mike, who had become partially paralyzed in a 1984 automobile accident, brought champagne to celebrate Roger's achievement.

Roger admits that he found it a bit anticlimactic not finishing at Katahdin. He added that he would not deny the value of hiking the whole trail in one season. "That has got to be an entirely different experience," he said. "Of course, north to south isn't as dramatic because you end up on a perch there (at Springer Mountain)."

One of the benefits that Roger found in walking the trail was the time it gave him to think. "What a place for thinking and planning," he said.

Women and Couples on the Trail

Though new as an 'endless footpath through the wilderness,' the Trail itself seems age-old, so naturally does it fit into its surroundings. Just a path, now through old clearings sweet scented with grasses in the sun, through dim forests, then up through scrub and out over bare mountain ledges, it seems it's been since the beginning; it seems it will be till the end.

Jean Stephenson, founding editor
of the *Appalachian Trailway News,*
"Impressions of the Maine Wilderness," 1941

FROM THE EARLY DAYS OF THE A.T., WOMEN HAVE HIKED THE trail, constructed and maintained sections, and helped hold hiking groups together. But among long distance hikers, women were rare until the seventies. And not until the eighties did women account for as much as a fifth of the thru-hikers. Before 1970, only three women had thru-hiked the A.T., and only two had done the trail alone. By 1993, more than three hundred women had thru-hiked the trail, but only one did it while pregnant.

Donna Satterlee's 1977 thru-hike turned out a little different than she'd planned. A month into her hike, she stopped at a clinic in Hot Springs, where her suspicions were confirmed: She was pregnant. At first, she thought she'd have to leave the trail, but the nurse-practitioner who examined her said, "It's fine if you want to keep hiking; just listen to how you feel." She found that by pacing herself, she could continue. After the ups and downs of north Georgia, the Stekoahs, and the Smokies, she was in good shape.

"If I had known I was pregnant, I probably wouldn't have started the trail, although I don't know for sure," Donna said. "If we hadn't done the trail then, we probably couldn't have done it until we retired."

Donna and her husband, Richard, occasionally left the trail and went home, and there she received her prenatal care. She read pregnancy books. "I felt pretty comfortable about it," she said. "In some ways, it was better than being at home. I got lots of fresh air and exercise."

They finished in late September, six months after starting at Springer. Six weeks later, Georgia Maine Satterlee was born. "If it had been a boy, we'd have called him Anthony Thomas. The initials would be A.T."

A high-school student now, Georgia likes her name. She's the only Georgia in her school, and people enjoy the story of how she acquired her name. And yes, Georgia likes to hike.

"All along, I felt I was slow compared to other thru-hikers," Donna said, "but in the White Mountains, we came across day-hikers, and I was hiking faster than they were.

"We made adjustments as we needed to," she said. "Balancing the pack was difficult with my stomach sticking out, so we sent my frame pack home, and I used my day pack. "

Donna tried hard on the hike to take good care of herself. "I didn't want to do anything that would harm the baby. If we needed to go slower, we did. My husband was always supportive. We'd rest a couple of hours at midday.

"My favorite places were the White Mountains and Maine. We passed through the huts at the end of the season, and they were short-handed and let us wash dishes and stay there. Near Mount Washington, we'd pass hut boys with their heavy frame packs, and they'd see me and say, 'You're the pregnant hiker.'

"Most people were friendly like that. Father Charles, who was just opening the Pearisburg hostel, said we were Mary and Joseph.

"One lady did write a letter saying, 'How could you do that?' But most people were supportive. We made a lot of friends. That's an important part of the trip.

"It was nice for us as a couple to be together. You have your ups and downs, but it makes you stronger.

"The memories of the trip are still vivid and basically good. The days that were miserable I remember less than the good days. The trail makes you aware of all the things you can do without. It helps you keep things in perspective.

"As a couple, we understand each other a little better. We've always gotten along well. After the trail, I knew him that much more. We always helped each other. If he'd chosen to go on ahead, I would have understood. But he chose to go slower and stay with me."

From the earliest days of the A.T. movement, women have been involved with the trail in many capacities, but only a small percentage of trail activists have been women. In the last decade, that has changed: Two of the last three ATC chairs have been women. In 1925, a woman, Harlean James, issued the call for the meeting that created the ATC. She remained active for decades, becoming one of the ATC's first four honorary members, along with another woman, Marion Park, who had been a key member of PATC. Jean Stephenson, who had a Ph.D. in judicial science, was founding editor of the *A.T. News* (in 1939), edited guidebooks, did trail construction and maintenance, and generally helped keep the ATC together for forty years. Ruth Blackburn, Anna Michener, Florence Nichols, Elizabeth Levers, and many others made important contributions to the ATC and its constituent clubs.

Since completing the A.T. in 1978–79, Cindy Ross may well have succeeded Grandma Gatewood as the most renowned female 2,000-miler. Cindy has written books on the A.T. and the Pacific Crest Trail, and she has written for *Backpacker* magazine. She also served as ALDHA coordinator. Cindy married another 2,000-miler, Todd "the Tramper" Glatfelter. Together, they have continued backpacking with their two children and set up a hikers' hostel in Pennsylvania.

Jan "Sacajawea" Collins has suggested several possible reasons why fewer women than men hike the A.T. For one, the trail is more dangerous for women. For another, women are generally smaller than men, yet still have to carry much of the same gear. This means they are carrying a higher percentage of their body weight. Jan believes that women are brought up to quit activities when they're painful and are thus more likely to drop out in the first few weeks of a thru-hike, before one is in top condition. Perhaps the Boy Scouts do a better job of preparing boys for backpacking the A.T. than do the Girl Scouts. Many male hikers get their start in the armed services, and fewer women serve in the military. Finally, women are probably less likely to start the trail without a partner, and partners are hard to find.

Over the years, many couples have married or honeymooned on the trail. Since thru-hiking is such an intense experience, it's natural that so many romances have blossomed on the trail. Mike Jones and his wife, Helen "Smiles in Our Hearts," who had met on the trail two years before, paused on one of their thru-hikes to get married in the parking lot of the Country Diner in Bastian, Virginia. At least two couples have been married at Trail Days in Damascus. Others have married everywhere from Springer to Katahdin.

It would seem that any couple able to endure the stress of a thru-hike would have a rock-solid relationship. Alas, such does not seem to be the case. The evidence suggests that A.T. marriages are no more durable than others in our society. According to Roly Mueser's survey, half the couples who complete the trail together split up fairly soon. Because many single hikers have trouble adjusting to life after the trail, it's probably at least as difficult for couples.

Leonard "Habitual Hiker" Adkins, who has been hiking with his wife Laurie "the Umbrella Lady" since 1982, said, "As a couple, we find it harder not to be on the trail. Other people say they're glad they have a job, so they have time apart. We find that on the trail, the more we're together, the better it is. In most couples, one partner will be a half mile ahead. We pretty much walk one right behind the other."

While it can be more difficult hiking as a couple, there are rewards. Dan Nellis finds that although he slows down when he hikes with his wife, "Kathy Backpacker," he enjoys having someone to share the experiences with. "Sharing chores, talking about fun things, exclaiming over the brightness of the stars—it's liberating and exciting to share that," he said.

"It makes the good times so much better and the bad times easier," said Ginny "Spiritwalker" Frost, who hiked the trail once alone and once with a partner. Others find that it's helpful to have someone with whom to share equipment and chores.

Some hikers, of course, have the problem of a nonhiking spouse. This requires sensitivity on both sides. Although not always the case, it's usually a wife or girlfriend who is back home.

Frank "Red Blaze" Shea had made plans to hike the A.T. a year and a half in advance. "I really wanted Katahdin more than anything in the world," he said. Then a few months before the trip, he met Stephanie Page, a non-hiker from Ohio who had never seen a mountain. Both realized it would be impractical for her to go along.

Stephanie met Frank a few times along the way and eventually began to

Walking the Appalachian Trail

understand what the thru-hike meant to him. "I wrote him a lot of letters, and I know that was really important to him," Stephanie said. "So even though I only talked to him once every two weeks, I felt very much a part of what he was doing. I had the map on my wall of where he was. It was a connection." Although she was lonely, she liked the changes she saw in Frank as the hike went on. He was calmer, more mature, less perturbed by petty problems. Now she wants to do the trail.

Ray Hunt and Collins Chew, formerly the ATC chair and vice-chair, hiked much of the trail together over fifteen years. When they did day hikes, their wives, Martha and Charlotte, would shuttle them to the trailhead, then shop or explore the area until it was time to pick them up. It worked well for all of them.

Many women do hike the trail alone, but most stress that they take special precautions. Kay Wood, who hiked alone at seventy, and Susan Gail Arey were two who chose not to hitchhike alone. Other women avoid road crossings when they are alone. Jan Collins and others recognize that the chances of encountering danger on the trail, although slight, are real, but they want to live their lives and are willing to take calculated risks. They do what they can to diminish the danger, then go for it. Most say that if they get bad vibes about someone, they move on. They avoid shelters near road crossings and don't broadcast their itineraries.

"Only a few times was I mindful of danger," said Connor "Carolina Cookers" Coward. "I just thought, if it's going to happen, it's going to happen and there's not a lot I can do. I'm not going to hide my whole life."

A few miles north of Damascus, Jan came across a naked man in the woods. "When I saw him, I thought he must be sunning himself. I cleared my throat, but he didn't move. My partners had gone ahead. I thought, 'I'm not going to go by this guy.' I backed up toward a dirt road. I walked down the road, and there he was in the bushes, putting his clothes on. Quietly, I turned around. He saw me and ducked down. I could tell he was hiding. I freaked. I thought, 'I'm dead.' I had to make a decision whether to throw my pack down and run for my life, or just run with my pack on. I just couldn't drop my pack. I started running down the trail in the opposite direction. I heard a noise. I thought it was him in the woods. I'd heard a deer running. I thought, 'What next?' As I came out by a little town, I saw a family fishing. The woman said, 'How are you?' I said, 'Not too good.' I started crying. She gave me a hug, and they took me into the village.

"I got such support from my partners. The Forest Service people were good about trying to track the man down. They finally caught him the next year.

"After that, I changed my hiking style. I had to hike with people. Now I hike by myself all the time, but I act like I'm with others."

Mary Ann Miller

*F*our of us sat on the curb watching the hikers' parade at Trail Days in *Damascus. With Mary Ann were her husband, Ken, and two-year-old son, Benjamin. Often the effects of a thru-hike are difficult to pinpoint, but here were a few tangible ones. Mary Ann, who lived in Warren Doyle's hometown of Shelton, Connecticut, started Warren's 1990 expedition alone. Ken was one of the two van drivers who supported the group.*

"I thought that hiking the A.T. was the most wonderful experience of my entire life," Mary Ann said. "I was free for the first time. All of a sudden I realized that I could do anything with my life."

Mary Ann joined one of Warren Doyle's group thru-hikes after seeing his slide show

For years before her thru-hike, Mary Ann had big family responsibilities. Her parents and two brothers had died young, and she had raised one brother and another brother's children. "I had always been the person everyone came to for help," she said. "I decided they were going to have to learn to get along without me for four months. I had never gone away, never done anything like this before. I found the first week that the mantle of responsibility that fell off my shoulders had weighed a ton." She added, "I had left instructions: There were to be no marriages, no births, no deaths while I was gone and that was the way it was."

Doyle's groups walk with day packs, keep to a strict schedule that permits few rest days, and hike an average of about 50 percent more miles each day than do other thru-hikers. The rigidity and extended togetherness are the opposite of what most thru-hikers prize. Many also worry about the impact of fifteen or twenty people on a backcountry trail that fewer than two hundred people a year complete; by other measures, however, long-distance hikers account for only a small percentage of the trail's use, and scout, church, and camp groups often use the trail for a weekend or longer.

For Mary Ann, though, the expedition was a great way to do the trail. An inexperienced backpacker, she enjoyed the support of other group members and the freedom from having to carry much weight. "All the backpackers that we met were struggling," Mary Ann said. "That's part of their experience, I'm sure. It means a lot to them. But our type wasn't a struggle. It was a picnic. It was like four months of absolute vacation."

The expedition members were able to hike with only day packs because a van, carrying the rest of their gear, met them nearly every night. Because of space limitations in the van, hikers had to keep their possessions in two milk crates.

Some hikers disdain adhering to a schedule, but Mary Ann found it liberating. "It freed you," she said, "because you didn't have to think about anything. You were going to go from point A to point B, whether it was fifteen miles or twenty-seven miles. That was what you did that day, so what else did you have to worry about? Nothing. And you knew you could walk that far. On the way, whatever you wanted to do, you could do. If you wanted to take a long time, stop at a store, nap somewhere for an hour or two, that was your prerogative. You had the freedom to do anything within the schedule. The schedule made it so easy to be free."

Doyle has his hikers hold hands in a circle at the start, finish, and key places in between. He considers it a powerful motivating force and a symbol of their determination to have the entire group finish. Only one "circle"—the 1978 expedition—was broken, and that remains a bitter memory for him. Members disagree on the circle's power, but people who see slide shows or videos of the trips retain the circles as a vivid image of the expeditions.

Hikers choose whether to join the circle and commit to staying together until the end. Mary Ann didn't join at first. Arguing with Warren at one prehike meeting, she said, "You're not being realistic." "This is not reality," he answered.

"There was dead silence in the whole room," Mary Ann said. "All the group members were there, and we just let that settle into everybody." Four members didn't join the initial circle on Springer Mountain. "Then we hiked for a week, and I joined the circle because he was right. It wasn't reality. Reality is waking up in the morning, making yourself breakfast, making the beds, maybe having to go to work during the day and living a life. Reality is not rolling out of your tent in the morning and having a deer walking by, and you can about reach out and touch it. Or walking through fields of flowers waving in the breeze. Or smelling a pine when you're walking through a pine forest. And being free of any responsibility."

For more than a year before the trip, Warren had the group take long practice hikes and attend meetings. He made the hikes difficult and warned repeatedly that the trip would be hard.

Mary Ann recalls her first long practice hike with the pride of a survivor. She got up at three in the morning to make the long drive to Virginia. During the day, they discussed the trip; not until eleven at night did they start the two-hour drive to the trailhead. At one in the morning, she was walking through the woods looking for a spot to camp. They were up at six, hiking again. "I remember thinking that I was going to die for sure," Mary Ann said. "There was no way to live through this experience." But the others helped pull her through. At the Bears Den Hostel, in Virginia, one of the women in the group helped Mary Ann into the shower. By that point, she was so exhausted she could barely stand. "As tired and sore as I was, I never was discouraged about doing it," she said. Instead, she'd get angry at Warren. "He'd make you so mad that you'd stomp off twenty miles in no time at all and the whole time you'd be thinking, I'm going to kill him. It fired you to go. He's amazing." People who attend Warren's week-long backpacking seminar or who go with the expedition say he effectively prepares them for the trail. Although some of the preparations may be unpleasant, those who come under his tutelage are much more likely to complete the trail than other hikers. Even for an experienced hiker, Warren's techniques can boost confidence. Albie Pokrob, who thru-hiked in 1978, joined Warren's 1980 expedition. Albie couldn't conceive of hiking fifty miles in a day, but doing it removed his previous idea of limits and he felt inspired to tackle other obstacles. "You thought, 'I could do that, maybe I can do this,'" Albie said.

At the beginning of the trip at Springer Mountain, Mary Ann was nervous and excited. The longest she'd hiked was three days. She knew she could do that, but she wasn't sure if she could go farther. "After the fifth day, I knew I could do it with no problem," she said.

During the preparations for the trip, Mary Ann and the van driver, Ken, became acquainted, and a romance blossomed. On the last practice hike in April 1990, Mary Ann arrived late at night at Hemlock Overlook-Center. She saw Ken, asked him a few questions, and they settled into a long conversation. "Now we're both getting wet standing in the rain," said Mary Ann, "and I said, 'I've got to get some shut-eye.' We were getting up at four or five to hike and it was real late. He says to me, 'By the way, what's your name?'"

"He was Mr. Romantic," Mary Ann said as Ken protested. "He would take me at night up into the woods, and there would be this huge rock in the middle of a stream someplace, and he'd sing and we'd dance. He brought me flowers. Just really romantic stuff the whole time we were out there." Laughing, Ken said, "I don't remember any of this."

At the end of April, Mary Ann flew to Atlanta to start the thru-hike. Since Ken lived nearby, he met her at the airport. She thought they'd go straight to Springer. Instead, they went to Ken's house for a Sunday family dinner. Ken's father drove them to Springer, grilling her the whole way.

In the beginning of the hike, Mary Ann became annoyed with Ken. She had grown friendly with another woman and was doing things with her. "He just seemed to be everywhere I was," Mary Ann said. "I thought, 'Can't he ever leave me alone?' But it was always stuff like, 'Come on, walk down here, there's a beautiful waterfall. Let's go up here in the woods and watch the sunset.' My mother taught me to always be polite. I was polite, but all the time I was saying to myself, 'What is the matter with this guy?'" "She was always after me," Ken said.

"It took a while, but he kind of grew on me," Mary Ann said. "At the end of the hike he came back to Connecticut for a while with me. Then I got a ticket to Georgia in the mail for Thanksgiving and met his family, and that's when he proposed. I packed up, and that was that."

Mary Ann and Ken were a source of humor to the other expedition members because of the creative places Ken found to pitch their tent. "It got to be a joke where our tent was going to be," Mary Ann said. Late one night in North Carolina, they decided that big roots made their campsite uncomfortable. So they picked up the tent, with their sleeping bags and other gear inside. They walked three quarters of a mile down a mountain in the dark and pitched the tent beneath the giant Wasilik poplar at Rock Gap, North Carolina. "It was scary for me because he knew where he was going, and I didn't, and I just had to trust him," Mary Ann said. "I knew we were going over water. I didn't know how deep it was or where to step. He would say, 'Put your right foot about three inches over and then jump.' I couldn't see anything, but we got there."

Her homecoming in Connecticut made Mary Ann more appreciative of her trail experience. Her thirty-four-year-old brother, who'd had several previous strokes, died a month after she finished the trail. It brought home to her that "life is short, and for some people, it's shorter than for others. If it's going to be short for me, I want to make sure I do what I want to do before it's all over."

After the trip, it was difficult for Mary Ann to relate to her co-workers. "When I came back, I had traveled much more than 2,167 miles. I had traveled mentally much farther than that, and everybody else hadn't. And so it was hard to talk to people sometimes." She was sad and surprised by people who were so concerned about things that seemed petty to her. It was disconcerting to realize that she had been like that, and she hoped she would not be that way again.

During our conversation little Benjamin had fallen asleep. Now well rested, he and his father would join Mary Ann on yet another springtime journey to Georgia, now home.

Elderly and Handicapped Hikers

In the woods, too, a man casts off his years, as the snake his slough, and at what period soever of life, is always a child. In the woods is perpetual youth. Within these plantations of God, a decorum and sanctity reign, a perennial festival is dressed, and the guest sees not how he should tire of them in a thousand years.

Ralph Waldo Emerson

THE GREAT DIVIDE IS SIXTY, ACCORDING TO ROLY MUESER, WHO hiked the trail at sixty-six. It's tough for someone over sixty to thru-hike in a single season. Older hikers average only ten and a half to eleven miles each hiking day. From age twenty to sixty the average is fourteen and a half miles. Because of lower mileage, it's hard for older hikers to finish the trail without hiking through big snowstorms and other treacherous weather.

"At sixty, it would have been a blast," said Kay "Grandma Kay" Wood, who eventually hiked the trail at age seventy in 1988. "I couldn't do it now," she said in 1993. "I do still backpack, however.

"I think I'm lucky. So many people would like to do it. Most people don't have the time. You're awfully lucky if you have the time."

A slender, cheerful woman, Kay Wood's involvement with the A.T. spans forty years. The trail used to run right by her house in Dalton, Massachusetts.

Last summer, at seventy-five, Kay was a volunteer ridge runner along the Massachusetts A.T., helping and educating hikers. By early June, she had already covered the route twice. A trail shelter not far from Dalton has been named in her honor, and she has been vigilant in making sure it's in good shape.

Kay eased into trail work after she began backpacking with her son in the late fifties. She noticed places where logging caused difficulties on the trail. She tried to have those situations corrected, even though she wasn't involved with any hiking groups. In the early seventies, she began maintaining an A.T. stretch near Dalton and became a volunteer coordinator. In her spare time, she climbed the one hundred highest peaks in New England.

With her children grown, she sold her big house, and then it seemed like the right time to hike the A.T. Over the years, she'd talked to many thru-hikers, which had given her an itch to hike the trail. She'd done stretches of it before, but she thought it would be fun to do the whole trail.

She hurt her knee in Virginia and panicked, thinking it was badly injured. After recovering, she came back in the fall and hiked Maine and New York. The following summer, she did Virginia through Pennsylvania, before developing shinsplints. She completed the trail in the fall.

"I'd never been in the South before, and I enjoyed seeing so many wildflowers, and the colors of the azaleas were so beautiful," Kay said.

As a lone hiker, the only thing she feared were stream crossings, which can be icy cold and slippery, with swift currents that make it easy to lose balance. "I loved Maine, all except the stream crossings. I picked August to hike there, thinking it would be dry. But there were a lot of thunderstorms, and the streams were high.

"I fell in a couple of times in Maine, where a couple of young hikers just bounced across. In one place, where the water goes over a dam, the other side is deep, up to your neck. I yelled for them, and they grabbed my hand and pulled me out so fast hardly anything got wet. I walked fast till I got to the next shelter and dried off.

"Farther north, I fell in face down and couldn't raise myself. I gave a big push and got myself out. I had a big bruise on my leg. I was finishing up a section and getting tired, and I would fall more."

Kay carried too much weight but couldn't seem to trim her load. "I didn't carry anything I didn't have to," she said. Much of the time she carried a two-week supply of food, since she avoided hitchhiking. At the start, she hiked five or six miles a day until she worked into shape. Later, she did three straight twenty-mile days on a rocky stretch in Pennsylvania; it was a mistake, because she hurt her legs there. She just felt good and wanted to keep up with some younger hikers. "It was stupid, but you get psyched up," she said. "I was feeling cocky."

Her only injuries were shinsplints and problems with her knees, nothing serious or permanent. She was never sick, though she did meet several hikers who were ill from bad water. "It's a nuisance to treat water, but it's worth it to not get sick," said Kay.

"I liked being alone," she went on. "While I walked, I wrote long letters in my head, and then when I'd get to the shelter, I'd be too tired to write them down. I thought about my kids, but I wasn't homesick. I was perfectly happy where I was. There was so much to see. A lot of hikers don't see what's close to them: the different types of trees, flowers, birds, and things.

"Grandma Gatewood stayed at my house in the sixties when she went up to the Long Trail. My girls were little then. I recognized her as she was hiking past. I asked if she'd like lemonade. She said she wasn't going much farther, so I asked if she'd like to stay. She had her little duffel bag and carried very little. She had a can of corned beef and just ate cold things. She had bunions and spent a lot of time washing her feet."

It's impressive when anyone does the whole A.T. But it's positively remarkable that so many elderly and handicapped people have hiked the two thousand miles. Most remarkable of all was the feat of Bill "the Orient Express" Irwin, the blind hiker, who in 1990 did most of the trail alone, except for his guide dog, Orient. No one on the trail that year could complain about much of anything without feeling sheepish. No matter how hard it was, it was harder for Bill. Yet, according to those who met him along the trail, Bill retained his equanimity in the face of thousands of falls, a broken rib, dreadful mixups, getting lost, and frequent danger. Even thru-hikers who can see are often poised on ridges, one step from oblivion, or climbing over barbed-wire fences, or crossing streams on jagged stepping stones.

A deeply religious man, Bill often said he was doing the trail to demonstrate his faith in God. Certainly, though, the trip also amply demonstrated Bill's courage, determination, and persistence in the face of seemingly insuperable obstacles.

Arthur "A. B. Positive" Batchelder, who helped Bill in Maine after finishing his own thru-hike, worried about Bill's safety in the cold fall weather. Arthur finally insisted on helping Bill around some stream crossings in late October, fearing that Bill would die of exposure. Arthur and Peter "Mr. Moleskin" Martel also helped to locate Bill on Avery Peak, where he was stranded by a big snowstorm. "In one day, he could fall a hundred times," Arthur said. "His legs were just big scabs."

"None of us could ever complain that year," said Luke "the Journeyman" Wiaczek. "We couldn't say we were having a hard time or we fell. Bill would come in, and his legs would be bruised and bleeding. He had no way of getting around it. But he was always up. He was definitely an inspiration to anybody."

"It was challenging enough for me," said Connor "Carolina Cookers" Coward, who hiked some with Bill. "I have no idea how he did it. If I hadn't seen him do some myself, I wouldn't believe it."

Ranking high among the most courageous and impressive hikers is Bob Barker, who has multiple sclerosis and thru-hiked with crutches and a heavy pack. Bob hiked the whole trail not once, but three times in the eighties and he, too, hiked alone. Like his friend, Bill Irwin, Bob displays tremendous determination. He has endured his share of falls and broken bones. Bob, too, is now blind, but he has continued to hike.

"I don't know how he does it," three-time 2,000-miler Bert Gilbert said. "The first time I met him, he was going up out of Kinsman Notch (in the White Mountains). He was using these two arm braces, and he was humping along. He carried an awful lot of stuff. He must have been carrying seventy-five pounds."

Bob has hiked the trail in both directions. On his second trip, in 1983–84, at age sixty-three, he spent 182 nights on the trail, averaging 12 miles a day, with a longest of 26 ½ miles. He wore out six crutch tips along the way.

Among the handicapped people who have done the trail: Jeff Lubman, who is deaf; Mike "Gutless" Schank, who lost part of his stomach and other organs to cancer; and Jack Eshelman, who had a hip replacement.

The oldest man to have hiked the trail, Ernie Morris, started when he was eighty-two and finished at age eighty-six. He continued backpacking until age ninety-two, when he hiked more than a week on the John Muir Trail in California's High Sierra with fellow 2,000-miler David Lipski. They left the trail when bears stole their food and destroyed their packs. Ernie died the following year, 1982, at age ninety-three.

He started his A.T. hike at Springer in 1972, but stopped at Rockfish Gap, Virginia, because of Hurricane Agnes, which devastated much of the Mid-Atlantic states. He returned to the A.T. in 1975 and finished six months later, three months after his eighty-sixth birthday. According to his daughter, Margaret J. Morris, in a letter to the *A.T. News,* he "loved every minute of it, even the scary parts, and always referred to it as 'the greatest adventure of my life.'" David Lipski wrote that Ernie used to say, "If you make demands on your body, your body will respond, within limits."

Paul "Bigfoot" Tourigny met Ernie Morris at Mad Tom Shelter in Vermont in 1975. Paul was doing the Long Trail with his nephew, John, and Ernie was finishing the A.T. Paul asked Ernie how old he was, and was just amazed to hear he was eighty-six years old. He was even more amazed to find out that Ernie's pack was as heavy as his own. Ernie generally kept his pack between forty and forty-five pounds, about one third of his own weight. When he started the A.T., Ernie also carried a fourteen-pound duffel bag.

Ernie believed in keeping in shape with proper diet and exercise, including exercising his mind. To do so, he would memorize things. That night, he kept Paul and John enthralled, reciting from memory Robert Service's poem "Dangerous Dan McGrew." Paul found Ernie methodical about his routines and disciplined about hiking his planned mileage each day.

Ernie was then living in Independence, California, at the base of Mount Whitney. At that time, he was the oldest person to have climbed 14,495-foot Mount Whitney, a feat he accomplished alone at age ninety. Paul has a picture of Ernie that same year climbing a tree to prune it for a neighbor.

After his first wife died in 1959, Ernie's blood pressure rose to 170. To lower it, he began hiking and climbing in the California mountains, eventually dropping it to 125.

Before he did it, Ernie had been planning to hike the A.T. for twenty-five years. "A lot of people are always thinking about what they are going to do," Ernie said. "I believe in making the most of each day, every hour, and every minute. You can't live tomorrow. You must live today." When he died, his ashes were scattered on the High Sierra trails that he loved.

Dr. Frederick Luehring hiked the trail in stretches and finished in 1963, at age eighty-one. At that time, he was the oldest person to have completed the trail.

Before hiking the trail, Luehring had a lifelong record of involvement in athletics. He played guard on the University of Chicago football team under legendary coach Amos Alonzo Stagg just at the time the forward pass was being developed. He was Princeton's first basketball coach and was an athletic director of the Universities of Nebraska, Minnesota, and Pennsylvania. A member of the International Swimming Hall of Fame, Dr. Luehring was secretary of the American Olympic swimming teams for the 1932 and 1936 games.

He hiked the A.T. over fifteen years, walking only in the summer. Dr. Luehring died in 1981 at age ninety-nine. Until a few weeks before he died, he walked daily, swam regularly, and chopped firewood. "I walk to live, and I live to walk," he often said. At ninety-two, he led a twenty-mile walk. At eighty-seven, he was picked up by police as he hiked the Long Trail. They thought he was too old to be there alone, but friends convinced the authorities otherwise.

Gordon "Old Man" Gamble hiked the A.T. at age sixty-six, despite arthritic knees. Gordon, who thru-hiked in 1980, pared his pack weight mercilessly. He planted a half dozen food caches in the South, keeping his pack light while he adjusted to the trail. He even wore heavily padded sneakers to lower his shoe weight. In his trail report to the ATC and the AMC, Gordon wrote, "The trail turned out to be quite difficult, much more so than anticipated. Had I realized that, in ascending and descending the 163 mountains along the trail, the footway would be so rough due to roots, rocks, boulders, and ledges, I doubt that I would have ever started."

But, he concluded, "Overall, I consider my first major retirement project a considerable success. I will cherish the memory of prolonged outdoor living in one of America's great wilderness areas. I also derive tremendous satisfaction from finding that I could cope with difficulties as they arose."

"Ramblin' Rose" and "Sourdough Bob" Goss of Michigan were nearing retirement. They had been acquainted with the A.T. for years, backpacking and car camping along the trail. "One year we started talking about doing the A.T.," Robert explained, "and we said, 'We'd better do it now if we're going to do it.'"

"The only time we'd get discouraged was at night when we'd get to the shelter. We'd be bushed and ask why in the world we're doing it. In the morning, we'd wake up refreshed and answer, 'Because we're enjoying it so much.'"

"We were doing it our way," Bob added. "We went a little slower than most people. That way, we got to hike with a lot of people for a few days."

"By the Whites, we were tough as nails and felt great," Rose said. "It was quite emotional to see Katahdin from the trail for the first time, to see the last mountain after you'd seen so many."

Nine thru-hikers finished on Katahdin the same day as Bob and Rose. Chuck "Woodchuck" Wood borrowed an American flag from the Monson post office and carried it to the top. "Strangers cheered," Bob said. It was quite a feeling. We fell in each other's arms and cried like babies. Neither of us is the crying type. Surely, it was a feeling of joy.

"Before the trip, people would ask, 'What do you expect to get out of that?' You can't really tell them. If you ask the question, you won't understand the answer. You have to have a feeling for the trail. Some of these things are hard to put into words. It was the most fantastic thing that we did in our life."

"I don't think you're ever the same people after hiking the trail," Rose said. "You realize what's important and what isn't. For six months, you get by with minimal clothing and food. You realize you've weighted yourself down with a lot of unimportant details. You start to appreciate the little things in life. You enjoy everything from a little bug climbing a leaf to a big grouse taking off. Nature is really what counts. Man-made things are not that important."

Tom "the Pennsylvania Creeper" Thwaites hiked the trail in 1990 after retiring as a physics professor from Penn State. The author of several Pennsylvania hiking guides, he said, "I was obsessed with mileage all the time, and that's a mistake. But I knew this was my one chance to do the A.T., and I wanted to make sure I'd do it.

"I was surprised at how tough the South was. There were no flat places till Watauga Lake in Tennessee. I was surprised at how tough Maine was, too." Over the last decade, the A.T. has been moved from logging roads and relocated onto mountains, making the trail better but harder. In Maine, near-constant rain made the trail slick, and Tom fell every day. "The roots were slippery, the leaves were slippery, even the rocks were slippery. There was no place safe to step," he said. "I had big bruises for months afterward."

Reverend Henry Childs pieced the trail together, finishing in his early seventies. An inspiration to younger hikers, he could be heard introducing them to Shakespeare or the philosophers as he traveled the trail. Strong but frail-looking, he exemplified how well hikers of all ages seem to mix on the A.T. If younger hikers mature during a thru-hike, then older hikers must become young. Steve "Offshore Steve" Gomez, who is in between old and young, said that during his eight years as a commercial fisherman, while still in his twenties, he felt old. Now, as a hiker, he feels young. Perhaps that's enough benefit for anyone.

Dick "the Old Hawaiian Mountain Goat" Davis

Exercise the body and it glows with vigor; exercise the brain and you stay alert; exercise the senses and enjoy all Mother Nature has to offer; open your heart and let in the sunshine of love for living and for those living, and you feel serenity.

Richard Davis, "the Old Hawaiian Mountain Goat"

In late April 1983, I took my wife, Frieda, on her first backpacking trip, a circuit of the eastern Smokies. It had rained for weeks, and snow was still deep at higher elevations. Frieda fell into a creek once and almost drowned, and was either drenched or frozen much of the time. One night, we stayed at Cosby Knob Shelter. A backpacker, Dick Davis, then sixty-two, was the first to join us. He was in more pain than any hiker I've ever seen. Frieda, an emergency-room nurse, marveled that he could hike at all.

Possibly no one has a more apt trail name than Dick "the Old Hawaiian Mountain Goat" Davis. Stubborn, resilient, stoic, he thrived where many others would have found the going impossible. Despite lifelong encounters with severe adversity, he cheerfully recounts his many adventures in a matter-of-fact delivery that belies his dramatic brushes with danger.

After completing the Pacific Crest Trail in 1980–81, he turned to the A.T. in 1983. Less than a month into his hike, he was walking near Clingmans Dome in the Smokies in eighteen inches of snow, when he slipped and twisted his knee, tearing muscles and ligaments. The next day, he limped down to the road and hitchhiked into Gatlinburg.

In town, a policeman pulled him over, and soon he was surrounded by six police cars. They searched him and questioned him. A man had been shot nearby, and Dick matched the description of the murderer. Finally, they realized they had the wrong guy.

After being cleared, Dick rested in town for a few days before returning to the trail. But the knee still bothered him a lot.

North of Hot Springs, he met a young man walking toward him. "Are you Dick Davis?" he asked. It was his nephew, and his brother was waiting at the road. So Dick spent a few weeks recuperating at his brother's home. "Knees take a long time. It's still recuperating," Dick said a decade later.

From Pennsylvania, he flip-flopped, skipping six hundred miles of trail by taking a bus to Woodstock, New Hampshire, to visit his boyhood haunts. He used ski poles to support his still troublesome knee. On Wildcat Mountain, his knee acted up again, and he rested another week.

He stayed overnight in a cabin in the Maine wilderness. On the trail the next morning, he felt pains inside of both arms, which soon passed down his trunk. "I knew I'd had a heart attack," he said. He lay alone on the trail for twelve hours, propping his feet up and reading and writing poetry. That night, he made it to a nearby ridge and camped.

In the morning, he saw a seaplane landing on a lake, but when he reached the lake, no one was there. He went back to hike the trail, and five days later he was at the base of Katahdin.

"It was such a beautiful day, I left my pack at the ranger station and started up," he said. On the way, he felt angina pains, which slowed him. Even twelve-year-olds were passing him. But he eventually did make the summit.

The next day, he caught a bus to Portland. He was in such bad shape that he didn't realize where he was until he reached the end of the line in Boston. The bus company let him ride free to Portland, where he was hospitalized for twelve days. At first, the doctors didn't think he'd had a heart attack. After hiking the PCT and much of the A.T. in the past three years, he performed a stress test better than anyone there. An EKG showed nothing. But an angiogram showed a coronary artery 100 percent blocked and another 80 percent blocked. "They didn't see how I could walk across the room," he said, "much less hike the A.T." In November, he had quadruple bypass surgery.

In 1985, he returned to the trail in New Hampshire. Hiking south from Mount Moosilauke, he became exhausted in the ice and snow. For a time, he was vomiting every few hundred yards. But by the time he reached Hanover, he was better and able to complete his hike.

Asked whether he ever thought of dropping off the trail, the answer was a quick and emphatic "Never!" He added, "Pain has never bothered me. I grew up with it."

As a youth, he had severe migraines, one after the other. At age fourteen, he lost his right eye. At sixteen, he cut off half his right foot when he fell onto a lumber saw.

His next major trauma occurred in 1950 in Hawaii, where Dick still lives. With a friend, he hiked up a ridge behind Schofield Barracks, and they filled their packs with wild oranges. Failing to make it back by dark, they spent the night huddled under a poncho. Descending the next day, they found a climbing rope in place. Dick said, "I tested it four or five times but didn't go to the top to see if it was tied. It wasn't, and he fell four hundred feet, landing on his back, with the pack of oranges helping to break his fall. Even so, he blew out five vertebrae, smashed his spinal cord, and received assorted other injuries. He lived but still has constant back pain.

He also had more than his share of accidents on the PCT. After picking up his mail near Mount Shasta, California, he was hit by the outside mirror of a potato chip truck, suffering a concussion. "It slowed me up for a while, but I went back to the trail and kept going until the weather turned bad," he said.

Later on the PCT, he had a backpacking stove blow up, and sat on an anthill. He had to plunge into an icy stream to rid himself of the ants.

Dick grew up on a small farm in New Hampshire, where his father worked in a paper mill. Dick worked on the farm before school, in the evenings, and on weekends. When he was as young as thirteen and fourteen his dad would place him in jobs working with lumberjacks. "The only way to get away was to run into the Lincoln wilderness. There was no Kancamagus highway then."

He'd take a blanket, a gun, a fish line, salt pork, and cornmeal, and explore the White Mountains. Dick, who is part Mohawk Indian, would watch the "tourists" on the A.T., then go off by himself before they saw him. "I was always intrigued by the A.T.," he said.

In the winter he'd take his six-dollar maple skis, secured by rubber bands since he couldn't afford ski bindings, and ski sections of the A.T. By the time he finished high school, he'd covered the whole A.T. in New Hampshire.

"I've always loved the mountains, the feeling of serenity and feeling close to the powers that be," he said. "Hiking the trails was the greatest experience of my life."

Dick's advice for new hikers is to "set your pace. Hike the way you feel. One day you might feel like hiking just six miles. The next day, maybe you'll feel like twenty.

"Remember that different people have different paces. I start off slow in the morning and go steady all day. Some people go in dashes and stops. At three or four in the afternoon, I'd pass young people who had left early in the morning like eager beavers. We'd camp together again that night. Everyone has to set his own pace so he'll be comfortable."

Despite all his mishaps, Dick at seventy-three is still cheerful and hard at work clearing trails in Hawaii.

Admiring Disciples of the A.T.'s Grand Old Man

Afoot and light-hearted I take to the open road;
Healthy, free, the world before me,
The long brown path leading wherever I choose.
Henceforth, I ask not good fortune;
I myself am good fortune.
Henceforth, I wimper no more, postpone no more, I need nothing.
I'm done with indoor complaints, libraries, and querulous criticisms.
Strong and content I travel the open road.

Walt Whitman, *Leaves of Grass*
(Inscribed on a statue at
Bear Mountain Zoo along the A.T.)

BACKPACKERS TEND TO BE ASCETIC AND STOIC. THEY SHRUG OFF pain and do not lust after creature comforts. Occasional company is tolerable, even desirable, but more than that and they can feel closed in, trapped. Ed Garvey, an early thru-hiker, is a notable exception. He's one of the most gregarious people ever to hike the A.T. During his 1970 thru-hike, people continually met him with food, drink, and various festivities. Garvey's hike was less of a lone adventure than a roving party.

Traveling Garveys: A trail family of devoted yet unworthy followers of "the most noble thru-hiking guru," Ed Garvey, who had friends meet him at road crossings with rides, food and (especially) good spirits during his groundbreaking 1970 hike from Georgia to Maine. It is toward the pursuit of these "good spirits" that all dedicated "Ed-Heads" are committed. Founded in 1992 on a northbound thru-hike by "Sprained Rice" and "Medicine Man," the group includes, in order of induction, "Fairhope," "Andy Bliss," "Trickster," "Phantom Engineer," "Pink Cloud," "Towanda," and "Orion." Honorary members include Jean Cashin and the guru himself. The group's official motto is "We are not worthy!"

Bill O'Brien, a two-time 2,000-miler, acquired his trail name, "Sprained Rice," in two parts. As a young Boy Scout he attended a banquet where "Rice O'Brien" was served, hence the nickname "Rice." After a bad fall in Maine on his first thru-hike, another hiker saw him limping along and changed it to "Sprained Rice." Bill is in many ways an embodiment of Ed's hiking spirit. Fun-loving and outgoing, Bill seems to know everybody on the trail and everything that's happening. "Bill is very much a contact person," said his partner, Andrew "Medicine Man" Sam. "Everybody he meets, he remembers their name. If they see him at Trail Days, he can tell them, 'Well, I met you at such and such a shelter or gap. He can tell them their trail name, their real name. It's amazing the memory he's got."

"The thing that keeps me coming back is meeting people out on the trail," said Bill. "It's such an intense experience. You like to think that you're on your own, but you're really not. You come to rely on contact with other people even if it's only for five minutes on the side of the trail when the other person's going the opposite way. You're deprived of normal human contact, so when you do have human contact it means so much more. It's the old deprivation story where you don't miss something until you don't have it. And that's why I think on the trail most people bond closely together. It's because you're in an isolation chamber. When you run across a fellow inmate, there's going to be a special bond. So to see these people again in the real world, it's always nice. It reminds you of the simpler life you led on the trail."

When Bill and Andrew were planning their 1992 thru-hike, they found that because they wanted to visit so many friends, they were going to have more than thirty mail drops, many of them at people's homes. (Other thru-hikers might average a dozen mail drops.) Bill and Andrew realized they would be partying with so many people along the way that the hike was taking on a "Garveyesque" quality. Early in the hike, Andrew developed the idea of a "Garvey Approved" stamp in a circle, modeled after the Good Housekeeping Seal of Approval. It would be used for things like shelters that would meet with Garvey's approval. Gradually, the idea evolved into "the Traveling Garveys," a group of people committed to emulating Ed's hiking spirit. New members generally were sworn in and given a copy of Ed's book, although, at the first induction, for Laurence "Fairhope" McDuff, they had to make do with a copy of a bird book. Bill and Andrew took the name "the Traveling Garveys" partly as a gag but mostly to honor the influential legend. No one has been more tickled by the Traveling Garveys than Ed himself, who seems to have found the attention flattering.

In March 1992, Andrew and Bill rode to Springer with two friends from Bill's previous thru-hike, "Long Legs" and "Crackerjack." Bill and Andrew started talking about the different meetings and mail drops they'd set up along the way. Bill said, "That's just what Ed Garvey did. He had people meeting him all along the way. We're the Traveling Garveys."

"It kind of stuck in our minds," Andrew said. "Then, in about the third or fourth shelter, we were signing the register, and for some reason I got this Good Housekeeping symbol in my mind. I thought, 'I'll just write "Garvey Approved," like the Good Housekeeping Seal of Approval.' I'd write 'Garvey Approved', then I'd circle it and put copyright 1992 on it. I did that in about two registers and kept on doing it without having any idea that it would snowball into what it did.

"Eventually, people started catching us and asking 'What is "Garvey Approved?"' We had Garvey-approved shelters, Garvey-approved toilets. The funniest thing that happened was they started doing spinoffs. Two guys hiking behind us started calling themselves 'The Graveys.' And another guy, the "Phantom Engineer," started approving bridges and buildings. If he liked it, if it was constructed well, he'd write 'Phantom Approved.'

> *Garvey Approved:* an acknowledgment of anyone or anything that facilitates a thru-hike. The Apple Valley Inn, Glenwood, New Jersey, is surely "Garvey approved."

Andrew's wife, Laura Sam, witnessed the induction of the first new member, "Fairhope," in Atkins, Virgina. "Andrew and Bill wrote up this oath that you'd have to take to be a Garvey and wrote out a certificate that was signed by the two of them to make it all official. Fairhope had to put his hand on an eastern bird book, pretend it was Ed Garvey's book, and take this oath to be a Garvey."

Later, Laura said, two women applied to be Garveys. Andrew and Bill had met the two women hikers at Trail Days, and they kept asking, "What is this Garvey stuff?" Farther north Andrew and Bill received a letter in the mail, a sort of resume, listing the good things they'd done and the places they'd been picked up by somebody, fed, and treated like a Garvey. The letter said they wanted to be Garvey Approved and enter the club. They were inducted at the 1992 ALDHA gathering in Hanover, New Hampshire.

> *Garveyism:* a style of hiking on the Appalachian Trail in which support personnel or trail angels are lined up in advance; pre-planned trail magic. Named for trail guru Edward B. Garvey (b. 1914) of Virginia, who had friends meet him at every road crossing with transportation, food, and spirits during his groundbreaking 1970 thru-hike.

Few people have had a more profound influence on the trail than Ed Garvey. His book about his 1970 hike, *Appalachian Hiker: Adventure of a Lifetime,* has been ubiquitous among thru-hikers ever since its publication. The mileage fact sheet included in the book was the forerunner of many publications that would address thru-hikers' practical needs. The first account by a thru-hiker to gain wide circulation, it introduced many prospective hikers to the trail. The hike itself, part of a surge of interest in backpacking and the outdoors, brought increased publicity to the trail. It also made Ed a celebrity in the A.T. community. At Trail Days and ATC meetings, people mob Ed like a rock star. They continually approach him to say how much his book meant to them, or just to meet him. And he clearly enjoys being such a positive influence on so many people.

The trail has been a major part of Ed's life since the early fifties. An Eagle Scout, he learned of the trail through the Boy Scouts, joined PATC in 1953, and six years later became supervisor of trails. He proudly describes a program he developed to repair and maintain the eighteen shelters that were the PATC's responsibility. In the sixties, he joined the ATC board, and soon became secretary. He spearheaded a drive to beef up ATC membership, which soon tripled. He also has effectively lobbied the federal government for A.T. funding and passage of the National Scenic Trails Act.

Ed has stayed close to the trail, continuing to hike, even doing three quarters of the trail in 1990, at age seventy-six. In late 1992, he had bypass surgery, but by the next summer, he was again hiking at a pace that would exhaust many younger people.

> *Garvey, Garveyed:* the act of garveying, as in, "We garveyed as soon as we hit the first road. If we don't garvey through-out Connecticut, we are not worthy."

Laura and Andrew
"Medicine Man" Sam

*I*t's not easy for a couple of any age when one is an avid hiker and the other doesn't hike at all. Andrew "Medicine Man" Sam, thirty, dreamed of a thru-hike. Laura, a high-school teacher and producer of high-school musicals would be staying behind at home in North Carolina. They had some difficult times, but both ended up happy with the trip.

Andrew "Medicine Man" Sam had wanted to do a thru-hike for years. As often happens, a tragedy gave him a special impetus. A registered nurse, Andrew worked with his best friend and frequent hiking companion, Mike Ward, in the intensive care unit at the University of North Carolina Hospital. One day in 1991, Mike complained of a pain in his lung. Andrew joked that the worst thing it could be was a pulmonary embolism. The next day, Mike was dead of the very thing they'd joked about.

Mike and Andrew had been inseparable, and Andrew was distraught. He realized that he should do a thru-hike while he had the chance.

"When Mike died so suddenly, it was really hard, and it left such an empty place in Andrew's life," Andrew's wife, Laura, said. "When he started talking about doing the trail, I thought it would be great. People were amazed. You'd mean you let him do that? 'Let' is not a word in our marriage. We support each other doing what we need to do. I've always been independent, so I wasn't afraid to be by myself. I only asked him for two promises: to write in his journal every day (and I'd write in my journal) and to please not stand on the edge of ledges. He kept his first promise. He did not keep his second promise. He'd send film back to be developed, and I'd look through the pictures and see where he'd been and be all excited. Then it'd be, 'Oh, God. He's on a ledge.'

"The hardest thing about being at home was that I'd look forward to his phone calls, and I'd get home, and there'd be a message on the answering machine from ten minutes earlier, and I knew I wasn't going to get another phone call for a week. It would drive me crazy. At the beginning, I'd get upset about it and cry. Towards the end, the last six weeks, I didn't see him at all, but I was okay by then."

Laura met Andrew several times along the trail. First at Trail Days, then for a week in Virginia during spring break. It was supposed to be another two months before she saw him in Connecticut at the home of his partner, Bill "Sprained Rice" O'Brien. Bill suggested instead that Andrew surprise Laura on their anniversary in June.

The day started out a miserable one for Laura. "I spent three and a half hours in the dentist office. I was getting a crown and it wasn't working out well. I'd had enough, and when I got home there was no anniversary card in the mailbox.

"A friend who knew that Andrew was coming had said, 'Come over to my house for a cookout that night. I don't want you to sit in your house by yourself.' I'd told her I was fine. But she'd insisted, so I'd said, 'All right. I'll come over.'

"The phone was ringing as I came in the door and my whole face hurt. I felt awful. It was my friend saying, 'Aren't you coming over?' I told her I felt awful. I said, 'I'll sit down for a while and if I feel better, I'll come over.' I got outside and let the sun hit my face. I thought, 'These people are trying to be nice. You're being rude. Take some aspirin and go over there.' I looked like hell because I'd been crying at the dentist. I didn't change my clothes, didn't put on any makeup, didn't comb my hair. I went over to their house and there was Andrew. It was the best surprise of my life." She added, "I told Andrew he's going to have a hard time topping that anniversary present. What's he going to do this year?"

Laura had difficulty adjusting after Andrew completed the trail. "It took me about three months to adjust to Andrew being back home, because I had everything in the house organized the way I wanted it. He came home and started messing up cabinets. Gradually, I got used to him being there again."

Laura found that after Andrew's return he was more relaxed and spontaneous. He claimed his work in the critical-care unit had demanded that he be structured. "After the trail," she said, "he was a lot more open to making friends. A lot more social. Less reserved."

Andrew, who returned to work two weeks after finishing the trail, felt he entered "the rat race" too soon. But the trail is still in him. He has visited Bill at Trail Days, which has made him realize how special that partnership was. "It made me realize how much I miss being with Bill on the trail," he said. "We hiked from Springer all the way to Maine. It was kind of unlikely. People split up on the trip. I don't think I realized as much as Bill did how much of a bond there was. We did have some separation anxiety at the end."

The trail, Andrew said, "renewed my faith in people in general. I don't judge people by their appearance as I used to. People with long beards, long scraggly hair, rough clothes—they were people to stay away from. But I saw so many people, including myself, with long beards and long hair. I'd look in the mirror and say, 'Oh, wow.'"

Trail Society—Values and Traditions

All you need in this life is ignorance and confidence, and then success is sure.

Mark Twain

T OBY "SON OF BILLY GOAT" WOODARD TIED A TOY COW TO HIS pack strap. His partner, P. J. "Random Vine" Dean, carried a stuffed bear. During their 1993 thru-hike, Toby walked a stretch without his pack and thus without his cow. He wondered whether to go back and do that stretch with his cow, so it, too, would complete the whole trail.

Hikers can be a sentimental, even silly, lot. Some hikers carry a seed, a pebble, or some soil from Springer to leave at Katahdin. At the 1981 ATC meeting in Cullowhee, Ray Hunt formed a group called SOTWFBWO (Society of Those Whose Favorite Boots Wore Out), a reflection of the attachment hikers have to their old gear. Its membership stabilized at one.

Figuring out the silliest thing that thru-hikers have ever done would be difficult, but one incident springs quickly to mind. Frank "the Merry Slav" Krajcovic was lying in the grass seven miles shy of the top of Mount Grey-lock, the highest point in Massachusetts. Three hikers approached with a watermelon that they planned to carry to the top and eat there. Frank joined them. One hiker carried the melon; the rest carried most of his gear. At the summit, they proudly displayed their prize, offering slices to everyone, because "even harder than four hikers carrying a watermelon up a mountain is for those same four hikers to devour it in one sitting." As it was, they ended up "with watermelon-shaped bellies," Frank said.

Every year, a few hikers become well known on the trail. In 1993, one who made his mark was "Low Rider." A harmonica-playing contortionist, he carried a walking stick festooned with salvaged garbage. In 1992, it was the Traveling Garveys; in 1990, Bill "the Orient Express" Irwin; in the mid-eighties, Dan "Wingfoot" Bruce. In 1980, there was Bob "O. D. Coyote" Pierson, who had a long, flowing beard, wrote long passages in the registers, and was the first thru-hiker to start (February 29) and the last to finish (November 17).

Speed hikers are a little more recognizable because they're so far out of the mainstream. Other hikers criticize them, saying they can't be getting as much out of the trail experience. Groups are criticized and lampooned, too, especially since most thru-hikers are strong individualists. Also criticized are people who stick rigidly to a schedule or who white blaze or blue blaze or yellow blaze, depending on one's point of view. For all of that, trail conversations tend to be much cheerier and more positive than those in the real world. After all, people on vacation should be happier.

Friendships spring up quickly and are incredibly durable. Hikers who know each other for only a few days feel closer than they do to some relatives. People of different ages, backgrounds, and occupations who would normally not even meet become like family. Some say it's like the bonds that spring up in military service, especially during combat or isolated postings. Dr. Lou "Tennessee Jed" Schroeder, with his wife, Dr. Janice Coverdale, has a medical clinic in Hot Springs. He thru-hiked in 1980 and compared the friendships to those that form among medical residents, who also undergo an intense experience.

Many hikers feel so strongly about the trail that they have their ashes scattered on it. Raymond Torrey, who helped build the first stretch of the A.T., had his ashes scattered in 1938 on nearby Long Mountain, New York, part of the Long Path, which he also championed. Rex Pulford, the father of Dorothy Hansen, died of a stroke while attempting a thru-hike, a long-held ambition. His remains and a monument were placed on the trail, not far from where he died. The remains of Howard Bassett, a 1968 thru-hiker, were scattered on the A.T. north of Jerry Cabin.

There is no completely satisfactory answer to the question of why people form such strong attachments to the trail. Jeff Hansen suggested, "That will always be a mystery to all of us. But I wonder if it's not just that people can have a sense of adventure and a sense of belonging all at once, and people miss both of those things in their lives." Dorothy Hansen added, "With other trails you could test yourself. You could get the adventure, but you couldn't get the camaraderie."

"You can't help but have a fondness for it if you've hiked even fifty miles of it," said Elmer Hall, proprietor of The Inn at Hot Springs. "I think it's one of America's really special institutions. It's quite amazing—this combination of public interest and private organization. It wouldn't have been possible without the government's recognition of it as a special resource back in the thirties.

Many hikers' most enduring memories have to do with other hikers. Communication on the trail is primitive but remarkably effective. The trail grapevine is a marvel. People going in different directions pass along news, as do those who live along the trail. Trail registers are the heart of A.T. communications. In these registers, hikers pass along news of what's ahead. They share philosophy, pithy comments, epic stories, poetry, cartoons, and complaints. Hikers can track the people ahead by the dates and contents of their entries. It all gives lonely hikers some companionship.

"On the A.T., it's a people trip," said three-time thru-hiker Leonard "Habitual Hiker" Adkins. "When you're a thru-hiker, for that summer you're going to be a special person. You're part of a moving community. You'll hike with someone for four or five days and meet them again in Connecticut or Maine, and it's like seeing an old friend. You're constantly meeting old friends. You form close friendships. Ninety-five percent of the people in my life now are hikers.

"I think the reason the A.T. builds friendships is that the trappings of different levels of society fall away. On the A.T., I've hiked with people for weeks and never known what they do to support themselves or even their real names. I've missed that acceptance of people back in society."

Although hikers welcome, even crave, some company on the trail, they are wary of large groups and crowded stretches of the trail. Shelters may comfortably hold four or five people on a rainy night, but six or eight can be crowded. One of the A.T. commandments is, "There's always room for one more in a shelter." But many backpackers have memories of being so crammed into a shelter that everyone had to turn over at the same time.

The more than 255 three-sided shelters are centers of A.T. social life. "I didn't use a tent because I really enjoyed the shelters, the community atmosphere of getting together at the end of the day and sharing stories," said Greg "Pooh" Knoettner.

Shelters never seemed more appealing than in Myron Avery's article,

"The Story of the Lean-tos," which appeared in the *PATC Bulletin* in 1942. "In the north it is a very simple matter. A floor is made of small poles, which are covered over with a deep layer of aromatic balsam fir boughs. These are renewed annually and a fir bough bed is a worthy rival, for the tired walker, to the best inner spring mattress."

Unfortunately, the custom of using fir boughs disappeared, but the uncomfortable poles, dubbed "baseball bats" by hikers, lingered until recently.

Because it's such an intense experience and they're so excited about it, thru-hikers seem to exist almost in a world of their own while on the trail. Sometimes, it's difficult for an outsider to penetrate. Even those like Roger Brickner or Tillie Wood, who've met many thru-hikers over the years, find that when big groups of them gather, outsiders tend to be excluded. Conversations dwell on shop talk: who's where and who's doing what, experiences along the trail and, of course, food. Thru-hikers find their experience so intense that it's often difficult to relate to those who are day-hiking or hiking the trail in pieces. Thru-hikers quickly become so close that outsiders often believe they are brothers or have known each other for years.

For as long as there's been a trail, the A.T. has attracted characters. Mark "Second Wind" Di Miceli said that over the last decade the number of characters has increased dramatically. Before, one might encounter one or two; now one might see a half dozen or more. A few of these people may be dangerous, but most add a certain color to the experience.

"You can spot the characters easily," said Tom "the Pennsylvania Creeper" Thwaites. "They're not dressed in uniform." One character he encountered was "Lothar of the Snake People." He saw snakes in subfreezing weather when no one else did.

Albie Pokrob recalled the first character he met on his 1978 thru-hike, "Ranger Mac." "He was impersonating a park ranger. I said, 'This is great. We'll learn about nature.' Then he got to telling some stories, and I knew he didn't sound like a ranger. At Wesser, he would say, 'The Stekoahs are a technical climb, and you need to get your pack weight down to twenty-five pounds.' He said he would go through my pack and give what he removed to needy hikers. When I finally left him, he said, 'You'll never make it through in this rain, and don't expect me to come and rescue you.' It was the last I saw of him."

Harry "the Indian" Thomas

*M*any people love the A.T., but only one has actually lived on the trail. Harry spent most of his adult life on the trail and found a wife there. Since October 1992, he and Jeanne "Fireball" have managed the American Youth Hostel lodge on the C&O Canal near Harpers Ferry, West Virginia, their way of staying close to the trail now that ailments limit Harry's hiking. They still labor mightily to complete their renovation plans. Photographer Mike Warren and I visited the hostel during an early March snowstorm.

Harry "the Indian" Thomas first came to the A.T. in April of 1965. When he finally left in 1988, after twenty-three years spent mostly outdoors on the trail, he was fifty-seven. He'd seen more of the trail and met more hikers than anyone. Near the end, Harry was seeing the sons of people he'd hiked with in the early years.

A Winnebago Indian, Harry grew up on a reservation in Nebraska. As a boy he spent much of his time in the woods and became an accomplished hunter and fisherman, as well as a master of other outdoor skills. Walking to school in subzero weather, he grew accustomed to a hard life. Later he "hoboed around," seeing the country and working odd jobs. While working in Saint Louis, he read about the A.T. and decided to try it. He never dreamed he'd spend so much time there. "I just thought I'd see what it was like," he said.

Harry, who first got on the A.T. at Allen Gap, North Carolina, spent most of his time in the South. His favorite spot was Roan Mountain when the rhododendron were in bloom. He also frequented the Smokies, especially in his early days on the trail when hiking permits weren't needed. Generally, he'd spend a few weeks in a place and then move on.

When he ran out of money or supplies, he'd work at odd jobs until he'd accumulated enough to return to the trail. "Jobs weren't hard to find," he said. For a decade, he traveled north each year to Elk Park, North Carolina, and Winchester, Virginia, to pick apples. For a time, he guided people on the trail, including Robert "Believe It or Not" Ripley. Other times, he would collect cans and redeem them for deposits, or rake under shelters to find money. Over the years, he made friends with many mountain people who would give him food or shelter. "They'd help me out," he said. "They'll share what they've got."

He supplemented his diet with edible plants and was accurate with a slingshot, which he used to kill rabbits and squirrels and frighten away skunks.

Much of his store of nature lore is self-taught. "It all comes naturally," he said. "You grow with it." At ten, he caught his first skunk. As a boy, he hunted and fished on the reservation with Lawrence Big Bear, learning much from him. "I used to watch him all the time," Harry said. "He'd never mark a tree. It was against our religion."

When he first started out on the A.T., he had only rudimentary equipment, including a Boy Scout pack and an Army blanket, but no sleeping bag. He never used trail maps or guidebooks, only road maps to identify towns where he could resupply. Sometimes, he'd make his own equipment or pick up discarded items. He made a pack out of a mailbag. He used nearly every possible kind of tent.

Sometimes Harry would carry a backpacking stove, but he usually cooked over a fire. "He was known for making the biggest meal on the smallest fire," his wife, Jeanne, said. "I've watched him make a fire when it would be pouring down rain, and you wouldn't think you could find anything dry. And I swear Harry could smell water. He'd find water where there wasn't any water."

He packed a heavy load, carrying what he needed to live on indefinitely. For a while, he even carried two packs that totaled eighty pounds. He carried a large supply of coffee and sugar in heavy plastic containers, because he didn't want to chance plastic bags breaking.

On a side trip along the C&O Canal, he once found an abandoned shopping cart. He put his pack in it and pushed it along the towpath for a hundred miles. Eventually, he lost control of the cart, and it toppled into the water. Scurrying to retrieve his pack, he saved everything but the coffee.

For company, he had three different dogs during his hiking career. He also had a pet crow for a time. It would alight near his campfire and nudge the lids off pots to see what was cooking.

At Humpback Rocks, Virginia, south of Shenandoah, he employed a big rattlesnake to keep people from bothering his pack while he went into town. He tied the snake to a tree, where it lay coiled beneath his pack. Nobody bothered his pack, and when he returned, he freed the snake.

In the early seventies, he became a shelter caretaker on the Long Trail in Vermont. He stayed there through the winter, the longest time he'd spent anywhere along the A.T.

During another winter, he camped out along the Maine A.T., with temperatures as low as fifty below zero. He piled on layers of clothing, but mostly he learned to adjust to the cold.

Another year, snow drove him off the trail in New York, when seventeen inches fell in one night. That spring, he hiked in Maine, and the snow was ten feet in places, high enough to cover the eye-level blazes.

Harry was camping on the side of Blood Mountain, Georgia, when he met Jeanne. Blood Mountain had been the site of a big Indian battle between the Cherokees and the Creeks. "Harry used to feel their spirits," Jeanne said. "It's a sacred mountain to him."

A resident of Florida, Jeanne had long read about the A.T. It became her dream to hike it, and after retiring, she decided to do it in 1987.

In 1988, Harry and Jeanne left the trail to get married in nearby Sylva, North Carolina. There are 107 steps leading up to the historic courthouse. "The condemned man always counts the steps to the gallows," Harry laughed.

That year they did parts of the trail, including a climb of Katahdin. While a rainstorm threatened, Jeanne waited on the tableland, a mile and a half from the top, and Harry went alone to the summit. She figured he'd be gone for an hour and a half, but people coming down said they'd seen him jogging on the Knife Edge. He was back in forty-five minutes.

"He wasn't doing the A.T. as an alternative to anything else," said his friend Jeff Hansen. "He was doing this because it was what he wanted to do more than anything else. It was the environment he operated best in and enjoyed the most.

"Harry didn't have a lot of financial resources, but if he ever needed things, he would always offer to contribute in exchange. That's different from most people. He didn't forget anybody who did anything for him."

"He was generous to a fault," Dorothy Hansen added.

"I think in a lot of ways, it's hard for me to think of the A.T. without thinking about people like Harry," Jeff said. "That's an aspect of the trail that makes it what it is."

"He was wonderful with [our children] Jamie and Chris," Dorothy said. "He spent a whole winter here, and he almost adopted them. When he and Jeanne were hiking in Maine, he made a little birchbark canoe and sent it in the mail for Chris. He came to visit a couple of months ago and made a slingshot for each of the kids."

With a droll sense of humor, Harry can joke about his Indian heritage. When he and Jeanne hiked the Oregon Coastal Trail, they crossed the Pioneer Indian Trail. Looking at the trail sign, Harry said, "Let me be the pioneer this time. I get tired of always having to be the Indian."

Over the years, Harry has overcome his share of injuries and ailments. A degenerative bone disease in his knees finally drove him off the trail. The legs got progressively worse after a fall near Newport, Virginia. Now he needs braces all the time, but he and Jeanne still walk the two miles into Harpers Ferry.

One time in the early eighties Harry had a small stroke while hiking the A.T. in southwestern Virginia. "His left side was paralyzed, but Harry doesn't give in to things," Jeanne said. He kept working with it for a week until he could get into town.

He also sprained his ankles on the trail. Once he hiked on a bad sprain for 140 miles without support. Finally, he got to a hospital, and the nurses were going to put him in a wheelchair. He said, "What do I need a wheelchair for? I just walked 140 miles on it."

Harry wants his ashes scattered where his close friend Howard Bassett's are, near Jerry Cabin along the A.T.

Asked if he had any regrets about spending so much time on the trail, he said, "No. I would like to spend more time on it. Maybe one day I'll be hiking again."

Animals

*Animals do not worry . . . they have no fear as to what may be
ahead when they are sick and . . . they just take each day as it
comes. . . . Apparently human beings are the only creatures cursed
with the ability to worry. . . . By the same token, maybe we are the
only ones blessed with the capacity for appreciation.*

Margaret A. Stanger, *That Quail, Robert*

THERE ARE FOUR CANDIDATES FOR MOST DANGEROUS LIFEFORM on the trail. Despite what many people think, bears and poisonous snakes aren't among them. The four are blackflies, mice, dogs, and people. Blackfly bites can make life miserable; mice can ruin food supplies; dogs can bite and foul water sources; people can commit mayhem.

Apart from those, encounters with animals are generally one of the joys of hiking the trail. After all, how often do most people have a chance to see a moose or a bear in the wild, or watch hawks and eagles soar, or listen to a loon or whippoorwill?

Rick Hancock swears that he saw a panther or mountain lion in eastern Tennessee. Rounding a bend, he came upon a brown wildcat. It turned its profile toward him before vanishing in the woods. It remains one of the most vivid images from his hike.

In Maine, Rick was staying with John Kuzniak at a shelter north of Monson. They were saying that only eight days remained until the end, and they hadn't seen a moose. Just then, they stood up and turned, and there was a moose on the trail thirty or forty yards away. "He was a humongous animal," Rick said. "He was so graceful, he drifted off the trail, and you couldn't hear him except for the faint crackling of the leaves. We had just gotten the words out of our mouths, and there he was." Moose have thrived recently, and now an estimated thirty thousand of the great animals live in New England.

On Albie Pokrob's 1984 hike, while he was on Mount Washington, Pete "Woulda, Coulda, Shoulda" Suscy told him, "There's a moose." Albie said, "Sure, sure. There's a moose on Mount Washington." But he looked out, and there, walking up the Crawford Path, was a big bull moose. The photo that he took appeared on the cover of *Appalachia* and friends ribbed him that he must have doctored it.

On her 1989 thru-hike, Nancy "Danny" Harrington and her companions were hurrying along the trail in Maine, when, she said, "A friend up ahead stopped and stuck his thumbs in his ears and wiggled his fingers. I thought he was doing a Three Stooges imitation. I wiggled my thumb on my nose." But her husband, Mike "Hago," said, "You dummy. He means moose up ahead." Sure enough, there was a moose not far away.

Rick Hancock saw several bears on his trip, and he heard at least one other. He was picking blueberries near the Vermont–Massachusetts border. "The whole patch just shook when a bear growled. I hadn't seen him, but when he growled, I figured there were other patches up ahead with no bears, and I put on my pack and got going."

Despite occasional sightings, hikers quickly learn that pretrail jitters over rattlesnakes and bears are overdone. Arthur "A. B. Positive" Batchelder spoke of the big scare when hikers first enter the Smokies and find shelters with chain-link fences to keep bears out. "The first night, every time someone got up you made sure they closed the gate behind them. I never saw one bear the whole time I was in the Smokies—twice that I went through. By the time I got to the other end, I didn't care if they closed the gate or not."

Ralph "the Hobbit" Goodenough saw six rattlesnakes and a bear on his 1985 thru-hike. He'd just seen the bear and two rattlers when he met a group of Boy Scouts hiking in Pennsylvania. He gave them a dramatic account of his adventures, and then they all started down the trail with Ralph in the lead. Within three minutes, Ralph came to a sudden stop, and three boys crashed into him. Ahead on the trail was a coiled rattler. Ralph showed the boys that the snake was afraid of them and just wanted to get out of the way. "I left them with a great memory," he said.

The Ice Water Spring Shelter, three miles north of Newfound Gap, in the center of the Smokies, is notorious for its resident skunk population. Nancy Harrington stayed there on a night when the shelter was full. A group of high-school girls camped outside, and a drunk slept on the floor without hanging his food. A skunk went for the Ramen noodles in the drunk's food bag, which woke everyone. The high-school counselor told them not to move. "Then we heard a growl," said Nancy. "Another skunk was trying to get the food away from the first skunk. I got really worried and stayed awake for the next couple of hours. It ended up with no spraying, but it was quite a night."

"My best memories are critters," said Jan Skadberg. One March night in Georgia, as she was near hypothermia, she munched on gorp in her sleeping bag to help warm herself. She recalls thinking, "Boy, the mosquitoes are bad." In a stupor, she swatted her nose to keep the bugs away. A hiker two sleeping bags away said, "I wouldn't do that, Jan."

"Why not?" she asked.

"Because you've got a skunk trying to get into your sleeping bag, trying to get at the gorp."

"Skunks are neat creatures," said Jim "Jimmy Bee" Bodmer. "They can sense from your voice that you're not going to hurt them. I'd talk real slowly and pleasantly, and they'd be on their way."

Pieter "the Cheshire Cat" Van Why hand-fed a red fox at Mollies Ridge Shelter in the Smokies. Nearby was the fox's den, and she was taking the food back to her kits. Although feeding a wild animal like that was risky, Pieter said, seeing a red fox was a thrill. But he will not do it again and recommends that no one else try it.

Perhaps even riskier was the time Frank "the Merry Slav" Krajcovic petted a porcupine in a swamp in Massachusetts. In his bare feet, Frank slowly waded through thigh-deep water, petted the porcupine, felt his quills, and fed him some wildflowers. "When I can get this close to nature, I am filled with gladness and reverence," Frank wrote in his journal. "I don't do it often but am always happy when I do do it. I did not feel threatened at all, and neither, I think, did the porcupine."

Ray Hunt was hiking with a group that stopped for lunch. People noticed that a chipmunk was slowly waddling about instead of darting here and there, as usual. The puzzle was solved when Darrol Nickel, a 2,000-miler from Tennessee, noticed that two of his apples were missing.

Another time, in Maine, Ray and his group came across some Canada Jays. "They hang around where people are and steal stuff. They look like blue jays, only gray. At an abandoned warden's cabin, we were eating lunch. The jays were picking up scraps and would even eat out of our hands. I had a sandwich in my right hand and a cracker in the left for the jay. He picked up the whole sandwich, and I still had the cracker. Everybody started laughing. I'd been had."

Dogs are perhaps the most controversial animals on the trail. They are prohibited in Great Smoky Mountains and Baxter Parks, and must be leashed in Shenandoah. Many hikers believe that they are a nuisance on the trail. And the trail can be a tough place for a dog, ripping up its paws and exposing it to wild animals. It's no fun removing porcupine quills from a dog or patching it up after a tangle with a bear. Skunks can leave a hiker with a foul-smelling companion. Moreover, you'll see much less wildlife while hiking with a dog.

In 1980, Al "A.T. Al" Sochard picked up two dogs at a railroad trestle north of Damascus. After Pearisburg, Keith and Lauren Robinson took "A.T. Dawg." But the other dog, which Al named "Trestle," stayed with him for the rest of the trail and for years afterwards. In the Mid-Atlantic states, Trestle had a skunk encounter about fifty feet from a shelter. Al didn't have anything that would neutralize the smell, and Trestle insisted on sleeping next to him. "It was a torturous night," Al said. The next day, someone gave him a can of tomato paste; he smeared it all over Trestle, and much of the smell vanished. But for the next few months, every time Trestle was wet, she smelled like a skunk again and took on a pink cast.

Trestle, a light dog at fifteen pounds, didn't like the water, as she demonstrated when she and Al reached the Kennebec River in Maine. The Kennebec is a one hundred-yard ford, the longest and one of the most dangerous on the trail. Trestle was perched high on Al's pack, but a third of the way across the river she panicked, jumped off, and swam back to where they'd started. Al continued across and dropped his backpack. On the far shore, Trestle was agitated, running back and forth, thinking that Al had abandoned her. After recrossing the chilly river to retrieve her, he put Trestle in his day pack and tied her in, with only her head sticking out. By this time, the river had risen, and Al had to swim partway. Just before they made it across, Trestle wriggled free and swam to the shore ahead of him.

Hikers like to tell friends and family back home how they became accustomed to mice running across their sleeping bags in shelters.

"The mice think they own the shelters," Ray Hunt said. "There's a resident population in every shelter. They ruin everything and eat only a little. It's really aggravating."

Frustration over mice has prompted some to take action. Hikers have carried mouse traps, but it doesn't put much of a dent in the rodent population. One person even carried a cat. Although it was probably the most effective measure, it was a heavy load: fourteen pounds of cat and one pound of cat food.

Paul "Bigfoot" Tourigny was nearly tagged as a serial mouse killer. On his first thru-hike, Paul had just met Karen "Littlefoot" Nevin at the Roan Mountain Shelter. The shelter was infested with mice, and they were so bold they would even emerge in daylight. He set up his mousetrap and caught several. Karen thought he was a monster. His response: "If you think of all the food in the world destroyed by rodents, you could feed the other half that's not eating." He continued trapping, despite her thinking that he was the worst person in the world. Eventually, though, they became good friends.

Luke "the Journeyman" Wiaczek recalls mice using his tent as if it were a playground apparatus. Lying in his tent after dinner, he heard a noise. At first, he thought it was sticks sliding down the side of the tent. Then he heard it again at two different places. For the next hour, mice ran up one side of the tent and slid down the other. "The mice finally settled down, but we laughed about that for days," Luke said.

Another mouse story from Luke: "We were hiking for a few days with "Little Red Riding Hood" and her dog, Shane. We woke up in the morning, and everybody had little piles of dog food stuffed in the toes of their boots. The mice must have been shuttling the dog food from the pack and stuffing it in the boots. Those crazy mice."

Like most hikers who frequent shelters, Luke learned to protect his food. He'd take an empty tuna can and suspend it upside down on a cord from a nail in the shelter rafters. The cord would go through a hole in the can (or plastic coffee-can cover or Frisbee), below which stuff sacks holding the hiker's food would be suspended. Mice could get partway down the string, but not around the can without falling. "You can't put food on the ground," Luke said. "If it's there, they're going to get it."

Insects of all types can make life miserable for a hiker, but blackflies are the worst. Said Henry Phillips: "At night it'd be ninety degrees, and you'd cover up in your clothes and swelter in your sleeping bag. Those bugs like to eat me alive. There were more flies in your food than food. I'd eat with the head net on and try to eat fast before any bugs got in. You'd spit and forget you had your head net on. I said, 'This is ridiculous.' People told me it's only going to last two weeks, but I said, 'This is going to be two weeks without me.'"

Ziggy

*J*im *"the Geek" Adams and Noel "the Singing Horseman" DeCavalcante had
similar adventures: thru-hiking the A.T. and paddling the Mississippi River.
They had talked on the telephone and corresponded over the previous three
years, but they never met in person until Trail Days in Damascus in 1993. I
caught up with them as Jim was revving up his motorcycle for the trip home.
Ziggy, his cat, had stayed home this time. "He's really a quite remarkable cat," Jim
said. "By the time he was one year old he'd been in twenty-five states."*

Sitting around a campfire in Pennsylvania one night, Jim "the Geek"
Adams hatched the idea of the "ultimate triathlon vacation."

An experienced white-water canoeist, Jim would paddle from Confluence, Pennsylvania, to New Orleans, walk the A.T., then bicycle from Maine
to his starting point, all in thirteen months.

Soon after Jim started paddling, a flood stranded him for four days in
Manchester, Ohio, where he acquired two-month-old Ziggy from a farmer.
A gray tabby with tiger stripes, Ziggy has only a two-inch stubby tail, as his
mother was a full-bred Manx.

In early October, a freak snowstorm hit the Ohio River. To keep little
Ziggy warm, "I'd put him in my life jacket, and he'd squeeze his head out
through the holes," Jim said.

Ziggy weighed three pounds when Jim started the A.T.; by the end, he
was a fourteen-pound contribution to Jim's backpack, plus another pound of
food.

Unlike most cats, Ziggy is not afraid of water. He waded in the Mississippi and caught small fish. Ziggy didn't have as good a record with birds, but

"he's hell on mice in the shelters," Jim said. His personal record was catching thirteen mice in the notorious Blood Mountain Shelter—and that was only the confirmed kills.

Ziggy wasn't intimidated by dogs, either. On the A.T., he chased them. "He was the aggressor," Jim said. He also chased coyotes and raccoons. Along the Nolichucky River, near Erwin, Tennessee, Ziggy chased the campground owner's two dogs. Jim had to go a quarter mile to retrieve them.

"I was always worried that he'd bother someone," Jim said, "but usually when I'd get to a shelter, people would say, 'We've already heard about him,' and they were happy to let him loose on mice."

Everyone wanted to see Ziggy or take his picture. He was the only cat they'd ever seen on the trail. "I'd have to try to keep him out of the sun, since cats overheat," Jim said. "If I stopped to talk, he'd start pacing on the pack, and when he was ready to move on, he'd bat me on the head."

Ziggy walked the trail for the first thirty-one miles. But when it started to rain, Jim put Ziggy on his pack, and there he stayed. In hard rain, Ziggy would sometimes hide under a log, making Jim search for him.

On the trail, Ziggy had ten different meows that Jim could recognize. He could tell when Ziggy was hungry, needed to purge, or was tired.

Ziggy ate mostly dry cat food. On the river, he also ate one can of wet food a week. On the A.T., he got no wet food until they reached a town. Jim generally carried a pound of food in a Nalgene jar.

Unlike fellow backpackers, Ziggy is a finicky eater. "His main people foods are green beans, popcorn, turkey, and roast beef. Of wet cat food, he'll only eat seafood," Jim said.

Of the 2,022 miles Jim covered by canoe, Ziggy was along for 1,900. He did all of the A.T. except for the Great Smoky Mountains National Park and Baxter State Park, which don't permit cats or dogs.

Jim used to be a paramedic. An incident in an ambulance prompted him to set his triathlon plans in motion. "A man wouldn't let me start an I.V.," Jim said. "He died of a heart attack. He was worried about AIDS. I told him this was single-use stuff, and forget about the AIDS. It was too late. I was crying. I couldn't believe how stupid some people could be. I said, 'That's it, I'm leaving,' and I gave notice."

On September 9, 1989, Jim launched his adventure from Confluence, Pennsylvania, by paddling down the Youghiogheny River to the Mononga-hela. At Pittsburgh, he entered the Ohio River, then the Mississippi, and went on to New Orleans.

On January 31, 1990, Jim and Ziggy reached New Orleans. "When we got to New Orleans, fifteen big tow boats greeted us with tooting horns," said Jim. "Construction workers were standing on buildings, shouting. It was the most wonderful feeling I've ever had. I felt, 'I've made it.'"

Jim wanted to finish paddling by Christmas, but bad weather delayed them. They were stuck in Arkansas for ten days when the Mississippi froze solid. Only 250 miles from the Gulf of Mexico, that part of the river rarely freezes. Jim felt he had to finish by February 1 if he wanted to have time to prepare for the A.T. He had to get used to walking again after paddling a boat all day. He also needed to rest, ship his boat home, order backpacking equipment, and submit reports to manufacturers for whom he tested equipment. While in Florida, he took a week-long canoe trip in the Everglades, before driving to Atlanta and starting to hike.

"I wasn't out to set any records," Jim said. "That's why I called it a vacation. I did have time limits to finish each section. That was so I'd be on the A.T. in good weather. Originally, I was shooting for one year."

At the start of his adventures, Jim, who is five feet six inches tall, weighed 212 pounds. By the end, he'd lost 57 pounds. "By Florida, I didn't have a belly on me," Jim said. "On the river I ate six thousand to eight thousand calories a day and lost weight."

Climbing Katahdin, Jim was "sad that the trip was over." The trip changed him more than he expected. As a paramedic, he became used to a high level of stress. Now, he feels more relaxed. But the adjustment after the trip was not easy. It was three months before he could stay in a crowded room. He often slept outdoors. "I got back October 6, and from then until Christmas, I camped out sixty days," Jim said.

Unlike many hikers, however, he wasn't depressed after the trip. He went to work right away on a two-hour slide show, which he's presented to many groups. "I was consumed with the slide show and excited about it.

"I miss the whole trip. Every day I think about it. It was wonderful, and I miss it [the trail] every day," Jim said.

Ziggy had some trouble adjusting, too. He's a camping cat. He won't stay indoors, except in cold weather. He still likes to go camping and hiking. Jim even claims Ziggy knows what the word "camping" means. "If he sees me getting out the backpack or the canoe, he follows me around until we go," Jim said. "We went camping recently, and he didn't want to come when we left. I figured he knows where we live; he'll come on his own. I went back the next day. He was still at the campsite. He loves camping."

Jim and Noel "the Singing Horseman" DeCavalcante were put in touch with each other through another hiker, Carol "Lagunatic" Moore. "I called and he got out his river map and we talked for an hour and a half, going over the map page by page," Jim said. "I told him where the good places to camp were, who to get help from, and what to watch out for."

"He sent me tips on the Mississippi River," said Noel. "I sent him tips on the Appalachian Trail. It was neat to correspond with him while he headed north on the trail and I headed south on the river."

Noel enjoyed the A.T. and has stayed in touch with the trail community, even serving as a consultant to ATC. The year following his hike he set out on another journey, this one a more solitary adventure. Noel paddled for three and a half months from the mouth of the Mississippi at Lake Itasca in Minnesota to the bayous one hundred miles south of New Orleans. He found paddling the Mississippi lonelier and mentally tougher but physically easier than hiking the trail.

Noel reminisced about his decision to make these trips. He said he had planned several adventures when he retired from the Air Force but had put them off. One evening at a party in New York he was discussing his plans with a friend of his son. The friend said, "You have these beautiful objectives and you're going to go back to work? Why don't you do these things now? Work later if you want to work." That night Noel examined his future in a new light. "That's when I decided, the hell with going back to work," he said. "I was going to hike the Appalachian Trail and go from there. And that's exactly what I've done."

Advice and Regrets

Now is the time to take possession of my life, to start the impossible, a journey to the limits of my aspirations, for the first time to step toward my loveliest dream. If I had only known then what I know now—but now I know enough to begin.

Hugh Prather, *Notes on Love and Courage*

I N FEBRUARY 1980, A SOUTHBOUND THRU-HIKER, "THE MONK," MADE an entry in the Gooch Gap trail register a day or two before finishing his hike at Springer. He'd hiked alone for forty-three days, sometimes through snow up to his waist. His advice: "Define your own trip in terms of quality, in terms of why, what you'll hope to learn and then, hike it. Don't let yourself 'hike' someone else's trip, and don't let others hike yours. And if the trip begins being something different than you anticipated, you'll know you're doing it the right way."

He went on: "I've really been hiking on pure excitement lately, but I'm not just hiking to Springer, I'm going home as well [after seven years]. I turned thirty on February 13 and the trip was sort of a present to myself. I never realized it would be the most profound experience in my life—it will have a vast effect on the rest of it as well. But now it's time to retreat, to pause, to understand what I've done to myself."

Southbound winter hikers are an especially tough, independent breed, putting up with extended loneliness and harsh weather, but the Monk's basic advice applies to northbounders, too. Some hikers end up regretting that others swayed them to hike faster or slower than they wanted, to blue-blaze, or to hurry out of towns. Enjoy people's company, the Monk is saying, but don't let them dictate the terms. There's a joy in companionship, but there's a price, too.

The most common piece of advice from veteran thru-hikers regarding the A.T. is "Do it." Few who've completed the trail regret it, and most regard a thru-hike as one of the highlights of their lives. "It's the most wonderful thing I've ever done," said Laurie "A Traveling Wilbury" Mack. "It was so incredible, I'd recommend it to anybody."

Thru-hikers can focus so much on finishing the trail that they forget to enjoy themselves along the way. Although you do have to be serious about your mileage to finish, many hikers wish they'd taken longer, made more time for people along the way, and done a few more side trips. Many regret not taking a full six months to do the trail. "A lot of type-A driven people now want to go back and enjoy the trip," said Connor "Carolina Cookers" Coward.

Pete "Woulda, Coulda, Shoulda" Suscy took his nickname from the common desire of thru-hikers to plan big hiking days. "We'd get up in the morning, and we'd say we should do twenty miles today, and we never would. Then sitting around the shelter at night, we'd say we could have if we'd wanted to."

Hikers offer conflicting advice about how much physical preparation to do before a hike. Physical conditioning doesn't hurt, but it's unclear how much it helps. Jogging and climbing steps are favorite pre-hike exercises, but some thru-hikers simply start slowly and get in shape on the trail. Besides, it's difficult to prepare for hiking ten hours a day up and down steep mountains with a heavy pack on your back.

"You have to get into hiking condition," said Mike "Hago" Harrington. "If you're going to do enough to get into hiking condition, you might as well hike the trail." He and his wife, Nancy, had run for years, but they found the muscles needed for hiking were altogether different.

Before her thru-hike, Laurie "Mountain Laurel" Potteiger worked as an office temporary in Washington, D.C. To get in shape, "I'd take my back-pack to these nice offices, and at lunchtime I'd strap my hiking boots on, put my pack on, and climb up and down thirteen flights of stairs. Some people I was working with had never seen a backpack before. People were just amazed at what I was doing."

Like many hikers, Mike Harrington emphasized the importance of having boots that fit and breaking them in properly. Every year, hikers endure unnecessary misery or drop off the trail because they don't take these simple precautions. Mike also pointed out that you can keep improving your backpacking skills as you hike the A.T. "There are always people on the A.T. who know more than you about hiking and are willing to help."

"The main thing is every ounce counts," said Joe "Cool Breeze" Fennelly. "First time thru-hikers always bring too much gear and have to mail it home. You need to keep in mind you're going to feel it every step of the way. Keep it light, simple."

"We were going into stores and asking how much it weighed before we'd ask how much it cost," said Mike Harrington.

The peculiar thing is that despite quantum improvements in backpacking gear in the last decade, pack weights haven't changed much in a century and a half.

It's hard to boil your life's possessions down to a tight, light bundle that fits on your back. For every technological advance that lightens a backpacking load, there seems to be a new piece of equipment to even the score. There is a never-ending conflict between the desire for creature comforts and for lighter loads, particularly when the extra pounds quell the rumblings in your belly. As Earl Shaffer put it, "Carry as little as possible, but choose that little with care."

The backpacker's dilemma is this: how to take sufficient creature comforts and emergency items without making it such a burden that you won't get there or it won't be fun. You need to prepare for medical emergencies, drastic changes in weather (snow is possible every month of the year on Mounts Washington and Katahdin), and extra food in case of injuries. Although the A.T.'s elevations are low, the trail passes through serious mountains, which deserve respect. These are not the Himalayas, but neither should they be trifled with. People who make the mistake of doing so suffer serious consequences. Sometimes the lighter gear or food may be more expensive. Most people weigh these tradeoffs continually.

A 1953 *PATC Bulletin* article entitled "So You Think Your Gear is Really Light?" says, "Going light is really an old concept that we 'moderns' have too often overlooked. No doubt Cain on his long trek to Africa was the first practitioner in this field!" The article refers to the "go-light" ideas of nineteenth-century outdoorsman George Washington "Nessmuk" Sears. His pack weighed less than thirty pounds, about the same as those of pioneer A.T. hikers in the 1940s and 1950s, who considered themselves lightweight backpackers. In his book *Woodcraft*, Sears admonished, "Go light; the lighter the better, so that you have the simplest material for health, comfort and enjoyment. My own load, including canoe, extra clothing, blanket bag, two days' rations, pocket ax, rod, and knapsack never exceeded twenty-six pounds; and I went prepared to camp out any and every night." To reduce your weight below Nessmuk's twenty-six pounds, you will probably have to rely on others, hike fast, and severely limit creature comforts.

An early ATC booklet, *Suggestions for Appalachian Trail Users,* stated that keeping weight down "cannot be over-emphasized. Learn what you can do without." A seminar at the founding ATC meeting in 1925 covered light-weight gear.

Charlie Trivett of Damascus recalls helping Susan Gail Arey when she hiked the trail in 1976. She weighed ninety pounds and her pack weighed forty-five. "I took her down to the post office," he said. "She was going to lighten her pack. She put a few things in an envelope, just a few ounces of stuff. She thought she was going to really lighten her pack. She couldn't understand it. Tears were coming out. She said, 'You mean that's all I'm getting rid of?'"

Of course, pack weight will fluctuate considerably. Water weighs two pounds per quart, and a hiker uses perhaps two pounds of food a day. Resup-plying for a week on the trail can add fifteen to twenty pounds. Wet gear weighs more than dry. Winter gear can add ten more pounds.

Hikers should carry plenty of water, or know where they can find it. This could be one to two quarts, depending on temperature and terrain. Some experienced hikers who know the area don't carry water, but that's risky. You can spend a miserable day without water, even endangering your health.

Information about how to prepare for a thru-hike is now readily available. Many detailed guides and videos have been produced in the past five years. Experienced hikers also are willing to give advice. ALDHA's gathering each October has workshops on various trails. And Trail Days in Damascus in mid-May is a good chance to visit with past and present backpackers.

Some people advocate a shakedown hike of at least a few days to try out your body and equipment. A hike that is a shorter version of the A.T. is Vermont's Long Trail. At 260 miles, with many difficult climbs, it might take three weeks to complete. Some thru-hikers have taken courses from Warren Doyle's Appalachian Trail Institute, the National Outdoor Leadership School (NOLS), and wilderness instructor Tom Brown. While the courses aren't essential, some hikers say they gained the confidence to do the trail, and new skills added to their enjoyment of the A.T. Information, books, and guides are available from ATC, P.O. Box 807, Harpers Ferry, WV, 25425-0807.

With so much information available, some hikers warn, there is a risk in overplanning. Stay as flexible as you can with your daily schedule, equipment, food, and goals, they advise. The passing seasons and changing terrain, as well as your own needs, will demand adjustments. For example, you may decide you don't want to do the whole trail. Keep in mind that a successful trip is one that you enjoy. Many hikers who did not complete the A.T. their first try went on to do many long hikes.

Proper attitude, desire, and commitment are essential for a successful thru-hike. Adjust to the trail instead of expecting the trail to adjust to you. Be positive; anticipate the good times ahead instead of concentrating on current misery. Know what you hope to accomplish and what you don't.

Before quitting the trail, sleep on it. One hiker advises waiting until the next town before making a final decision. If you don't miss the trail after forty-eight hours in town, perhaps it is time to drop off.

Don't worry about finding a partner for an A.T. thru-hike. Show up at Springer at peak time, and you'll find plenty of potential partners. Laurie Mack, who separated from her partner after a few weeks, recommends not picking anyone ahead of time. "You don't need a hiking partner. The best place to find one is on the trail."

Don't go too fast for your capabilities. If you're not sleeping well and not recovering in the morning from yesterday's hike, you may be pushing too hard. Experienced backpackers conserve energy whenever they're not hiking, hardly moving a muscle without good purpose.

Be sure to inspect your injuries right away and take corrective action. Untended injuries can get worse. Many hikers who let their blisters fester have been forced to drop off the trail. Wash your socks and feet frequently; use tape and moleskin when necessary. Recently ibuprofen has emerged as the nonprescription painkiller and anti-inflammatory of choice on the A.T.

Many hikers aren't prepared for the expense of a thru-hike. A rough rule of thumb now is $1 to $1.50 per mile. A lot depends on a hiker's tastes and how much time he spends in towns.

"Save enough money before the hike so you can splurge in town," advises Bob "Sweet Pea La Foot" Hill. "I was constantly worried about having enough money. You should be able to splurge in towns. That can make the difference in terms of your enjoying the trip. I would have enjoyed the trail more if I'd had the money."

Henry Phillips, a former teacher, said, "It would be great for kids to do the trail right out of high school. It would give them an edge on everything they do for the rest of their life. It's a shame more people don't do it."

Some advice for parents and friends: Keep in touch. Letters, cards, packages, and telephone calls from home are an important connection to the outside world.

New hikers should bear in mind that when they get information on distances and difficulty from people along the way, it will often be wrong. One problem is that miles seem longer on ascent than on descent. Sometimes, place names can mislead a hiker. Agony Grind and Rattlesnake Mountain can strike terror into one's heart, but the reality is that Agony Grind, although steep, is short, and you are unlikely to see anything slithering at Rattlesnake Mountain.

Three useful trail items are gaiters to keep socks and lower legs dryer and cleaner, plastic coffee-can lids to foil mice trying to reach suspended food bags, and mosquito netting to deter man-eating bugs. Pieter "the Cheshire Cat" Van Why carries a ten-ounce bugproof "sleep screen." Laurie "the Umbrella Lady" Adkins, who has hiked all over the country, advocates an umbrella as the best rain protection. Most hikers, however, prefer the traditional rainsuits and ponchos.

Most thru-hikers hitchhike at least a few times to towns for supplies. Exercise caution in accepting rides. Try to look as clean and presentable as possible before sticking your thumb out. Keep your backpack nearby, and look like a hiker. Many people near the trail know that hikers hitchhike and are used to giving them rides. As an alternative to hitchhiking, it's sometimes possible to request a ride from someone in a parking lot.

Give some thought to adjusting to life after the trail. It may require almost as much preparation as the thru-hike. In the excitement of hiking the A.T., the aftermath is often ignored.

Rick Hancock says to remember that every day is not going to be fun filled, but that "you're out there to enjoy yourself. It's your hike. It's no one else's. Those days when you only feel like hiking five miles, just hike five miles. Don't get into that trap where you feel you have to get to this shelter or that campsite."

"Just go, just do it," said Luke "the Journeyman" Wiaczek. "Don't get bogged down on the hows, the whats, or the whys. Just go. That all comes into focus when you do it. When you get out there. There's no amount of advice or training or planning that anybody can offer you. Once you get out there, you'll learn it. And that's part of the fun, the learning process. Just go, and let me know when you go. I might want to join you," he said.

Above all, don't break stride, don't backtrack, and don't step in any wet cowpies.

Mark "Second Wind" Di Miceli

If anyone is a natural thru-hiker, it might be Mark Di Miceli. Just as some people have a special aptitude for baseball or the piano, so do some people flourish on the trail. A five-time thru-hiker, Mark came to the A.T. in 1983 and did his last trip in 1990. He lives along the Hudson River north of New York City. In the course of a four-hour discussion, our conversation shifted swiftly from Indian arrowheads along the trail to the best hiking socks to the meaning of life.

"When you have a successful thru-hike on the A.T., it's like a jewel inside of you, and whatever you do afterwards, no matter how bad things get, you've always got that jewel that you can take out," Mark Di Miceli said. "Maybe it's just a shelter you spent one night at out of the rain, and you were happy that you were dry, or maybe it's just a turn in the trail, and you don't even remember where it was. Maybe it was some time you were sitting under a tree having some cold water. But that's your jewel, that's the oasis in your head that you can always pull out when times get tough. It's a wonderful thing to have."

Mark says the key to enjoying the hike is learning to pace yourself, especially on hills, which you should climb slowly but steadily. Anticipate the pace you'll be going by the top and keep that the whole way up. That way, you won't wear yourself out, you won't get frustrated, ultimately you'll make better time, and you'll build yourself into better shape. Most people, he says, race up a mountain, walking until they are huffing and out of breath. Then they stop, catch their breath, and run another hundred yards up the mountain. "It's self-defeating," he said, "because every mountain you come to is a headache more than a pleasure." His beginning pace feels slow, but he won't have to stop. If you have to stop to catch your breath, he suggests, you're walking too fast. When you're in good shape, you should be able to walk from the bottom to the top of every mountain on the A.T. without stopping. He says, "I'm not saying don't stop. But don't let the mountain break you. Stop when you want to stop. And once you do that, it becomes money in the bank. You know when you get to any mountain, that mountain belongs to you. It's a good feeling. It's the whole key to backpacking, when you know how to pace yourself.

"I didn't do it automatically. I used to kill myself. I was a real bang-your-head-against-the-wall guy. I used to run up every mountain. 'Mountain, here I come.' It was not intelligent." Then one year, he learned his lesson. A policeman had been killed on Snowbird Mountain, just north of the Great Smokies, and the killer was on the trail. Helicopters flew overhead. Mark decided to hike with a couple for safety. "What more could a guy who just killed a cop want than somebody walking through the woods with all the provisions he needs to survive?" Mark said. The woman in the group was the slowest, so she set the pace on the climb. "I forced myself to walk slow, and I noticed I didn't get as tired walking from the bottom to the top of a mountain. I said, 'Boy, that's it. That's the whole key to this gig.'" Mark believes that poor pacing drives many people off the trail. They end up hating to hike.

To become an efficient backpacker, Mark recommends reading as much as you can about backpacking. He also suggests studying other people on the trail. Most of the best hikers do just that, he said. It requires humility, but they refine their techniques and learn about the most practical gear. "Most people on the trail learn through trial and error. They go through a lot of changes, adjusting their pack and things like that. You've got to eat your pride and say, 'I made a mistake.' I've seen guys walk in the worst boots because they paid two hundred dollars for them. They're custom-made, so they have to be good. 'I don't care if bones are sticking out from my skin, these boots have to be good.' It's ridiculous. You have to stay flexible and open to new ideas."

Mark warns that many people trim their pack weight too much. "Life is like a string on an instrument," he said. "If you've got it wound too tight, you're off. If you've got it too loose, you're off. There's a happy medium where it's absolutely perfect." Cut too much, he said, and you'll feel great for the ten hours hiking with only five pounds on your back. But, he said, "When you get to camp at night, you're going to be hurting. You're not going to sleep comfortably. You don't have a good mattress because you wanted to save six ounces. Every person has to find out where that perfect pitch is for him."

Mark didn't find the perfect pitch until his second thru-hike, when he hiked alone. "That's when I concentrated more on the weight I was carrying. I went down too low. I wasn't comfortable in camp. It depends what you're trying to do. If you're trying to enjoy hiking twenty to twenty-five miles a day, then you're going to want to carry a certain amount of weight. If you want to hike fifty miles a day, then it's important to carry less weight. So I figured it out. I balanced it out to where it was good for me."

On his first thru-hike, Mark actually gained six pounds of body weight. Most hikers lose between ten and twenty-five pounds on a thru-hike, and forty-five is not unprecedented. Less than 5 percent of thru-hikers gain weight during their hike. A marathon runner, Mark was running ten to twelve miles a day, five days a week, and fourteen to seventeen miles the other two days. He was in such terrific physical shape that his thru-hike was easier than his other activities. "It was a vacation," he said.

Not everyone will be in shape to run a marathon before starting the A.T., nor need he be. Still, Mark advocates getting in the best shape possible before hitting the trail. He finds that running improves stamina and toughens feet. Once your feet are tough, he suggests wearing two pairs of nylon socks while hiking. The socks are cheap, dry quickly, and reduce blister-causing friction. Each pair of socks lasted him a thousand miles. He suggests clipping toenails weekly to avoid wear and tear on socks. He also recommends having sufficient time and money, so you don't have to rush and scrimp.

Mark is security-conscious on the trail. "The rule of thumb is, no matter how many miles you've walked, if you get to a shelter and something tells you, 'This is not kosher,' whether it's raining or snowing, just go on." He's also wary of telling anybody where he's spending the night, unless he knows the person well.

He saw the trail change over the seven years he hiked it. "It's gone from a country lane to a superhighway," he said. By his fifth thru-hike, more odd characters were along the trail. He reminisced wistfully about the early days on the A.T.: "When the first guys hiked the trail, there were no facilities for them. That was hard. Now it's the opposite. Now you've got basically hot-dog stands on the trail. There was a time with a happy medium, a nice amount of outside help, but the trail wasn't ridiculous, either. Now, you've got some nicer shelters on the trail, no leaky roofs. The water sources are clean. It's a tradeoff."

Mark came up with the trail name "Second Wind" on his second thru-hike. The name has multiple meanings: There's a spiritual reference to his being a born-again Christian, as well as references to his second thru-hike and to the idea of pacing himself on climbs.

Like most repeat thru-hikers, Mark learned to cultivate a proper trail attitude. "I learned a long time ago," he said. "You never argue with the logic of the trail. It's a losing battle. You have to be flexible. You're not going to change the trail. You have to do the changing. You have to adapt to whatever the trail is."

Mark is a purist who believes in hiking every inch of the trail, even the least attractive sections. "You need a backdrop," he said. "If all you have is Mount Katahdin and Smoky Mountains, you don't know what 'great' is. It's like having a white star in with fifty other white stars. It doesn't have any significance. The Italians used to drink bitter wine. They'd take a shot of it before they'd eat dinner. It's garbage. But everything you eat afterwards is twice as sweet because you have that bitter taste in your mouth. On the A.T., the rainy days help you appreciate the sunny days. If you just have the sunny days, you take them for granted.

"You're going to have to hike when you're no longer having fun. That may be through three months of smoldering, bug-infested, God-forsaken weather. It could be raining every day. But you've got to always keep your goal in mind: to hike the Appalachian Trail. If you stick with that goal, you won't skip trail, and you'll put up with what you've got to put up with. If you went to a store to buy something, wouldn't you want the best that you could get? When you talk to people and tell them, 'I hiked the Appalachian Trail,' they want to hear the best that they can get, too. They don't want something that has holes in it. They want it to be pure. I'm not saying everybody accomplishes that, but that's what everybody should strive for."

For Mark, the trail is not a way to elude problems back home. "You can't avoid life by going on the trail. It's a change, and you have to adapt to it. But essentially, you do the same things on the trail as you do in everyday life. Do you think your needs have changed because you're on the A.T.? You no longer need companionship? You no longer need water? You no longer need shelter?"

What sends most people off the trail is their inability to deal with themselves, Mark said. "When you're with other people, you don't have to think about yourself. You have diversions. But when you're alone, you have to face it: 'Hey, I'm not in shape. I'm not prepared for this trip.' There's nothing to take your mind off it. The loudest thing on the trail is your thoughts. You can't avoid them. There's no place to go, no place to hide. Rocks and trees get monotonous after a while. Your thoughts are always there, always eating away at you. Loneliness is one of the major reasons people get off the trail.

"After thirty days of being on the trail, I no longer thought of things at home. I thought of things that happened to me on the trail. For the first thirty days, I'd be thinking about my car or going fishing. After thirty days, all I thought about was that shelter back there. After ninety days, I felt a one-ness with the woods and the trail. I realized when I called home, I was no longer part of their life, either. I was the guy who was away hiking."

One last piece of advice from Mark comes in the form of a cautionary tale. On his first thru-hike he hiked twenty to twenty-five miles a day. In the Presidential Range of the White Mountains he pushed too hard one day, doing the kind of thing that has hurt many hikers so much that they had to drop off the trail. With a partner, Mark walked twenty-seven miles from the hostel in Crawford Notch to Pinkham Notch, one of the A.T.'s toughest stretches. They had been planning to stay in Madison Hut and arrived there at dinnertime. But the hut was full with a camp group, and Mark and his partner were turned away. That left them a rugged seven-mile descent to Pinkham, much of the way in complete darkness. "We were beyond tired," Mark said. "The adrenaline started to flow and we were running on raw energy. We were walking by feel and we were walking fast. We got to Pinkham at ten. That was my longest day. It was ridiculous. My knees hurt for a month after that."

Katahdin: The Holy Mountain at the End of the Trail

I didn't know whether to laugh or cry when I got to the last blaze—so I did both!

Steve Bruce, 1984 trail report to ATC

THERE ARE MANY PLACES TO FINISH THE APPALACHIAN TRAIL, but only one place to complete it: Katahdin. "Having Katahdin at the end of the trail is almost like it was a plan by the creator of the universe," said Irvin "Buzz" Caverly, superintendent of Baxter Park since 1971. If there is one regret of people who do the trail southbound, in bits and pieces, or flip-flopping, it is that they didn't end at Katahdin. Robie "Jumpstart" Hensley said, "There's something magical about Katahdin from the time when you first start counting the miles. It's my Shangri-La, the end of the rainbow. I lost a little of that feeling when I flip-flopped. Then I had to look at Harpers Ferry as my goal."

An unsigned article in the Myron Avery collection at the Maine State Library, entitled "Katahdin—An Inspiration" says, "I dwell in the shadow of Katahdin—Maine's superlative mountain . . . If the concept of a wilderness can be reduced to any specific illustration, it is probably best typified by the impression of its lonely mountain, reached only by a long journey through the wilderness. This is the meaning which Katahdin has had through the centuries for those who journeyed to its summit."

The common translation of *Katahdin* from the Abenaki Indian language is "greatest mountain," and arguably it is. When Dorothy Hansen was deeply discouraged during her thru-hike, her father wrote to her: "Remember, there's no Holy Grail at the end. It's just another mountain." "But there is a Holy Grail at the end for a lot of people," she said.

The year that Dorothy hiked, entries in registers of shelters for hundreds of miles discussed whether many thru-hikers missed the point of the trip because they were too goal oriented. They hike twenty-five miles a day, trying to reach the end too quickly. And in the process, some suggest, they don't enjoy the trip. Someone wrote that the ultimate test of whether a thru-hiker is hiking the trail for the right reasons, for the journey rather than for the end, would be to hike to Katahdin Stream Campground, reach the base of Katahdin, and quit without climbing the mountain. That way, you would see if you did it for the journey or for the goal.

"I don't think I would have been constitutionally capable of doing that," Dorothy said. "There were times when the only thing that kept me going was the thought of standing there on top of Katahdin."

In 1972, after hiking from Georgia to Maine, Lowell Nottingham was halfway up Katahdin when he decided to turn around, saying, "There would be nothing to look forward to" if he completed the climb. The *A. T. News* reported that 1988 thru-hiker Daryl Binney stopped at Abol Bridge, fifteen miles from the finish. His dog, Janson, had come with him the whole way, and because his dog couldn't enter Baxter State Park, he didn't want to either. "I couldn't imagine climbing Katahdin without you," he told Janson.

Katahdin is exactly a mile high, counting the thirteen-foot stone cairn there. The A.T. has higher mountains but none as impressive; it towers over the landscape for miles. Millinocket, the closest town for A.T. hikers, is only five hundred feet above sea level. An early guide to the A.T., written by Myron Avery, describes Katahdin as a huge massif, appearing different from every direction. He wrote, "The casual climber, who thinks he has seen all after he reaches Baxter Peak, knows little of the wonders of Katahdin. It is a mountain not for a one day's trip but for many days and to which the traveler will return again and again with increasing pleasure and enthusiasm."

Katahdin is also the centerpiece of Baxter State Park, which must remain "forever wild," by the terms of a gift from Governor Percival Baxter to the people of Maine. Besides money, Governor Baxter inherited from his father, who had been mayor of Portland, a sense of public service and philanthropy. For more than a decade, he tried to convince the state legislature to protect Katahdin and its environs. Finally, he decided that he would have to do it himself. Over the next four decades, he pieced together dozens of acquisitions, two hundred thousand acres in all. Describing his efforts in a March 1931 letter announcing his initial donation of Katahdin, Baxter wrote, "It has long been my ambition to have the state of Maine own Mt. Katahdin for to my mind that mountain is the grandest and most beautiful of all the natural attractions of our state."

A decade before, on January 27, 1921, while serving as president of the Maine Senate, Baxter gave a memorable description of Katahdin in a speech to the Maine Sportsman's Fish and Game Association. "The scenery of the White Mountains in New Hampshire is tame and ordinary when compared with that of Mount Katahdin and the range beyond, and Katahdin is not unworthy of a place among the great mountains of the world . . . The grandeur of the mountain, its precipitous slopes, its massive cliffs, unusual in formation and wonderful in coloring cannot be surpassed or even equaled by any mountain east of the Mississippi River."

As a condition of his gifts, Governor Baxter stipulated that the park "shall forever be left in the natural wild state, shall forever be kept as a sanctuary for wild beasts and birds." In a 1944 speech he described acquiring the land and setting up the park as his life's work. And he continued, "The works of men are short-lived. Monuments decay, buildings crumble, and wealth vanishes, but Katahdin in its massive grandeur will forever remain the mountain of the people of Maine. Throughout the ages it will stand as an inspiration to the men and women of this State."

It's one thing to decree wilderness; it's another to interpret that vision, especially decades later. Making the park accessible to some recreation has meant building campgrounds and some primitive roads. How much recreation to allow remains a point of contention. In 1993, the park authority voted to continue the ban on motorcycles, and one commissioner suggested that "the day should come when no motor vehicles are allowed [in the park]."

If anyone else has ever loved Katahdin as much as Governor Baxter, it was Myron Avery.

It was probably inevitable that two strong, opinionated men who loved Katahdin would eventually differ on how to protect it. At first, Avery welcomed the donation. He wrote a letter to Baxter, calling it a "very generous and farsighted act." By 1933, proposals were surfacing to make the area a national park or forest. Avery favored federal intervention. He worried that Baxter's initial donation did not include enough land to adequately protect Katahdin. He worried also that the state wouldn't adequately fund park maintenance. But Baxter successfully fought the national park, and Katahdin stayed with the state.

Henry David Thoreau has been closely linked to Katahdin in people's minds ever since his 1848 ascent, one of the first recorded climbs (although he failed to reach the summit). He popularized the area with an account called "In the Maine Woods." Approaching Katahdin from the Aboljack-nagesic ("Abol" for short), he wrote, "Seen from this point, a bare ridge at the extremity of the open land, Ktaadn [sic] presented a different aspect from any mountain I have seen, there being a greater proportion of naked rock rising abruptly from the forest." He found it "certainly the most treacherous and porous country I ever traveled" and so wild that "the tracks of moose . . . covered every square rod on the sides of the mountains."

In a further description of Katahdin, Thoreau captures what may be the distilled essence of the Appalachian Trail itself: "The mountain seemed a vast aggregation of loose rocks, as if some time it had rained rocks, and they lay as they fell on the mountain sides, nowhere fairly at rest, but leaning on each other, all rocking-stones, with cavities between but scarcely any soil or smoother shelf."

Ironically, Thoreau never made it to the top of Katahdin. He climbed a difficult route in a thick fog and remained well short of the summit. He waited a long time for his "cloud-factory" to clear, but then decided to descend so he could catch up with his hiking party. As he walked down, the sky opened up and he got a magnificent view of the surrounding lake country. In his account, he said that one who earlier visited this spot compared it to a "mirror broken into a thousand fragments, and wildly scattered over the grass, reflecting the full blaze of the sun." (Frequently this phrase has been incorrectly attributed to Thoreau. A 1993 article in the *A.T. News* by Eric Pinder traces it to an 1847 article in the *Bangor Courier* by J. K. Laski.)

Arthur and Linda Belmont have been running the store and campground at Abol Bridge, the northern end of the one hundred-mile wilderness, since 1978. Linda finds that the hikers are grateful "for the least little thing." The northbounders, who are within a few days of finishing their hike "are elated; they want to party." And she finds they've changed during their stay in the woods. One father, she remembers, walked right by his hiking son and didn't recognize him. Busy at the campground, Linda has been to Baxter State Park only once in all the seventeen years she's been at Abol. "Someday when we move from here, I'm going to come back and see what the big draw is," she said.

For months as a thru-hiker heads north on the A.T., people ask him where he is headed. He answers Maine, and at first it seems as distant as the moon. Then, after months of walking nearly every day, in a little clearing, he crosses over from New Hampshire and the end no longer seems so distant. In a few weeks Katahdin appears as a small speck on the horizon. For more than a hundred miles, it continues to grow until the huge massif is straight ahead. Many thru-hikers spend their final night on the A.T. at Daicey Pond, with Katahdin looming large above the water. From there, it is a flat two-mile walk to the base of the mountain.

Sharon "April Fool" Rise came upon a high-school outing on one of the mountains in Maine. "I went by them, and they asked me how far I was going. I said I'd done the whole thing so far, and they stood up and gave me a standing ovation."

Expressing the ambivalence many hikers feel at the end of their hike, Robie Hensley wrote, "The weeks seem to pass so quickly. I'm anxious to get home, yet I regret leaving this trail I've grown to love."

"I felt sort of finished and sort of not really finished," said Ken Miller, who thru-hiked in 1989. "Now what do I do? That was the question most of the people up there were asking."

At Katahdin, "I was really sad," said Jan "Sacajawea" Collins. "I didn't want it to end. You're either elated to be there or sad to have it end. I have pictures of people crying on top. People were sitting on the Knife Edge contemplating the trail. We arranged a picture with arms up in triumph, but it was a prop. They were so sad."

The first time she completed a thru-hike at Katahdin, Ginny "Spiritwalker" Frost felt "pure happiness and utter euphoria. Until that time, I had never been that happy in my life." The second time, she was a little sad because it was "the ending of a lot of really good things."

For Frank "the Hawk" Logue, climbing Katahdin at the end of his thru-hike was "without a doubt the best morning of my life." He, his wife, Victoria "the Dove," and Peter "M&M" Scal had decided on a predawn climb to finish their 1988 thru-hike. As they crossed the tableland, a mile from the summit, a cloud covered the very top. "As we approached the summit, the cloud exploded," Frank said. "Two minutes later, the sun appeared. It could not have been more perfect."

John "Oliver Twist" Newman completed the trail in 1989 with Noel "the Singing Horseman" DeCavalcante. "I felt elation, sadness, regret it's over," John said. "My big emotional moment was at Rainbow deadwater. All of a sudden everything hit me. My dad had died in 1982. I started the trail in 1983. I started crying. I could not stop. It was so bad, I couldn't even see the trail. The journey was dedicated to the memory of my dad. Every day, I thought how much he would have enjoyed the trail.

"At Rainbow deadwater I felt I'd done the whole trail. At Baxter Park, I changed from a few days before. Nothing would have stopped me then. I would have carried Noel or Noel would have carried me."

David Field

*I*n the A.T. community it takes a lot to stand out as being exceptionally devoted to the trail. David Field clears that hurdle with ease. A fast-talking professor of forestry, his exuberance for the trail is contagious. And few people have had as much to do with charting the current route of the trail in Maine, which most thru-hikers consider the finest stretch of the entire A.T.

David Field is a different type of 2,000-miler. For thirty-six years, he's been maintaining the same stretch of trail on Saddleback Mountain, and building shelters and relocating trails throughout Maine. Added up, his trail-work hikes in Maine alone have totaled well over two thousand miles. A former president of the Maine Appalachian Trail Club (MATC) and a current ATC board member, his roots go back eleven generations in Maine. Since at least 1804, his ancestors have lived near the base of Saddleback. He is a direct descendant of Darby Field, who in 1642 was the first person recorded as having climbed Mount Washington, one of the outstanding exploration and mountaineering feats of the seventeenth century.

"After thirty-six years of clearing the trail on Saddleback, you acquire a proprietary feeling towards it," David Field said. "You're personally embarrassed if the trail isn't in good shape. You feel bad if someone says something bad about it. It's sort of a peer-pressure thing. But it's more than that. I think I'd keep it in good shape even if there weren't any hikers there."

"There's a social angle to it," he added. "You enjoy being out working with friends. I have friends in my hometown, and I have people at work that I'm friendly with, but the closest friends I have are in the Maine Appalachian

Trail Club and the Appalachian Trail Conference. Working with people for years and years, you really get close to them."

As the E. L. Giddings professor of forest policy at the University of Maine, David has combined his work and avocation all his adult life. His first job was with the Forest Service in the White Mountain National Forest out of Gorham, New Hampshire, "which to me was hog heaven, right in the shadow of the Presidentials. I love the woods, so the A.T. gives me an excuse to be out in the woods."

Although David loves to hike, he's been so occupied with trail work that he hasn't even hiked all of the A.T. in Maine. "I've always been intrigued by the idea of hiking the whole Appalachian Trail, but I've never seen any way to do it," he said. Nevertheless, he's been around. He's hiked stretches of the A.T. as far south as Springer. He was overseer of the trail in western Maine for ten years, and he hiked that 120-mile stretch regularly. He's spent most of his time on the relocated sections of the trail. He's never hiked the Barren-Chairback Range, one of the trail's most remote sections, because it's still close to its original path. "Every summer I say I'm going to do that, but there's only so much time. If you spend all your time working on the trail, there's no time to hike."

As a teenager, David started doing trail maintenance almost by accident. A hurricane in 1954 hit Bigelow and other mountains in western Maine. He and his brother, Michael, noticed the damage while they were hiking. Bringing tools from home, they came back to clear the trail. In one day alone, they took out 250 trees that had blown down across the trail. They didn't know about the trail club, but they recorded what they did in a register at Horns Pond. Eventually, they received a letter from the MATC acknowledging all they'd done and asking if they'd like to join.

David's roots at Saddleback go back even further. His hometown of Phillips is at the base of the ridge, and he first climbed the mountain when he was eight. Since then, he's been up the ridge more than a hundred times. He has an old letter that refers to his great-grandfather, who, after returning from the Civil War, would climb Saddleback to pick berries. His grandmother talked about climbing the mountain in long dresses and high-button shoes, and sleeping there under a tarp in a thunderstorm.

David gradually became more involved with the MATC. He became an officer in 1968 and served as president from 1977 to 1987. He first joined the ATC Board of Managers in 1979. In the mid-seventies the trail in Maine was poor, he said. Most of it was still on old logging roads, and much of the rest was on land owned by a few large paper companies. To improve the route and protect the trail corridor, land had to be acquired; eventually, two thirds of the trail in Maine was relocated. New shelters had to be built along the new route. In 1978, the club built its first shelter without the uncomfortable "peeled-pole" floors; David recalls carrying boards up to that site.

In the late seventies, David made a conscious decision that the Maine A.T. was where he'd make his mark in the world. "I decided this is going to be it. I'm not going to be able to do other things because this is going to take so much time," he said. "It took more time than I thought it was going to. A lot more."

David still teaches at the University of Maine, where he served as department chair for five years. He also taught at Yale School of Forestry. His work in management planning and policy development for MATC and ATC fits right into his professional work. He teaches forest management, economics, and planning, and his research covers similar topics. Currently, he's studying the financial implications of forest biodiversity. His argument is that when you manage a forest for diversity of species, it is more profitable as well as biologically beneficial. The idea is that "enlightened self-interest is going to accomplish more than regulation, so far as private forest lands are concerned." He finds the tentative results encouraging. "What I've just described," he said, "is portfolio theory, straight from the business school. But it goes back to folk wisdom."

Speaking of his leadership style, David said, "More than a few times as president, I did things I thought needed to be done and didn't worry about the democratic process," he said. "I can get impatient. You just need strong leadership sometimes, or people sit around on their thumbs trying to decide what to do forever. So you say, 'Okay, we're going to do it this way, and you go do it.'"

Maine has always been a rugged, beautiful place for a trail. With its immense forests, pristine lakes, blueberries, and moose, it's the favorite part of the A.T. for many hikers. There has been a steady stream of people willing to work hard to make that trail possible, but none have worked any harder than David Field. It took a hurricane to get him on the trail and working thirty-eight years ago. It will likely take more than that to get him to stop.

Life after the Trail

Raised on the Illinois prairie, I still see with awe every mountain and valley, forest, ledge, and bald, mountain brook and noisy cascade. . . . I have nothing but happy memories of my Appalachian Trail hike—and what a store of them I have.

Phyllis Darnall, 1984 trail report to ATC

FOR FOUR TO SIX MONTHS, YOUR WORLD CONSISTS OF FOLLOWING the white blazes. It's hard but simple. Your life boils down to a routine tightly focused on the basics: food, shelter, health, companionship, and natural beauty. Your only possessions are the few you can tote on your back.

Then, all of a sudden, you're done. You've climbed the final mountain. You've achieved the goal that seemed hopelessly far away only a few short months ago. Instead of that simple focus, you now have none. As Pete "Woulda, Coulda, Shoulda" Suscy puts it, the blazes in real life are harder to follow. You have the biggest appetite of your life, which will persist for up to two weeks after you finish. You're in the best shape of your life, but that won't last long when you stop spending ten hours a day climbing mountains with a heavy pack on your back.

After a thru-hike, things that everyone else takes for granted seem magnificent to you. Turn on the tap, and fresh water comes out. Flush toilets. Staying clean is a snap. Garbage cans nearby. Refrigerators are nice. But you must adjust to whizzing around in cars after months of two-mile-an-hour days.

You are not the same person as the one who began in Georgia last spring. You try to explain, but you have little more success than you did last winter when you tried to explain why you must do this. You mention the good times you had with "Rerun," "Cool Breeze," and "Sprained Rice," and your family only wonders why these people don't have real names. You say that sometimes you had the best days of your life and on other days suffered the most exquisite misery you have ever endured. But every day, good and bad, is etched firmly in your memory. It was a time when you lived fully, a time of adventure and stimulation. A time when you tested yourself and found that you liked the answer. A time when you reached inside and found that you were made of stronger stuff than you ever thought possible. You had your dream and you lived it. You are relieved that it is over, sad that it came to an end, proud that you did it, and grateful that you had the chance. And you wonder, how have I changed? What will I do now? And perhaps, will I ever again do this trail, this hike, this adventure?

After more than two thousand miles on the trail, you can expect to undergo some personality changes. A heightened affinity for nature infiltrates your life. Greater inner peace. Enhanced self-esteem. A quiet confidence that if I could do that, I can do and should do whatever I really want to do. More appreciation for what you have and less desire to acquire what you don't. A childlike zest for living life to the fullest. A refusal to be embarrassed about having fun. A renewed faith in the essential goodness of humankind. And a determination to repay others for the many kindnesses you have received.

"If you haven't had an intense experience on the trail, you missed something," said Mike "Hago" Harrington. "It has redirected the way I'm living my life. I'm working less and hiking more."

"I quit teaching in 1985," said Henry Phillips, who hiked the trail in the early eighties. "I hear a lot of teachers complain but keep doing it. I would have never quit before the trail. I realized now's the time to do something different. I'm selling welding supplies, and I enjoy it a lot more. Being on the trail an extended time gives you a different perspective. Little things don't bother you as much, like a train being a little late. The trail put me at ease."

"I had been a C.P.A., now I'm a mailman," said Dick Potteiger. "I learned that the less stuff you carry, the more you enjoy your hike, and that carries over into life. We got rid of the big house and simplified our life. The trail slowed me down and gave me new directions." By the time thru-hikers finish, "they have a lot in common," Dick said. "It mellows everybody out.

It redefines their values. I always thought I'd like to do other things but now I'm trying to figure out how to do the A.T. again. I don't know of anything that compares to an A.T. thru-hike."

"My fellow thru-hikers told me that I seemed to enjoy thru-hiking more than anyone that was out there that year," said Laurie "Mountain Laurel" Potteiger, who married Dick a few years after her hike. "I definitely was gung ho about it. I knew I wanted to work here [ATC]. The trail and thru-hiking has meant so much to me, I couldn't understand people who would say, well this is one of many goals I have, and after I do the A.T., I'll go on to something else."

"I have more memories than there were miles," said Mitch "Breeze" Keiler. "I'm more excited now about the trail than when I started. Such a great experience is earth shattering. You can't conceptualize what a change in your life you'll have from hiking the trail. You change one step at a time." Mitch said he never returned to the corporate world and has instead become an outdoor educator.

Hiking the trail has had a tremendous effect on her life, Laurie "a Traveling Wilbury" Mack said. She felt she could do anything after her thru-hike. She even helped build a cabin for herself. "The idea for the cabin happened on the trail. I would not have had the confidence before the trail to attempt something like that. I'd have said, "It's a good idea, but . . . So instead, I just did it."

For many people, the end of the trail signals a new struggle. Disorientation and mild depression are common soon after finishing. Those who lack firm attachments, such as job or mate, seem to suffer the most. Some dislike that their achievement is not celebrated in the real world. Susan Gail Arey found that her finely polished wilderness-survival skills were of no benefit— or relevance—in her office job. "It hurt to be away from nature," she said. "I would hear paper crinkling and think a mouse was after my food. It was like shell shock. I would see a white mark and think I had to follow the blazes. People don't tend to understand."

"You're almost apart from society," said Wayne Gross. "You're not in tune with things when you go back."

"At the end I felt strange and numb and disoriented," said Ralph "the Hobbit" Goodenough. "In the shower, watching the last of the trail dirt run down the drain, I cried and cried. It was wonderful." At first, Ralph felt cut off from the trail community. Now, he said, "I go back to the trail and feel part of it, even when I hike short distances."

"After I got off the trail, I had a horrible adjustment, really bad," said Laurie Mack. "I was feeling that no one understands me. I was alienated from everyone, almost like I was a spectacle. Last summer, a friend from the trail and I were talking about adjusting, and he said he's just starting to be comfortable talking about his trail experiences."

"The first night back, I sat on the couch," said Leonard "Habitual Hiker" Adkins. "I was vibrating. I called a friend, drove fifty miles, and camped out in a wilderness area. I'd hear newspapers rattling and think it was a mouse. My first few nights, I took a pad out on the front porch and slept out there. Now, I'm able to come home after a trip without having those adjustment problems.

"I didn't realize it was the Alcoholics Anonymous slogan, but I adopted it: 'Accept each day.' Change what you can change, and accept what you can't. It made a difference in my life. I was fighting things. When life throws you that curve, you accept it. If it's something that could be changed, it should be changed. I realized I can pretty much do what I want to do. If I try something and fail, at least I tried."

A year after her second thru-hike, Ginny "Spiritwalker" Frost says she still hasn't adjusted. "It's hard. It's always hard. It takes three to six months to get your life together again. All of a sudden, it's gone. There's a huge hole in your life. When things weren't going well, I'd indulge in trail memories and trail dreams," Ginny said. "I keep it alive because I want to."

In 1991, a year after his thru-hike, Arthur "A. B. Positive" Batchelder hiked the A.T. in Georgia. "We met a guy who'd hiked the trail ten years before, and he's never held a steady job since. He said his record was a year or two. He just could not get into that routine of every day the same place."

Pete Suscy ended his 1984 thru-hike with six other people. Six months later, none had permanent homes or full-time jobs. Two were in South Carolina, trimming trees and living out of a pickup truck. One was in Europe on a peace march. One was living in a garage. Pete himself had advanced from sleeping outdoors in subfreezing weather on the campus of the University of Maine to a caretaking job that permitted him to sleep in the greenhouse.

"Did the hikes change my life?" said Albie Pokrob, one of Pete's 1984 partners who also hiked the A.T. in 1978 and 1980. "How could they not? The lifestyle, learning to be patient, dealing with so much weather. I learned that all those things will pass. If it's cloudy now, it's always sunny ahead. My whole outlook in life is pretty much determined by that first thru-hike." He's gone on to mountaineering, climbing Denali in Alaska, and working at weather stations on Mount Washington and in Antarctica.

"When I left the A.T., I was in the best shape of my life," said Rod Kinley, a 1973 southbound thru-hiker. "But it was disappointing being separated from my [trail] friends. I was upset by it. It would have helped if we'd had a club (ALDHA), like they do now."

Greg "Pooh" Knoettner was another thru-hiker who found his post-trail adjustment difficult. "I expected to come back into society and be much more well adjusted and not take things too seriously, because that's the way I'd been on the trail. But I got back to the real world and was just overcome by how superficial it is and how many stupid little things you hear all the time. I guess I was bitter.

"I couldn't get a job. But I adjusted and I learned to be happy with less. I started getting more outdoor jobs. Now I feel perfectly well adjusted. I don't know if I've lost that special feeling that you have right after getting off the trail, or whether I've been able to reconcile that special feeling with the way the world really is and accept it."

Introducing his girlfriend, Juliana, whom he met while working at Harpers Ferry, Greg laughed and said, "The trail just seems to keep bringing great things to me."

On the trail, he said he "matured a lot, became more easygoing and accepting, just mellowed a lot. I was a type A, probably still am, but a mellower type A, reformed."

The end of the trail was a "really tough time" for Scott "the Mountain Beaver" Beavers, who hiked in 1992. "I thought I'd hike the trail and then go right back. It didn't work out that way. I didn't work for three months, and I didn't have a place to live for two months. The first night I slept alone in a house, I had a feeling of despair. I was back into the mainstream. The experience was over."

Dick "Lo-Tec" Cieslik hiked the trail over two summers. After the first year, "I had a deep depression when I had to go off," he said. "I felt disassociated from the rest of the world. I had a bad time the whole next year." Now that some time has passed, he's happy he did the trail. "Most people would say it's the best thing they ever did," he said. "It's a way to see the U.S. in a very special way, in the backcountry. You see it like the pioneers did. By the end of the trail, you can walk through a brick wall, you're in such good shape."

Some hikers have a hard time putting their sleeping bags away. Many are reluctant to sleep indoors, and those who do often end up in a sleeping bag on the floor. Some are startled for weeks by the sound of flush toilets and other loud noises.

A.T. memories remain vivid long after the hike. People who can't remember what they had for breakfast can recall details of their A.T. adventure two decades later. It's rare to find a thru-hiker who doesn't think about the trail at least a little each day for the first few years after the long walk. Many hikers describe trail flashbacks. One minute they're shopping for frozen pizza, the next they're on Roan Mountain.

Ross "Ridgerunner" Geredien, a 1989 thru-hiker, said that weather changes take him back to different days on the trail. "I can remember almost all of the 150 days on the trail," he said. After a while, some memories fade and names and places blur, to be replaced by a more general feeling for the trail. But even after decades, many details persist. Earl Shaffer and Gene Espy still speak of people and events on their thru-hikes more than forty years ago, and they make it sound like it happened yesterday.

Four years after his hike, Ross finds that he's still adjusting. The hardest part was beginning college right after his thru-hike. "There were ten thousand people in an urban environment. In the dorm, I felt real enclosed." He expected to interact with people as he had on the trail, but he learned some hard lessons. "I trusted people that manipulated me," he said. Like many hikers, he found it difficult to explain his trail experiences to others. But finally, he stopped talking about the trail and got on with his school life. He eventually found like-minded people to share his experiences. He now believes that the trail prepared him well for life.

More than a decade after his thru-hike, Rick Hancock says that when he sees an A.T. slide show "I get a lump in my throat and a tear in my eye." Rick retired his pack to "a place of distinction. When I was on my own in an apartment, I kept it in the living room as a conversation piece."

"I still think about it almost every day," said David Bally, a 1989 thru-hiker. "Lately, things pop into my head, like flashbacks. Just boom, I'm there. It's always a happy thought. I don't have any bad memories of it at all. As painful as the blisters were, the good outweighed the bad for sure."

After the trail and the abrupt change to a more sedentary life, a thru-hiker can expect to undergo some physiological changes, too. Many suffer through periods of listlessness and lack of focus. Psychologist Thomas McKnew draws parallels to long-distance runners. He says that the "runner's high," the result, at least in part, of the body's production of endorphins, may be applicable to thru-hikers, too. The morphinelike endorphins, one of the body's responses to pain, are credited with inducing cheeriness in the face of adversity. Maybe that's why thru-hikers seem to be such an upbeat, energetic lot. After a thru-hike, the switch to a relatively sedentary lifestyle can throw a body for a loop. If exercise tends to cheer people up, the reverse may also be true.

The biggest post-hike adjustment, however, is psychological. "So many hikers expect to find out the answers to their problems or at least to hone in on them and get them in perspective, but that doesn't always happen," said ATC's Jean Cashin. "Sometimes, they come off the trail, and they're more puzzled than ever with what they want to do with their life."

Although most thru-hikers adjust inside of a few months, some endure prolonged struggles. A handful have permanent problems. No one has studied the severe cases, but there are scattered stories of people who became unbalanced after the trail; one hears of reports of schizophrenia and other serious ailments. It is reasonable to assume that people who are already severely troubled or prone to mental illness when they arrive at the trailhead might get a push in that direction from such an intense experience.

Some hikers adjust by remaining active in the trail community. Some simply continue to backpack; others maintain trails or become involved with clubs. Reese "the Sagwagon" Lukei, Jr., has served on the ATC board of managers. He, along with fellow 2,000-milers Ned Greist and Les Holmes, helped to develop a Boy Scout backpacking merit badge. Reese has been active in the American Hiking Society since 1977. Currently, he's in charge of developing the American Discovery Trail from the Pacific to the Atlantic. He hopes this will become the backbone of a national trail system comparable in scope to the Interstate Highway System.

Another A.T. hiker, Rick Hancock, succeeded Reese as head of the Tidewater Appalachian Trail Club. "I'm still on the trail as often as I can be," said Rick. "The knowledge that I gained I'm sharing with others. I'm trying to give something back for the pleasure hiking gave me."

Dorothy Hansen

*F**ew people have closer ties to the A.T. than Dorothy Hansen. A 1979 thru-hiker, she has been operating the Mountain Crossings at Walasi-Yi Center, Neels Gap, Georgia, with her husband, Jeff, since 1983. That same year her father, Rex Pulford, died of a stroke on the A.T. while attempting a thru-hike. One morning I talked with Dorothy and Jeff, leaning over the counter of their store as hikers and other customers, their children Jamie and Chris, and their cat, Custard, drifted in and out.*

Living on the trail can be a mixed blessing for a thru-hiker, but Dorothy Hansen has no qualms about it. The A.T. has long been in her blood. From the time she was nine years old, her family traveled north from their home in Yankeetown, Florida, to hike along the A.T. During their summer-vacation trips they'd do three- or four-day hikes along the A.T., over the years totalling about a thousand miles.

Despite her backpacking experience, Dorothy didn't come to the trail well prepared in 1979. Jeff, who has advised many thru-hikers and saved many trips over the last decade, said Dorothy was an unlikely candidate to complete the trail. She had a homemade backpack, with a frame constructed of copper pipe soldered together. Her straps had no padding. For shelter, she had only a poncho, so her down bag was soaked each of her first four nights on the trail. Dorothy hiked in tennis shoes because she could find no women's hiking boots to fit her wide feet. In her favor, she carried a light load. Jeff said, "What Dorothy had was an awful lot of was stick-to-itiveness."

Of her thru-hike, Dorothy said, "I did it because I wanted to be alone, to answer some questions about myself. I'd always wanted to be a hermit, and I wanted to see if I could be alone for five months. But I started in April, and there must have been one hundred people on the trail headed for Maine. So I quickly realized it wasn't going to be a hermitage. In fact, I remember writing home to my parents after the first week that I felt like I had to take a walk to get away from taking a walk, it was so crowded out here. I quickly realized that that was what was going to keep me going, that there were so many wonderful people out there. Instead of reinforcing my desire to be a hermit, it opened me up and made me more of a social creature. Everyone's so friendly and outgoing. As soon as they find out what you're doing, they just bend over backwards to take care of you.

"I came out of it with a real feeling of indebtedness. I wanted to repay everyone for the kindnesses. I remember my parents saying that if someone does something nice for you, the way to repay them is not necessarily to do something nice for them, but for somebody else. So it's nice to pass along some of what was done for me."

Toward the end of her walk, Dorothy was hiking with two other women when she saw Katahdin for the first time. They were all so happy to have the end in sight that they took off their packs and shoes and began dancing. One of the hikers slipped and dislocated her kneecap. She had to be flown out by helicopter, thirty miles from the end. "I think that put the fear of God in all of us," Dorothy said. "From there on, we were almost too careful."

Lesson learned, Dorothy was able to complete her thru-hike at Katahdin. "I remember writing in my journal that I felt like lemmings out there. It's almost a biological urge to hike to Maine."

Having talked to a number of repeat hikers, Dorothy said, it seems that "after the second or third time, it just gets better and better. Jeff doesn't understand that, perhaps because he hasn't hiked the trail. To him, you've done this trail once, why not go out and do the Pacific Crest Trail or the Continental Divide Trail or the Long Trail? Why keep doing the Appalachian Trail? But I remember feeling when I got to the end that if I had the time and money, I would have hiked forever. It wouldn't necessarily have had to be the Appalachian Trail. But you do develop a love of the trail itself as an entity. People call it an escape. I'd say it's a running towards, rather than a running away from. I can understand just wanting to do that forever. You just feel so good about yourself."

Although Jeff hasn't done an A.T. thru-hike, he's an expert outdoorsman. He went to forestry school in Oregon and then led outdoor-education programs in the West and Alaska. For five years, he spent 200 to 250 nights a year backpacking. He became director of an outdoor school in northern Georgia. That's where he met Dorothy, who worked there after her thru-hike.

Jeff said that when he led six- or seven-week outdoor programs, they'd spend the last day or two talking about re-entry into the other world. He'd tell the hikers that no one but their immediate peers would be able to relate to their experience. "You have these experiences that mean more to you than anything you've ever done in your life, and you'll bring them up at the dinner table and get blank stares back—at best."

"It was the hardest year of my life after I finished the trail," Dorothy said." I remember thinking, 'Why am I not out there where the world makes sense? Where my priorities are straight and I'm doing what I want to with my life. Part of it is that you need to talk about it and share what you've done with other people, and nobody cares.

"I had one week from the time I finished the trail till graduate school. I was a teaching assistant in a little cubbyhole with no windows or anything. Graduate school is such an artificial society. And all of a sudden going from the great realities of food, water, rest, and life to schedules and academia—it was really hard. I remember riding back and forth to school on my bike with tears rolling down my face, thinking 'What am I doing here?'

"Growing up, I'd always felt a little bit of a misfit, that I didn't fit in. I think I came out of the A.T. still feeling a little bit of a social misfit in terms of the world at large, but you feel like you almost have a community of misfits—strong individualists—and it feels okay. You feel confirmed in your individuality."

The aftermath of the hike wasn't all pain and disorientation, but also some powerful positive feelings. "Part of it is short-lived," she said. "You come out of it with the feeling that no matter what I wanted to do, I could do it because I had done that [trail]. A few years later, that starts to wear off after the world has a chance to get at you, but there's an inner core that stays there. You know you have done something wonderful. And no matter what happens from there, you've always got that. You can say, 'By gosh, I did it.' A feeling of self-worth, of accomplishment, and also there is something— I'm agnostic, maybe atheist—but there is something about being out there that makes you feel holy. Not necessarily in a religious sense, but part of something bigger than yourself.

"I remember walking along a ridge and seeing a beautiful rainbow through the mist. It was the most beautiful view I'd ever seen in my life, and the birds were singing, and I remember saying, 'Thank you.' I didn't know who I was saying thank you to.

"Sometimes when you're in the middle of business and life as usual, you think, 'What's it all about?' You're born, you live, you die. What's the big deal? But when you're out there, you know why you're there, and you feel grateful to be there."

Dorothy's father, Rex Pulford, attempted a thru-hike in 1983 at age sixty-two. "When I thru-hiked, my dad did it vicariously with me," Dorothy said. "And when he retired, he decided he wanted to do the whole thing. He started off real early. It was March 13, which at the time was early. He ran into a lot of snow, but he had a good hike. On Max Patch Road, there were six inches of snow with high winds, so they took refuge from the trail. By the time he got up to North Carolina, he'd run into a group of people that he was hiking with off and on."

At a clinic in Hot Springs, he had his blood pressure checked because he'd always had high blood pressure. It was lower than it had been since he was a teenager. On April 21, he hiked north from Hot Springs. After eating lunch at the Rich Mountain firetower with a group of hikers, he hiked a short distance north and a quarter-mile past Hurricane Gap died of a stroke. "When he fell," Dorothy said, "he must have called out. One of the young men who was just ahead of him came back and tried to resuscitate him but had no luck."

The hikers he'd been with decided to take his walking stick to Maine. They took turns carrying it, and eventually, his walking stick made it all the way. "I sometimes wonder where it is," Dorothy said. The hikers also carried his journal, taking turns making entries. But Dorothy and Jeff haven't seen that, either.

Dorothy's mother, Betty, had been meeting Rex every few days to bring supplies and help with chores. After Rex's death, some people who lived close to the trail offered her a place to spend the night. "There were a lot of hikers there," Dorothy said. "It was a sad occasion, but my dad had always loved hikers and hiking so much and I think all of us kept looking over our shoulders expecting to see him walk in. It was one of those things he would have liked so much, a gathering of really neat people. I've always said that when I go, I'd like to go that way, doing my life's dream.

"He'd always wanted to do the whole thing, ever since we first started [doing short sections]. Sometimes I wish he'd been able to get a little closer to Katahdin before he died, but then in a way that might have been worse. To be a few days from your goal and not make it."

Later, with Sam Waddle's help, they erected a monument for Rex near Hurricane Gap. A half circle of irises borders the monument, and sometimes a hiker will plant wildflower seeds there.

"My mother never hiked the trail herself but always loved the trail and wanted to do things for hikers," Dorothy said. "When she got permission from the Forest Service to put a memorial stone up, she decided that instead of a vertical monument she wanted a flat stone. That way, when the hikers come through, they'll have a place to cook a pot of hot chocolate or something. It's a continuation of that desire to help."

Suggested Reading

A. T. Trip Planning

Bruce, Dan. *The Thru-Hiker's Handbook.* Harpers Ferry, W. Va.: Appalachian Trail Conference, 1993

Chase, Jim. *Backpacker Magazine's Guide to the Appalachian Trail.* Harrisburg, Pa.: Stackpole Books, 1989

Cook, Joe and Monica. *Appalachian Trail Companion.* Harpers Ferry, W. Va.: Appalachian Trail Conference, 1994.

Logue, Victoria, and Frank Logue. *The Appalachian Trail Backpacker's Planning Guide.* Birmingham, Ala.: Menasha Ridge Press, 1991.

Whalen, Christopher. *The Appalachian Trail Workbook for Planning Thru-Hikes.* Harpers Ferry, W. Va.: Appalachian Trail Conference, 1992.

A. T. Journals

Brill, David. *As Far as the Eye Can See.* Nashville, Tenn.: Rutledge Hill Press, 1990.

Flack, James M., and Hertha E. Flack. *Ambling and Scrambling on the Appalachian Trail.* Harpers Ferry, W. Va.: Appalachian Trail Conference, 1981.

Garvey, Edward B. *Appalachian Hiker II.* Oakton, Va.: Appalachian Books, 1978.

Hensley, Robie. *Appalachian Trail Journal.* Chuckey, Tenn.: Robie Hensley, 1992.

Hodgins, John. *An Appalachian Trail Sketckbook.* Batavia, N.Y.: Hodgins Printing Co., 1984.

Irwin, Bill. *Blind Courage.* Waco, Texas: WRS Publishing, 1992.

Ross, Cindy. *A Woman's Journey on the Appalachian Trail.* Charlotte, N. C.: East Woods Press, 1982.

Sands, Mary. *Appalachian Trail in Bits and Pieces.* Pittsburgh, Pa.: Dorrance Publishing Company, 1992.

Shaffer, Earl V. *Walking with Spring: The First Thru-Hike of the Appalachian Trail.* Harpers Ferry, W. Va.: Appalachian Trail Conference, 1983.

General A. T. Books

Bates, David. *Breaking Trail in the Central Appalachians.* Washington, D. C.: Potomac Appalachian Trail Club, 1987.

Chew, V. Collins. *Underfoot: A Geologic Guide to the Appalachian Trail.* Harpers Ferry, W. Va.: Appalachian Trail Conference, 1988.

Fisher, Ronald M. *Appalachian Trail.* Washington, D. C.: National Geographic Society, 1972.

————. *Mountain Adventure: Exploring the Appalachian Trail.* Washington, D. C.: National Geographic Society, 1988.

Hare, James R., ed. *Hiking the Appalachian Trail.* Emmaus, Pa.: Rodale Press, 1975.

Warren, Michael, and Sandra Kocher. *Appalachian Trail.* Portland, Ore.: Graphic Arts Center Publishing Company, 1979.

Appalachia Books

Brooks, Maurice. *The Appalachians.* Boston: Houghton Mifflin Co., 1965.

Douglas, William O. *My Wilderness: East to Katahdin.* San Francisco: Comstock Editions, 1989.

Frome, Michael. *Strangers in High Places: The Story of the Great Smoky Mountains.* 2d ed. Knoxville: University of Tennessee Press, 1980.

Hakola, John W. *Legacy of a Lifetime: The Story of Baxter State Park.* Woolrich, Maine: TBW Books, 1981.

Kephart, Horace. *Our Southern Highlanders.* Knoxville, Tenn.: The University of Tennessee Press, 1984.

Ogburn, Charlton. *The Southern Appalachians: A Wilderness Quest.* New York: William Morrow & Co., 1975.

Waterman, Laura, and Guy Waterman. *Forest and Crag.* Boston: Appalachian Mountain Club, 1989.

General Outdoors Books

Brickner, Roger, K. *The Long Island Express: Tracking the Hurricane of 1938.* Batavia, N. Y.: Hodgins Printing Co., 1988.

Fletcher, Colin. *The Complete Walker III.* New York: Alfred A. Knopf, 1987.

Hart, John. *Walking Softly in the Wilderness.* San Francisco: Sierra Club Books, 1977.

Schimelpfenig, Tod, and Linda Lindsey. *NOLS Wilderness First Aid.* 2d ed., Harrisburg, Pa.: National Outdoor Leadership School and Stackpole Books, 1991.

Tobias, Michael Charles, and Harold Drasdo. *The Mountain Spirit.* Woodstock, N. Y.: The Overlook Press, 1979.

For further information:
Appalachian Trail Conference
P. O. Box 807
Harpers Ferry, WV 25425-0807
304-535-6331

Important Dates in A.T. History

1879 Benton MacKaye born in Stamford, Connecticut.

1899 Myron Avery born in Lubec, Maine.

1900 Benton MacKaye graduates from Harvard, climbs Stratton Mountain, Vermont, and ponders a long-distance trail.

1921 MacKaye article proposing A.T. appears.

1922 Trail construction begins in Harriman Park, New York.

1923 First section of trail dedicated at Bear Mountain, New York.

1925 Appalachian Trail Conference founded in Washington, D.C., with Major William A. Welch as chairman.

1926 Arthur Perkins becomes ATC chairman.

1927 Potomac Appalachian Trail Club founded, with Myron Avery as president.

1931 Avery officially begins his twenty-one-year tenure as ATC chairman.

1933 Avery and others put trail through Maine's one-hundred-mile wilderness.

1936 Avery becomes first person to walk the entire trail.

1937 A.T.'s final link completed August 14 between Spaulding and Sugarloaf Mountains in Maine.

1938 The "hurricane of the century" closes large stretches of the A.T. in New England on September 21.

1939 Mary Kilpatrick becomes first woman to hike the entire trail.

1948 Earl V. Shaffer becomes first thru-hiker.

1951   Trail reopens with completion of a six-mile stretch near Priest Mountain in Virginia; Gene Espy becomes second thru-hiker; Chester Dziengielewski and Martin Papendick become first southbound thru-hikers.

1952   Myron Avery dies; Mildred Lamb becomes first woman thru-hiker.

1955   Grandma Gatewood, first woman to thru-hike alone and continuously, completes first of three hikes of the trail.

1957   Grandma Gatewood and Dorothy Laker thru-hike.

1958   Justice William O. Douglas completes trail.

1964   Grandma Gatewood becomes first person to complete trail three times.

1965   Earl Shaffer is first to thru-hike in both directions.

1968   National Scenic Trails Act gives the A.T. federal protection and funding.

1970   Ed Garvey thru-hikes and spurs interest in the trail; by 1970, sixty hikers have completed the trail.

1971   First brother-sister thru-hiking team, Cathy and Sam Johnson, completes the trail.

1972   First meeting of 2,000-milers at ATC conference in Plymouth, New Hampshire.

1973   Warren Doyle thru-hikes in sixty-six and one-third days, fastest hike yet; Ed Kuni becomes first to hike trail twice in successive years.

1975   Ernie Morris, age eighty-six, finishes trail; Ned Greist finishes his last section of trail after starting in 1928; Warren Doyle leads first group expedition.

1976   A.T. founder Benton MacKaye dies at age ninety-six; 1978 amendment to Scenic Trails Act provides greater support for A.T.; John Avery thru-hikes in sixty-five days, twenty-one hours.

1980   Michael Cogswell thru-hikes at age six.

Important Dates in A.T. History

1982   Bob McGhee is one thousandth 2,000-miler; Alf Loidl becomes first Australian thru-hiker.

1983   Steve "Yo-Yo" Nuckolls hikes A.T. three times in succession.

1984   Phil Goad completes first round trip in one year.

1987   Dan "Wingfoot" Bruce's Golden Anniversary thru-hike marks fifty years since A.T.'s completion.

1989   Judy Barksdale is two thousandth 2,000-miler.

1990   Bill "Orient Express" Irwin is the first blind hiker to complete trail; Ziggy becomes first cat to cover whole trail; a record 212 hikers finish the trail; David "Trekker Tree" Bradley succeeds in finding ice cream on or near the trail for ten straight days near Harpers Ferry.

1991   David "the Runner" Horton completes trail in fifty-two days, nine hours, forty-one minutes. Scott "Maineak" Grierson finishes in less than fifty-six days. Bonita Heeton becomes first woman to complete the trail twice in succession.

Index